STEPHEN BROOK'S

Maple Leaf Rag

'I confess that before I made these journeys across Canada, I subscribed to every prejudice going. . . . Canada in my mind was perceived as dull, decent, excessively forested, culturally barren,
politically timid, utterly overshadowed by its mighty neighbour to
the south. . . . On the rare occasions when I was required to think
about Canada at all, it was impossible to do so without smugness. . . .

Whether I was able to shed my prejudices, and with what fresh
ones they were replaced, it is for readers to decide.

I opened the map of Canada and searched for the closest point to
Britain. It was Gander, the celebrated refueling stop. So to Gander I
went.'

VINTAGE DEPARTURES

Stephen Brook

Maple Leaf Rag

Travels Across Canada

VINTAGE BOOKS

A Division of Random House   New York

First Vintage Departures Edition, June 1988

Copyright © 1987 by Stephen Brook

Library of Congress Cataloging-in-Publication Data
Brook, Stephen.
Maple leaf rag.
(Vintage departures)
Includes index.
1. Canada—Description and travel—1981–   .
2. Brook, Stephen—Journeys—Canada. I. Title.
F1017.B76   1988   917.1'04647   87-40423
ISBN 0-394-75833-1 (pbk.)

Author photo © 1988 by John Kegan

Manufactured in the United States of America
10 9 8 7 6 5 4 3 2 1

Contents

Acknowledgments

Canada is such a vast and daunting country that without the help of numerous individuals and organizations, my visit would have been far less fruitful. I am most grateful to Air Canada, Via Rail, the Greyhound Bus Company, Northwest Territorial Airways, and the Alaska Marine Highway System, all of whom provided me with transportation, a precious commodity in Canada. Other organizations, including Tilden and Budget Rent a Car and Pacific Western Airlines, also gave me valuable assistance. The following hotels, all members of the Best Western group, offered me comfortable accommodation: Village Park Inn in Calgary, Harbourview Motor Inn in Nanaimo, BC, Glacier Park Lodge, BC, Macies Ottawan Motel in Ottawa, Heritage Inn in Moose Jaw, and the Westwater Inn in Regina. Ross Woloschuk of the Ambassador Motor Inn in Edmonton was especially generous and helpful. I also received kind hospitality at the Vancouver Centre Travelodge and the Edgewater Hotel in Whitehorse. Many local tourist associations – including that of Manitoba, Travel Arctic, and the Greater Vancouver Convention and Visitors' Bureau –were extremely helpful, as were a number of Quebec Regional Tourist Associations. George Sinfield of Yukon Tourism was an invaluable guide. My thanks too to Raven Tours of Yellowknife, Hydro Quebec, and to the many officials both at Tourism Canada in London and at the provincial houses here in London who responded to my endless inquiries. I also wish to record my irritation with Canada Post, an organization that believes it is a matter for congratulation if it succeeds in delivering a letter in under two weeks.

John and Elizabeth Fraser ensured that wherever I went in Canada there would be somebody willing to talk to me. Barrie Chavel was the kindest of hosts in Toronto, as were Nicholas and Thea Hoare in Montreal and the Duff family in St John's, Newfoundland. My thanks too to Shane O'Dea in St John's, and the many other individuals all over Canada who entertained me, informed me, and smoothed my path. David Crane took the time to discuss the intricacies of free trade and other economic issues with me, and I am also grateful to Jay Myers for reading the manuscript and removing errors and oversimplifications.

S.B.

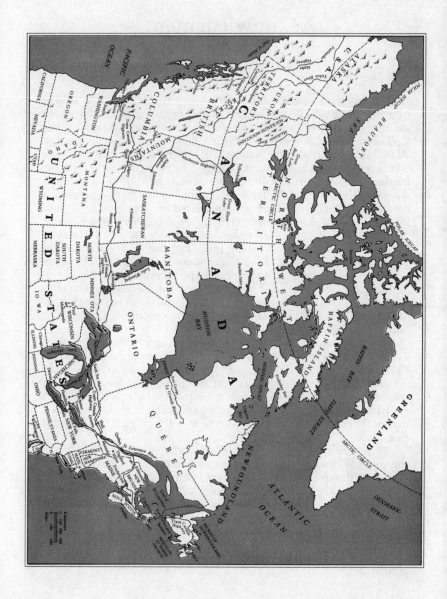

Introduction

In the early 1970s I was working on the editorial staff of the distinguished American magazine *The Atlantic Monthly*. I was copy-editing a long political analysis of Canada, and checking for errors. The author had casually identified Ottawa as the capital of Ontario, a statement I didn't question. As everybody knows – no? – Toronto is the capital of Ontario and Ottawa the capital of Canada. After the article, complete with error, appeared in print, I had to eat humble pie for a week, and it was not considered tactful for me to observe that not a single one of my eminent colleagues had spotted this frightful mistake.

I doubt that either the British, represented by two of us on the magazine, or the Americans, represented by the rest of the staff, have dispelled much of their ignorance since then. Americans on their way to Canada, it is joked, still strap skis to the roof racks in July, and the British can only place Canada on the map if they have relatives who live there. If as many people lived north of the 49th parallel as live below it, then perhaps the world might take more notice of Canada, but with a mere 25 million people inhabiting the second largest country in the world, it is not surprising that Canada has made a fairly small dent on the consciousness of more populous nations.

I confess that before I made these journeys across Canada, I subscribed to every prejudice going. Despite dim memories of good meals in Montréal restaurants and of the charming roofscapes of Québec City, Canada in my mind was perceived as dull, decent, excessively forested, culturally barren, politically timid, utterly overshadowed by its mighty neighbour to the south. Moreover, the majority of Canadian expatriates of my acquaintance shared this view of their native land. On the rare occasions when I was required to think about Canada at all, it was impossible to do so without smugness. Since the British are the former proprietors of the establishment, we can only observe it, as we observe India or Australia, with lofty and slightly contemptuous fondness. We applaud Canada's virtues, such as its consistently dutiful performances within the United Nations, and commend its moderation, but in general the state of Canada does not command much of our attention or concern. It is simply not that important. All these attitudes, symptoms of the imperialist hangover, formed part, if not the whole, of my own mind-set as I prepared to travel across Canada.

There, I have grovelled enough. Whether I was able to shed my prejudices, and with what fresh ones they were replaced, it is for others to decide.

I opened the map of Canada and searched for the closest point to Britain. It was Gander, the celebrated refuelling stop. So to Gander I went.

Part One

Newfoundland

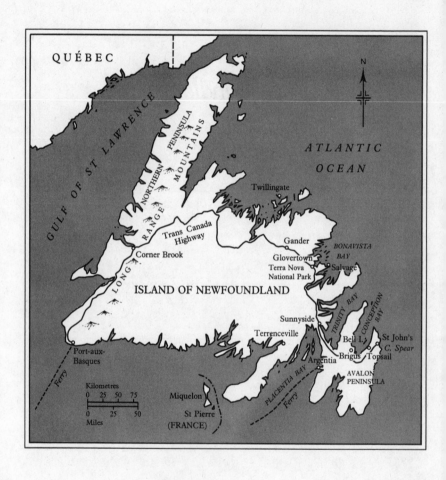

1

Life is Hard, Then You Die

Forty years ago aircraft couldn't take a deep enough breath to allow them to jump straight from Europe to the major North American cities, so they paused in Gander. Despite its antiquity, the airport still looks makeshift, its flat huts desultorily arranged among the woods and lakes of the Newfoundland interior. It livens up, I was told, when the homeward-bound Aeroflot flights come in, and Soviet diplomats head into town to pick up some satin underwear and Japanese circuitry before returning to the land of GUM.

I rented a car and prepared for a leisurely drive down the Trans Canada Highway to the capital, St John's. As I turned onto the Highway, I had my first lesson in negotiating Canada: from A to B it's always twice as far as you think. On my map, Gander and St John's seemed to be neighbouring towns, pinpricks on the Rorschach blot of eastern Newfoundland. But, as the sign on the Trans Canada reminded me, the cities are 320 km apart. (For some reason, Canada has embraced the metric system, though half its citizens seem in surreptitious revolt against it. Even in Québec I would be told that a village was *trois miles d'ici*. I shall stick with the old system so as not to take advantage of the reader. Distances, and broad expansive Canada is kitted out in statistics of distances, can sound too easily impressive in kilometres; it will reduce the glare somewhat to speak of miles. St John's, then, is 200 miles from Gander. And however I measured it, it was still going to take me four hours to get there.)

I left Gander in a July drizzle, and arrived in St John's in drizzle. Some of the inlets of Trinity Bay were spanned by bridges of cloud and fog, and near the hamlet of Sunnyside the sun dutily performed for forty seconds. The landscape, stunted spruce and featureless lakes and ponds fringed by berry-laden bushes, provided no distractions from a speeding car, but the firmament did its best to entertain. Pancakes of black cloud raced across the sky in front of banks of white cloud, and behind the puffy cumulus

5

were scattered, just here and there, postage stamps of blue sky to taunt me with the expectation of better weather, an expectation that visitors to Newfoundland soon learn to discount. The road keeps to the interior much of the way, avoiding the fogs that loiter along the coast, puffing up when the Gulf Stream currents collide with the Arctic waters coming down from the north.

At St John's I learnt that the hotel where I'd intended to stay had burnt down the previous winter, so I spent the night instead at an externally attractive but internally depressing Tourist Home. A Tourist Home differs from a hotel in that visitors are constantly reminded that they are staying in the home of a stranger. Rules are pinned up in every room. At another tourist home in St John's – I sampled a few of these establishments on Newfoundland – a scrawl above the bathroom door implored the user, 'Please Flash WC After Each Ease', as though the average tourist was a nomadic tribesman unacquainted with the technology of the water closet. Tourist Homes are also guarded by fearsome landladies who always loom unexpectedly from doorways to greet you cheerily and make you feel guilty for carrying a six-pack of Labatt's up to your room (where not expressly forbidden by printed notices) and for bringing in wetness and mud from the sodden world outside. Most Tourist Homes are manically decorated with religious paintings, statuettes on ledges, and travel posters bright with sunshine, a visual lament for an absent friend. All the furnishings are in deep colours: green sofas are pushed back against maroon walls, and the edges of gangrenous green bedspreads lick carpets of Mediterranean blue. Moreover, the provincial government, clearly wishing to deter tourists from ever setting foot on Newfoundland, has seen fit to impose a 12% tax on all hotel rooms. After I left the island someone told me that tourists can claim an exemption from the tax, but since no tourist has ever been informed of this it's a sublimely useless provision. If it's true, you read it here first.

Weary, I was glad to settle into even my padded cell of a room. The wall on either side of the window was draped with heavy curtains, while the window itself was covered only by a single net curtain, as though it were more important that the walls get a good night's sleep than that the guest should do so. In the morning I rose early – jet lag disguised as enthusiasm – and splashed across the road to where my car was parked. I was puzzled to find a parking ticket attached to the windscreen, and even more astonished to read that it had been issued at 3 a.m. While the burghers of St John's were dreaming of papayas, insomniac meter maids had been sloshing through torrential downpours in search of stationary yet law-breaking vehicles. My offence? I had parked on the side of the road due to be cleaned – also, it appeared, in the middle of the night. Nowhere on the street was there any sign to warn motorists of these strange municipal habits. It did not seem entirely reasonable for St John's to expect me to *guess* that it cleaned certain sides of certain streets at roughly 4 a.m. on Friday mornings, and my spirits rose as I sniffed the makings of a good row. At City Hall, I demanded to see the city clerk, who at that moment was immersed in an economic development committee meeting. Since it's not every day that an irate Englishman jumps up and down in the anterooms of City Hall clutching a sodden $2.50 parking ticket, the good official promptly abandoned the economic wellbeing of St John's and ducked out of the meeting to assure me that charges would not be pressed. I could leave the city with my record unblemished.

These trivial diversions were, it seemed, keeping Newfoundland at arm's length from me, just as Newfoundland itself kept Canada at arm's length from Europe. For Newfoundland was in fact the Firstfoundland, and by 1500 its abundant cod fisheries were regularly skimmed by European vessels; their crews tramped the quays of St John's long before the first colonies of New England and Virginia were founded. The principal occupation of Newfound-landers remains what it was in 1500: cod fishing. There has never been much agriculture on the island, and I never actually laid eyes on a single farm. The main crops include turnips, cabbage, and potatoes – not the makings of a great cuisine. There are some local dishes, but few restaurants offered them. I did sample fish and brewis, a mess of boiled salt cod, biscuit, and crisp salt pork which demonstrated that a whole is often an improvement on the sum of its parts.

The colony was intended to be an outpost, not a settlement, and immigration was forbidden. But many who came only to fish did stay on and put down new roots. Ninety-six percent of the settlers came from Devon or southwest Ireland. Apart from a small and very wealthy merchant class, the settlers formed an egalitarian society: everyone fished and almost everyone was poor, thanks to the merchants' expedient of keeping the work-force permanently indebted to them. By 1829 the indigenous Beothuk Indians were extinct. British immigration ended in the 1840s and the population pattern has scarcely altered since.

To survive, Newfoundlanders had to be adaptable. Despite the dominance of the fisheries, theirs was a pluralist economy. In winter the men would go sealing on the ice or head for the game-filled woods. Many families maintained two homes, one for summer, one for winter, the one by the shore, the other among the inland forests. When times were hard and work was scarce, men would leave the island in search of employment. That pattern too has remained unaltered: during the oil boom in western Canada in the 1970s, thousands of 'Newfies' headed for construction sites in Alberta. Some returned to the island after a year or two, but many others stayed on the mainland.

Until fairly recently the fishing industry was scattered among the 1300 outports huddled among the innumerable coves and inlets of the jagged coastline. Most outports could only be reached by boat, and up on the Northern Peninsula and in other remote parts of this remote island, the isolation was considerable. Even so, the sense of community was more marked than the sense of isolation. Communities would join forces for seal hunts and other activities. World War II dealt the first blow against this way of life. Naval and air bases sprouted on the island and provided fresh and more rewarding jobs. Until that time fish and produce, rather than dollar bills, had been the principal tokens of exchange in the outports; now a cash economy became the norm. Improved communications led to increased mobility, and to further emigration. The Greenpeace campaigns of recent years against sealing have, Newfoundlanders insist, had a punishing effect on the economy, for sealing was one of the few ways in which fishermen, whose incomes were as unsteady as the waves, could supplement their earnings.

Newfoundland, with its dispersed population of 560,000, has always been chronically poor. Even today its unemployment rate is appallingly high – about 20%, officially. The discovery of offshore oil will undoubtedly bring economic benefits to the island, but the extent or longevity of those benefits is open to question. In 1933 Newfoundland went bankrupt, and for the next decade the self-governing territory reverted to colonial status. To end this state of affairs, some Newfoundlanders urged union with the United States, but the idea fizzled out, and the British pressed the Canadian government to bring Newfoundland into its federal system. In 1948 a referendum voted in favour of Confederation, thus making Canada 'complete' from sea to sea for the first time. But it was close. The margin was 51% to 49%.

Confederation has benefited the island greatly. Newfoundland's trading position improved and its people became eligible for the generous Canadian welfare system. The island may have remained poor (in the interior I spotted a car bearing the following grim bumper sticker: LIFE IS HARD, THEN YOU DIE), but nobody dies of starvation any longer, as they had earlier this century. On the debit side there was a feeling of impotence within the federal structure, since Newfoundland is entitled to a mere eight seats in the House of Commons. Before the bankruptcy of 1933, Newfoundland had enjoyed the same relationship to Britain as the rest of Canada. It had been an independent dominion, with its own coinage and stamps. Consequently Confederation entailed a grievous loss of status, a dwindling to dependency. But there was no real choice. From an economic point of view, Newfoundland was simply not a going concern. Even today 40% of provincial revenues are disbursements from Ottawa. The majority of the islanders are far better off than they were before 1949. Economic development, however, was pushed at the expense of the fisheries. Many outports became ghost towns as fishermen moved to the towns in search of greater security. The welfare rolls grew and many islanders continued to leave for the mainland, never to return.

My few glimpses of St John's, though rain-smeared, had sufficed to show me what an attractive little town it is, but I decided to take advantage of a promised improvement in the weather to visit some outports. It took some time to clear a path through a suburban ooze of gas stations and warehouses to the village of Topsail on the other side of the peninsula. 'Peninsula' is not a useful word in Newfoundland, where almost every settlement, except Gander and Corner Brook, is situated on a peninsula. A whisker of land near Sunnyside leads from the mainland to the starfish-shaped Avalon Peninsula, with its many arms reaching out into the sea. A few miles across the grey waters rose the purple-black cliffs of Bell Island, the site of the world's largest iron ore mine until it was declared exhausted twenty years ago.

Tucked along the side of the bay are many sheltered villages such as Avondale, cheerful little places no doubt surviving more as dormitories for St John's workers than as self-sufficient fishing villages. Some, such as Holyrood in the throat of the bay, have become small summer resorts, though the rain was now falling again and there was no sign of bucolic activity. I continued up the west side of the bay to Brigus. Its cosy wood-frame houses and barns were deposited to no apparent plan on the rocky treeless slopes that defined the little harbour, where small fishing boats twitched in the wind. On one side of the harbour rose two churches, and on the other a lane of stately high-doored houses, an elegant touch, these captain's houses, bringing a note of New England prosperity to what would otherwise resemble a purely Hebridean scene.

A few miles up the coast, along the Port de Grave peninsula, a finger of land pointing into the bay for seven miles, fierce winds howled over the rock and rapidly skimming wavelets scuffed the sheltered harbour waters. Squarish wooden houses squatted among the lichen-smeared rock like stumps resisting the wind. At the tip of the peninsula in Hibbs Cove, neat yellow fences were hung with fishing nets, and a squad of goats nibbled glumly along the ledges of a cliff.

Failing to find a room for the night at any of these outports – there's nowhere to stay – I returned to the Trans Canada and drove for many miles before finding a motel just off the highway. I checked in at seven, seconds before the dining room closed. After a hasty meal I retired to my adequate but depressingly functional room, pulled a chair to the window and gazed at the trailer trucks parked outside.

In the morning I drove on to the narrow wrist of land that attaches the Avalon Peninsula, past the settlement of Come by Chance, once an oil refinery town and now defunct, and moved through the uneventful interior to Terra Nova National Park. This area was once smothered beneath glaciers, which left souvenirs of their grinding progress by strewing huge boulders over the landscape. The resulting wooded hills and rocky outcrops provide an excellent habitat for all manner of mosses and bog plants, including rare orchids. On this drab morning the view from the fire tower on the summit of Ochre Hill was of broad low hills, and, flung around the horizon like discarded cigar tubes, the silvery fjords of Bonavista Bay. Popular response, as recorded in the visitors' book, varied according to weather and peer-pressure. 'Great . . . beautiful . . . fantastic . . . exhillerating . . .' gave way two days later to 'So so . . . all right . . . never saw nothing like it . . . fog – can't see a thing . . . lovely view of fog'.

Just north of the park lies Sandringham, which, despite its name, is an unevocative place, with no whirring of partridges or yapping of corgis to evoke the Mother Country. From here a road leads towards another toe of land that juts into the bay, the

Eastport Peninsula. Here the pretty outport of Happy Adventure has stood by the bay since 1710. Neat white houses, their roofs red or blue or green, are arranged haphazardly, though there is a logic to their distribution, since most do face the harbour. Alongside the wharf stand the sheds of the Happy Adventure Sea Products Ltd. Here passersby can buy lobster at $4 a pound and salmon for less. Inside the main shed a conveyor belt bounced red plastic baskets stacked with cod past a line of women who cut, skinned, boned, and weighed the fish, before moving the portioned cod to another corner of the plant where it was vacuum-packed and frozen. It was −20° in the freezer room, and the men inside peered at me from beneath heavy hoods.

Out on the dock a crew about to set off in the *Lori Geraldine* confirmed that this had been a terrible year for cod, though it had little effect on prices which are negotiated by the union before the season begins – with a precautionary 'reopener clause' in the event of a major fluctuation. When I asked the captain where all the cod had gone to, he shrugged. 'Wish I knew.' And cast off. Fisheries department officials in St John's asserted that such shortages as did exist were localized, but Richard Cashin, head of the largest fishermen's union, said cod catches were 40% down and the inshore fishery should be declared a natural disaster. A fisherman from the Northern Peninsula claimed: 'There's nothing hardly. Most of the fish is all dragged up.' Yet two years later, the cod industry was booming again.

Newfoundlanders are not the only men out on these waters searching for cod. Portuguese, Icelanders, and Norwegians, among others, scour this part of the Atlantic too. Fortunately for the local fishermen, the industry was resuscitated by the proclamation of the 200-mile limit in the 1970s. Now increasing concern was being voiced over the introduction of factory freezer trawlers, which process the fish on board instead of waiting to get the catch back to shore. Their introduction would certainly result in the loss of many jobs in shore-based plants and on conventional trawlers, though it's argued that such jobs are mostly part-time. The older methods still survive, for fisheries officials detected a move, at least in the crucial US market, away from fresh-frozen fish to either fresh fish or pre-prepared fish, such as 'fish nuggets' and fillets in sauces. Factory trawlers couldn't cater to these expanding markets. The Newfoundland fisheries may be adapting themselves to market changes, but they still cater exclusively to wholesalers. Apart from the small shack at Happy Adventure and,

I dare say, one or two more such places in accessible outports, there is no retail fish market in Newfoundland. If you don't catch fish yourself, chances are your neighbour does and will sling a cod or salmon over the fence on occasion. So there's no real need for a fish market, though in St John's I did find a butcher who also stocked salmon, cod, goat, seal 'carcas' and seal flippers, a local delicacy.

Newfoundland lacks the gentle touch. Its landscape is elemental, dulling one's fancy with its misty monotony. Its waters are grey and cold, and as late as July icebergs still come drifting down from the Labrador coast. Although the interior, much of it mountainous, is abundantly forested, there are none of the majestic rainforests so liberally scattered over western Canada. Instead stunted fir trees, mostly spruce, bow and cringe beneath the relentless winds, their roots scrabbling for nourishment in the veneer of soil that coats the harsh granite of the island. Newfoundlanders cling to their chosen spaces. Outport houses are dotted almost randomly around the harbours; gardens are small, lawns uncommon. In the towns, except where pattern-book suburbia has taken hold, the houses are packed tightly together in terraced streets. Nobody seems to desire solitude in Newfoundland; isolated cabins on the shores of lakes are invariably summer cottages. Indeed, a half dozen cottages overlooking a bay is sufficient to constitute a community. Newfoundlanders huddle together to protect themselves and each other from the merciless inhospitality of the environment.

The rawness is overwhelming: a rawness of climate and landscape, and of a dependence for survival on the caprices of nature. It is only in recent years that the rudimentary tokens of modern civilization – roads, cars, television, banks – have reached the outports. Before their arrival, life must have had an unyielding sameness. Of course Newfoundland life is easier than it was. Even in an outport, the basic comforts and some luxuries are accessible and affordable. But in visiting rural and coastal Newfoundland it was the constraints of the life that remained constantly in my mind; the pleasures of such an existence – the camaraderie, the relief when the ice breaks up in spring, a successful hunt, a local dance, an afternoon of berry picking in the pallid sunshine – such pleasures remained resolutely beyond my imaginative grasp except in the abstract.

At the tip of the Eastport Peninsula is the beautifully named outport of Salvage. Electricity and a road only arrived here within the last forty years. It is reached at the end of a marvellous drive along the peninsula, with views onto the islands of Bonavista Bay at every turn. Salvage, probably the oldest continuously inhabited settlement on Newfoundland, clusters round a number of small coves and, while the road links them all, the fishermen's houses tend to be set back from it, either ranged along the rocky headlands above the shore, or placed down by the water close to wooden jetties. The simple two-storey Lane House, backed against the hillside, is now the museum, a jumble of powder horns, shot bags, iron pots, a harmonium, a stringless guitar, fish jiggers (the curved hooks commonly used in these waters), and household implements. On the walls are coloured portraits of Queen Victoria, Edward VII, George VI and his consort. A large black stove stands downstairs but the bedrooms were never heated. It was a grim place even in summer.

An old man stood near the door. I never worked out whether he was a curator or just enjoyed waylaying the occasional visitor. He was garrulous in the extreme, but an absence of teeth and an impenetrable accent made it difficult for me to decode his utterances. He was proud of the 'gons', of some ancient eye goggles ('thet one thah, see'), and a century-old compass that had come from his father's dory on Grand Bank. His humour was laconic. Referring to the downpours that had soaked Salvage as well as St John's, he remarked: 'Had a drop of rain yesterday – two inches.' Although a retired fisherman himself, he couldn't get too excited about the paucity of fish this year. 'The cod, some years'll be t'ick, other years not so t'ick. This year's no squid neither. We fish from beginning May month till near Christmas, then a lot of us'd go to t'woods or t'oicefields. Last wood I cut was in '70. Didn't feel so good, so I gave it up.' He spoke warmly of his reasonable pension, since when his father and grandfather had retired in the days before Confederation, when the average annual income was $300, they had only had a pittance to live on. Times were hard now, but they had been infinitely harder then. But a price has been paid. Many of the more remote outports, especially on the Northern Peninsula, were, in effect, closed down, their inhabitants resettled in 'growth centres', projected sites of factories that often failed to materialize.

I walked over to the Ocean Breeze Lounge for a beer. Even at 4 in the afternoon the place was busy; groups huddled around large tables and all talked at once. Many of the women, young as well as old, were obese, and the same seemed true in St John's. Perhaps it was caused by a constant diet of fried foods and a lack of exercise – bleak windy Newfoundland is not the ideal place for a hike, despite the abundance of wilderness parks, and there are no squash courts in Salvage. I couldn't understand the accents of the younger villagers either – just the odd phrase or two.

Fortunately the dedicated traveller here is aided by *The Dictionary of Newfoundland English*, a scholarly tome compiled both by checking printed sources and by encouraging talkative folk, such as the old fisherman at the Lane House, to gabble into a tape recorder. In St John's I went to see George Story, the principal compiler of the dictionary, and he told me that idioms that vanished from print in the eighteenth century were still encountered in recordings made in the 1960s. Common occupations, such as fishing, sealing, hunting, trapping, and berrying, encouraged the development of a rich local vocabulary, and the relative isolation of many outports had kept the dialect, expressed in the most distinctive accent in Canada, alive. Moreover, since the overwhelming majority of the population shared the same linguistic heritage, certain archaisms, such as the 'May month' I heard in Salvage, or 'new suit of clothes', still persisted in everyday speech.

Some miles inland at Glovertown I came face to face with local whimsy. The front yard of Ackerman's Hospitality Home was crowded with wooden profile cutouts of cute animals (bunnies, bears, ducks), a motionless menagerie that never needed feeding. A line of flags, including a Union Jack, flying high from posts attached to the fence, struck a curiously ceremonious note, as though heads of state were in the habit of dropping by. Though the interior decoration at Ackerman's was, as elsewhere in Newfoundland, the visual equivalent of a box of cheap chocolate creams, the place proved comfortable and friendly. Just as the house exhibited a kaleidoscopic variety, so too its inhabitants played many parts. The casually dressed young woman who greeted me on arrival later appeared wearing a smart police uniform. Mr Ackerman himself will provide a number of essential services. Should you be taken ill while in Glovertown, Ackerman's Ambulance Service will get you to the hospital, and should you die, Ackerman's Funeral Home will do a nice job with the embalming.

After my hurried meal the night before, I decided to feast at the best restaurant in town. The menu featured Chinese food and thoughtfully provided descriptions of the dishes on offer. 'Loved by young and old' applied to quite a few, as did 'loved by millions' (which was the higher commendation?). Curries were, without exception, 'very popular in South Asia'. The special that night? Sweet and sour seafood nuggets with chicken fried rice. A glance at my neighbours' plates showed that the rice was walnut-hued with soy, and the colour of the fish sauce exactly matched the red leatherette chairs in the dining room. I couldn't face it, and ordered instead fried cod tongues, oysterish in texture and slippery on the throat. I had travelled 2500 miles for this?

I was glad to get back to St John's. The prettiness of some of the outports seems accidental; a conscious aesthetic impulse was surely the most muted of motivations when, centuries ago, the settlers raised their houses along the rocky coast. In St John's, in contrast, the old town is determinedly pretty. The town is ranged along, and sprawls behind, the west side of St John's Harbour, a magnificent sheltered inlet guarded at its entrance by the fortress high on Signal Hill. John Cabot was the first European to sail into the harbour since the Vikings, who founded a settlement on the Northern Peninsula that may well be the legendary Vinland. Cabot came on St John's Day in 1497. Sir Humphrey Gilbert followed in 1583 and laid claim to this land as the first British colony.

Of the earliest buildings here, little or nothing remains, for St John's was frequently devastated by fire in the nineteenth century. The worst conflagration raged through the town in 1892. With each rebuilding different architectural features – gables in 1846, mansard roofs in 1892 – were adopted, leaving a patchwork of stylistic layers. The streets close to the wharf, Water and Duckworth, are filled with commercial buildings, some of which now house shops and restaurants and some small theatres, not to mention an extraordinary number of inns, as befits a sailors' town. It's along the terraces behind Duckworth, and in the ridiculously steep lanes that climb the hillside head on, that St John's domestic architecture is seen at its best. Gower Street is a delight, with its handsome three-storey clapboard houses prettily painted in bright colours, deep blues and greens enlivened by contrasting window trim, though these jolly decorative schemes are relatively recent, for during the last century the houses would have been painted in uniform colours.

There is an interesting rivalry in St John's between the two major religious foundations. The Anglicans got here first; their original structures perished in the 1846 fire, to be replaced by

Gilbert Scott's neo-Gothic stone cathedral. This distinguished building is, however, clearly upstaged by the thrusting towers of the Roman Catholic basilica of the 1840s, a church that still astonishes by its size. The Catholics cheated, of course, since a glance down the hill at the Anglican cathedral shows that one of the churches has to be liturgically incorrect in its orientation. The basilica is the culprit, but by bending the rules the architects gave their building a splendid site that still dominates both town and harbour. The Catholic community remains prominent in the town, and has a reputation for enlightened attitudes; one resident muttered to me that it was only a matter of time before the clergy opened an abortion clinic in the basilica basement.

Some of St John's modern buildings are quite good too, including the City Hall, though its concrete terraces are not universally popular. I was taken into the Mayor's Office – His Honour was out for the morning – to inspect the mayoral chair, a gift from Dublin, and the mace, a gift from Ayr. In the council chamber I was shown, one by one, a series of paintings depicting the seal hunt. The long, dangerous expeditions onto the ice in pursuit of pelts are now a thing of the past, though the inshore seal fishery still continues as fishermen, in search of meat rather than furs, make day trips by boat or foot. In the old days, as these paintings depicted, up to one hundred men would set off in steamers to hunt the seals. It was awful work: the pay poor, the shipboard accommodation crowded and uncomfortable, the work itself hard and perilous. It was not uncommon for men to freeze to death on drifting ice. But this occasional work helped make ends meet, especially in the long winter months when there was little else to do. Modern Newfoundlanders tend to restrict their discussion of this now defunct practice to the economic implications of its demise. Seals, the fishermen argue, destroy nets and lines and consume colossal quantities of fish as their numbers grow unchecked. Newfoundlanders are not slow to elaborate all the arguments for regular culling, but the peculiar barbarity of doing to death an infant still dependent on its mother is glossed over. Seal meat, which apparently tastes like fishy venison, remains relatively cheap, and had I been in town in May I could have gate-crashed Murray's Pond Country Club's regular Flipper Dinner and Dance. The most popular way to prepare seal flipper is to bake it with vegetables and top the lot with a pastry crust. I digress.

Perhaps the most striking modern building in St John's shouldn't really be described as modern at all. Fires, decay, and occasional bouts of land speculation have left gaps along some of the old streets, and the city has adopted a policy of building 'infill' housing. This fills the gaps with modern versions of the old wooden clapboard houses that would once have stood there. These struck me as immensely successful, since the new houses are not slavish imitations of the old, but variations on a theme. From a distance they blend perfectly into the streetline, but from close up it's evident that these are new houses, traditional in style but employing modern materials and techniques. Such is the skill of the designs that the new houses never sink to pastiche. It's not only the attractive streets above the harbour that have been well maintained. Down by the quay itself, where I would wander for an hour each day, some old commercial buildings have been well restored. The dockside Murray Premises from the mid-nineteenth century once housed offices and fish storage facilities. The exterior is of plain whitewashed masonry, but inside the splendid timber-frame construction has been exposed. Inevitably, this block of prime real estate is now filled with pricy restaurants and boutiques, but it also incorporates an attractive small museum.

One day a large Polish cruise ship pulled into the harbour, and disgorged a few hundred Montrealers into the streets for a few hours. Behind it were moored two Spanish trawlers that had been impounded after being caught fishing, allegedly, within the 200-mile limit. There was always some activity down by the water, as well as in most of the old pubs along Water Street, some affecting on the exterior to be more scruffy than they truly are; there are also fashionable bars, the kind that insist on a 'dress code'. And here and there I found touches of far California, as in the following advertisement for a workshop pasted up in the Arts Centre window: 'Designed to free creativity, through a series of carefully graduated exercises – mainly writing but also using drawing and dream imagery. Participants will construct their own personal mantra and mandala. No special skills in writing or drawing are required. This is an excellent method for artists and writers (especially those suffering from "writer's block").' I found this wonderfully enlightened in its willingness to liberate those who have no artistic skill from their inability to create. I wanted to attend – what's $20 when you get to construct your own mantra? – but it was for women only. I went to the pub instead, where I was able to confirm that a substantial proportion of bespectacled Newfoundland women favour dippy glasses. The sides of the glasses whisk along the horizontal until an inch before the hinges, at which point the plastic genuflects to form a vee. It looked like a fashion that had peaked in the 1950s and had, for no obvious reason, enjoyed prolonged life as an archaism.

And then I went to dine with the O'Dea family, whose vowels are still as Irish as their name, though they have been in Newfoundland for generations. Free-flowing gin and wine helped accommodate me to island life for another evening, and the dinner was excellent. We were joined by a local surgeon, Frank Duff, and after dinner by his wife Shannie, the deputy mayor of St John's. She was full of tales of bizarre goings on at a ceremony she'd attended at the Viking site at L'Anse aux Meadows. 'Had you heard that at Port au Choix, a fishing village just down the coast from L'Anse aux Meadows, they hold an annual beauty contest and the winner is crowned Dragger Queen? It's true. Absolutely true.'

After dinner Shannie drove me up Signal Hill to admire the view. The hill was heavily fortified during the Napoleonic era, and it was here that Marconi received the first transatlantic wireless message in 1901. With the lights of St John's glinting to the west and hulking Cape Spear, North America's most easterly point, to the southeast, the view was certainly splendid. Many others had driven up the winding road to enjoy it too, though we were the only visitors who actually stepped out of a car. 'The Hill is a National Historic Park,' explained Shannie, 'with one of the highest visitors' rates in Canada. Not that this has much to do with the historic significance of Signal Hill. It just happens to be the local lovers' lane.'

As the deputy mayor drove me back to yet another hospitality home, she took pity on my plight and invited me to install myself in one of the many spare rooms in the Duff mansion. The prospect of escaping from my boxy little room with the non-natural-fibre sheets was irresistible, so the next morning I moved into a basement wing chez Duff. The household consisted of at least four Dufflings, twenty-five children from neighbouring houses, nomadic domestic servants, two dogs, and assorted tennis partners. Over the next couple of days I explored not only St John's, but the microcosm of the Duff house, and I am confident that I met at least half the inhabitants, many of whom wore traditional Newfoundland dippy glasses.

That evening I went to have dinner with Gertrude Crosbie. One could be forgiven for believing that Newfoundland was, and perhaps still is, the feudal domain of the Crosbie family. Various commercial enterprises bear the name, leading St John's law firms are stuffed with Crosbies, and Brian Mulroney's Minister of Justice is the formidable John Crosbie, himself a contender for the leadership of the Progressive Conservative Party until he appeared to be making disparaging remarks about the proud French-Canadians of Québec, and that was the end of that political ambition. During the following months Mr Crosbie found himself embroiled in two political scraps. He was accused in effect, of nepotism, since certain government business appeared to be ending up in the hands of his relatives in St John's – though it must be hard to assign any legal work to a Newfoundland law firm without tripping over a Crosbie or two. Then, in October 1985, John Crosbie seemed to suggest, in the wake of the Tunagate saga, of which more in later chapters, that the Prime Minister's Office lacked political savvy. Nobody seriously disagreed. However, the next day Crosbie snarled and growled and insisted his words had been taken out of context, and so forth; the networks obligingly replayed the interview with the minister, which confirmed that Crosbie had said exactly what everybody had thought he had said. Crosbie still wouldn't see it that way, and the nation had the pleasure of hearing him refer to the press as 'you buggers' on CBC News. A bit of a brute is Mr Crosbie, but even his opponents acknowledge his intelligence and ability.

On Mrs Crosbie's wall there hung a genealogical chart, which I studied when no one was looking, but I wasn't able to work out exactly who was related to whom. Four of her children sat down to dinner, plus various spouses and infants. I gathered that I was perching that evening on a fairly stout branch of the family tree. Seated opposite me was a dapper young man from Toronto, who had come to St John's as an oil consultant after a spell of a few years on Prince Edward Island as a strawberry farmer. The man was clearly a city slicker, and I couldn't picture him in dungarees raking whaleshit into the fertile soil.

It must be a tradition among the *grandes dames* of St John's to take overseas visitors on nocturnal tours. Mrs Crosbie was appalled to learn that I hadn't yet visited the Battery, and after dinner she ushered me into her car and drove back into town. We took the road up Signal Hill, but after a few yards turned right and appeared to be heading straight for the narrows. Instead we came to a maze of lanes that crawled along the side of the cliff. These lanes were so tight that when another car approached, one vehicle would have to back up to allow the other to pass. The houses, many of them scarcely more than shacks, were arranged higgledy-piggledy wherever their foundations could get a grip on the rock. The Battery looked like a spruced-up squatters' camp. Although the houses themselves were unpretentious, their setting was spectacular, and the Battery had the additional merit of being within easy walking distance of downtown St John's while feeling quite separate from the city. Cautiously we made our way down to the lower levels and crossed onto the South Side of the harbour that faces the main town. We drove up to The Brow, high on the flanks of the hill. This used to be an unsavoury quarter, but new houses have replaced the squalid ones, and the community has become quite fashionable on account of the panoramic view across the harbour onto the old town. We descended, then took the road past the wharves and the few old houses still standing near the water, and on past the oil tanks and warehouses. After the 1892 fire the city ordered all oil installations to be moved to the South Side, where an accident would be less likely to destroy an entire city. The road, ever narrower and increasingly rutted, wound on past the fish processing plants and out onto the spur of land that encloses the harbour narrows opposite Signal Hill. Out through the channel glided a handsome white schooner, a most unlikely vessel to be making for the open sea late at night.

Incongruities such as these were causing me to feel increasingly attached to St John's. It was more than picturesque. There was a richness of social structure here that gave the place life: the grandees such as the Crosbies (Gertrude's family came from a similar background and had owned the Murray Premises in its commercial heyday), the university folk like the O'Deas, the mixture of old salts and busy lawyers crowded into the Battery, the young professionals eagerly restoring the old houses downtown and crowding into the fern bars at night, the bemused foreign sailors roaming Water Street in search of a good time, and the swarms of landladies, shopkeepers, and small-time merchants. Like all good cities, St John's kaleidoscopically took on different aspects when viewed from different angles, and its personality shifted as the light and the weather changed, which they did all too frequently.

The Hibernia oilfield 193 miles east of Newfoundland was first discovered in 1979. Local business people grew overexcited and there was an immediate wave of land speculation in which many people got their fingers burnt. It is unlikely that any oil will be extracted before the early 1990s, but in the meantime everybody is arguing about the benefits the oil business will bring the islanders. It's already clear that it won't do much to reduce unemployment on Newfoundland. Many managerial jobs will go to outsiders, such as the strawberry-growing consultant I'd met at dinner, though the provincial government is trying to secure most of the service jobs, such as cleaning and catering, for local people.

The great row over jurisdiction – namely, who owns the oil, the federal or the provincial government? – has been settled by an act of noblesse oblige in which Ottawa has decided to treat the oil as Newfoundland's. There are also arguments about the rate of extraction. The provincial government favours a gradualist approach, hoping to spread out the anticipated prosperity; while the federal government, urged on by St John's businessmen, can't wait to get their hands on the first oil bucks. The social impacts are already being felt. The first BMW, Porsche, and Jaguar dealerships had recently opened up in St John's, a sure sign that executives, hitherto scarce, are moving in. Until oil was discovered, there was little reason for anyone, other than the occasional federal official on assignment, to come to live here. Now there are many newcomers, oil executives and technicians who want more sophisticated entertainment than St John's has offered hitherto.

After my Crosbie dinner I had a Crosbie lunch. At a Duckworth Street restaurant Gertrude's son Bill, a lawyer, introduced me to a few recent arrivals. There was an ebullient CBC television correspondent who'd come to Newfoundland a year or two before and adored the place, despite the climate, treasuring its homogeneous native culture, in particular the 2500 folk songs collected in recent years. The fourth member of our party was a Brazilian oil engineer, who demonstrated, with his high degree of cynicism, why Newfoundlanders are right to be wary of outsiders. He looked forward, he told me, to a Mideast war. 'It would be great for oil,' he reassured me, 'as it would convince the Canadians to set a floor price so as to guarantee a local source of supply. And that will lessen our worries about the high cost of extraction.' It seemed that the big oil companies, so much more powerful than the provincial government, were playing games with the province. Rumours had been going round St John's that some companies might withdraw members of their staff. This implied threat of a partial pull-out was intended to increase pressure on the provincial government to let the oil companies operate at their own pace. The truth was worse: by 1987, as oil prices remained low, most companies had pulled out altogether.

In the evening I dined at the Duffs'. Frank was in charge of the barbecue. I was in charge of pulling the corks. Dinner was, shall we say, informal. Just as I was beginning to miss the presence of a Crosbie at the table, in walked two more. Barbara Crosbie made up in ebullience for her husband's attachment to silences. Although she was disparaging about some aspects of Newfoundland life, she did have a bizarre affection for the place and considered that most Newfoundlanders sold themselves short. Which was why she didn't care for 'Newfie' jokes, the Canadian equivalent of Polish jokes. Individual Newfie jokes were indeed funny, but she could easily do without the genre. I remarked on the fact that most collections of Newfie jokes are published on the island itself. It was hard to imagine Irish jokes pouring out of Cork, but Newfoundlanders had cunningly appropriated the genre and thus diminished its power to strike home. (Alternatively, their eagerness to exploit their reputation as mentally under-nourished hicks could be seen as further confirmation of the stupidity derided by the jokes.)

It had been a sunny day and I remarked on the phenomenon. (Some crazy Dutch balloonists had been cooling their heels in a St John's park for weeks praying for weather suitable for their ascent, and they had another month to wait. Their transatlantic flight was brief and ended up in the ocean, needless to say.) Barbara confirmed the rarity of the event. The first six months of the year were 'dire' and 'spring' simply means that freezing temperatures gradually give way to damp, drizzle, and fog dense enough to close the airport for days. As late as June that year, the temperature had been at freezing point. 'Every year we wait for spring, even though we know perfectly well it will never come.' Late that afternoon, when the sun was still shining, I'd noticed that the entire Duff household had done a costume change and re-emerged in shorts and halters and sandals, as though suddenly transported to North Africa for the day. Optimism could be defined as a Newfoundlander changing into shorts.

My repeated conjunction with Crosbies, like a wonderfully propitious astrological chart, reinforced my impression of the tightness of Newfoundland society. (Some months later, back at home in London, I invited some Canadian friends to dinner. Unexpectedly, they brought with them an additional guest. Another Crosbie, I need hardly say.) Shannie confessed that, despite her political eminence, she was still seen by many as an outsider – or, in local parlance, a 'come from away'. 'It's very difficult to succeed in Newfoundland politics if you're a come from away. One of my grandparents came from St Pierre' – an island just south of Newfoundland that is still a French colony complete with a gendarmerie – 'but at least I had the sense to marry a hundred percent Newfoundlander.'

It was getting late, this evening's crop of Crosbies drifted home, the children, who appeared to have been hosting an orgy in the den, mooned off to bed, yet the evening still seemed incomplete. Of course! What about my nocturnal excursion? Shannie, without so much as a hint from me, provided it. She was giving a party that weekend and had asked a friend who grew strawberries on another part of the island to air freight some crates to St John's. Would I mind coming out to the airport to help transport the produce back to the house? The whole story was preposterous, but I never say no to a jaunt. The penalty for my doubts was having to lug half a dozen crates of strawberries from the terminal to her car. Back at the house I dipped some of the fresh juicy berries into the last of the red wine.

It was dawning on me that the great advantage of having to endure so uncompromising and harsh an environment is that it seems to nourish the bizarre. A black car may be dark but it shows up all the scratches. Canadians, despite the splendid efforts of Stephen Leacock and Mordecai Richler among others, are not known for a highly developed sense of hilarity, but that is the precise quality I was encountering on Newfoundland. Was it humour or desperation that prompted the choice of the carnivorous pitcher plant as the provincial flower? And it was hard not to smile on learning that Brian Peckford, the provincial premier, received more death threats than any other Canadian politician. No demands, just threats. Shannie Duff, tall and firm-jawed, may often have looked as though her favourite occupation would be swinging a machete at a political opponent, but she proved excellent company, as had almost everyone I met on the island. Even the Salvage fisherman would, no doubt, have had me in stitches had I been able to understand what he was saying.

I spent my last hour in St John's having coffee with a courteous old gentleman who recalled for me the days before Confederation when Newfoundland still enjoyed Dominion status, even though bankrupt. He and his wife had never travelled west for their holidays, but had spent them either in New England and New York, or across the ocean in England. Newfoundlanders do, he admitted, feel some affinity with the other maritime provinces, but they don't much like Québec people and suspect that central Canadians from Ontario look down on the islanders. As he talked, something occurred to me.

'All this time you've been referring to Canada as though you weren't part of it, as though it were a foreign country. But you've been part of the Canadian nation for almost forty years now.'

'It's true,' he said. 'I guess we don't really feel Canadian here. We're Newfoundlanders first.'

'But you are part of Canada?'

'I guess we have to accept it.'

Part Two

The Maritime Provinces

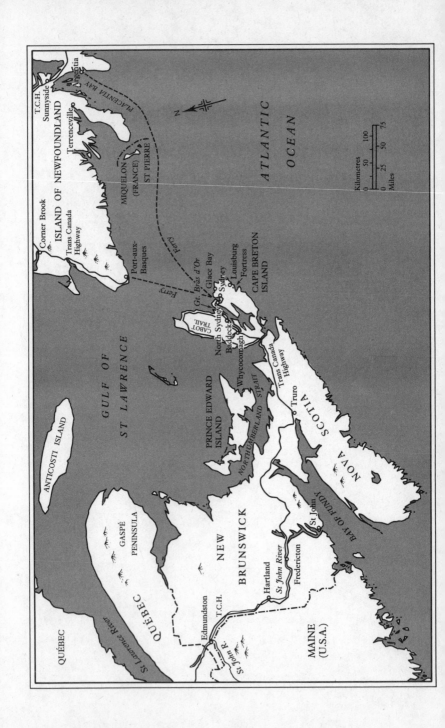

2

No Jobs, Just Weddings

A ferry service leaves from Port-aux-Basques at the southwestern tip of Newfoundland for mainland Canada. I hoped to get to Port-aux-Basques by taking the slow coastal ferry from Terrenceville, east of St John's. This would take me to some extremely remote communities, many miles from the nearest roads, along the southern shore. All I had to do was get to Terrenceville, a mere 150 miles from St John's. The only way to get there from the provincial capital is to take an afternoon bus which passes within ten miles of Terrenceville, tramp those miles encumbered with luggage, and, since there is no hotel at the outport (naturally), sit up all night on the docks until you board the ferry, which departs at 8 a.m. Clearly no tourist was ever intended to use the coastal ferry. It existed, reasonably enough, solely as a means of communication between remote outports, and was not instituted to amuse visitors in search of an inexpensive coastal cruise.

I admitted defeat and took the direct ferry service that makes the 266-mile journey from Argentia to North Sydney. Under a brittle blue sky flecked with high cloud the *Ambrose Shea* pulled out of Argentia and steamed slowly past the dumpling-shaped islands of Placentia Bay and out into open sea. The breeze was too keen for comfortable sunbathing, but on the top deck children played quoits and shuffleboard while their well-wrapped elders, wearing parkas advertising the 1985 Argentia Mixed Darts League, took strolls. When the light failed – which it did spectacularly as a creamy green and orange sunset flung itself across the horizon – the children scrambled down to the Kiddies Corner (*Coin des Petits*), where they were strenuously amused. Adult entertainment was provided in the bar, where a guitarist was singing: 'In a good old Newfie outhouse when it's twenty-five below . . .' A 'dayniter' – a reclining seat, so called, I assume, because night is indistinguishable from day on an overnight crossing – in an upper lounge gave me a passable night's sleep. By morning the bright teenage girls who'd chatted so brightly over their hip of beef at dinner the night before looked droopy and straggle-haired, though the knots of Québeckers and Acadians who gathered in various corners seemed chipper and unmarked by eighteen hours at sea.

The ferry slinks into Nova Scotia along Cape Breton at North Sydney, a useful destination only for motorists. A bus links North Sydney with the larger town of Sydney, but only every two hours. No attempt was made to meet the ferry, and it was only by flagging down on spec an ancient vehicle, subsequently identified as the Sydney bus by an illegibly pencilled noticed taped to the windscreen, that I avoided a two-hour wait at the roadside. I found a modest but acceptable hotel close to the bus station, and rapidly installed myself.

I had come to Sydney, which is on no one's list of tourist attractions, solely to visit its steel plant. Like other manufacturing industries, steel making in the Maritimes had long been a depressed industry, and Cape Breton has long suffered from grievously high rates of unemployment. Coal and steel were the principal industries but both were in decline, and forty mines had closed between 1921 and 1966. I had written in advance to the steel works about my impending visit, but when I telephoned the plant to confirm that I had arrived, the response was less than overwhelming. Nevertheless I made an appointment to see one of the managers and set off to visit the plant.

In 1784 Cape Breton had become a separate colony with Sydney as its capital, inhabited by Loyalists who, disturbed by anti-British agitation in New England, had moved north. Those independent days came to an end in 1820, when Cape Breton merged with neighbouring Nova Scotia. Nothing remains today to remind visitors of Sydney's ancient prestige, though for a factory town it struck me as surprisingly pleasant. The bay acts like a broad audience to the stage of the town, giving it a shoreline of shopping streets and residential neighbourhoods, among small parks and gardens. Even the downtown section has a suburban quality. Sydney seemed muted, as though it woke every morning and took a collective dose of Valium. People were friendly – the bank teller chatted eagerly about her desire to visit England some day, motorists glided to a halt whenever a pedestrian stepped off the pavement, ladies on flower-arranging duty at a local church smiled cheerily as I peered down the nave – but the energy level of the town seemed low as I walked to the steel works. The plant is approached over a causeway that crosses some unappetizing tidal mudflats popular with local birds. When it was built in 1901, the steel plant was the largest in Canada. Iron ore was sent down from Labrador and Québec, and local coal supplies and good shipping connections helped the plant to prosper. The population of Sydney grew from 3000 to 20,000, and today 115,000 people live within a fifteen mile radius of the town.

Set apart from the chimneys and storage sheds of the plant itself was the four-square brick administration building. There were few people around, but eventually I was directed to a manager's office. He told me about the plant, about changing markets and the need to adapt to them. The corporation was not thriving, and the workforce, which had stood at 4000 ten years ago, was now reduced to 1200.

When I asked the manager whether it would be possible for me to tour the plant he looked at me with astonishment.

'There isn't a great deal to see.'

'Surely . . . a large plant like this . . .'

'But we've been closed since the end of June.'

This was news to me. Setbacks to Canadian manufacturing industries are not routinely reported in the British press. Even though I had ample excuse for my ignorance, I still felt foolish, and immediately understood why the plant managers had not been anxious for me to pay a visit. The managers were hoping to rehire the bulk of the workforce in October, and it was costing the Corporation $2 million a month to keep the plant idle.

Most of the largest enterprises in Canada are crown corporations. Because of the size of the country, it was not feasible in the nineteenth century for private capital alone to undertake the mammoth projects needed to turn Canada into a modern nation. Most of these projects were underwritten by the provincial and federal governments and administered as crown corporations. The railways were the most important, and controversial, example. The practice continues into the present century; Air Canada, for instance, is a crown corporation, though private airlines are allowed to compete with it. The Sydney Steel Corporation was in private hands until 1967, but became a crown corporation under provincial ownership as the only alternative to closure. The Corporation is now dependent on the federal government for approval of its costly modernization and diversification schemes, while at the same time the federal government, which owns the railways, is its largest customer.

The layoffs that summer were simply one more blow to the already punishingly depressed local economy. In 1984 a colliery fire in nearby Glace Bay had cost over 1300 jobs, and two heavy water plants, which were losing $125 million a year, were also marked for closure. Earlier in the year 30% of the workforce had been unemployed (at Glace Bay the official rate is 55%), and these additional closures would increase the rate significantly. Nor did there seem much reason for hope in the future; the news that a new mine would be opening seemed encouraging, but if energy prices remain depressed, this development too could be in jeopardy. There are few new industries on Cape Breton sprouting to take the place of those tottering towards extinction, even though politicians were encouraging new industries by offering them ten years of immunity from taxation.

In the evening, people emerged from their houses in search of entertainment. On Charlotte Street teenage girls too young to enter the bars giggled in doorways and corners, heads of families led their brood into Chinese restaurants for dinner, and men with sour faces and beery breaths swirled around the downtown bars giving muted signs of jollity that flickered grimly rather than merrily. I entered Jasper's Family Restaurant. It was almost empty. I find these American-style establishments depressing enough in the United States, but infinitely more so in other countries, where they register as a triumph of the bland over the imaginative. At Jasper's, the meal was served in reverse. First I was offered tea or coffee; I demanded a beer. Then, after I'd been catechized on the subject of dressings, I was brought a salad. This I left untouched, following my European habit of consuming salad after the main course. This baffled the waitress, who assumed that I had rejected the salad as inedible (a plausible interpretation), and I had to restrain her from removing it. Of the food I remember nothing, only the paraphernalia that surrounded it: the unadventurous lettuce leaves, the rolls of reconstituted blotting paper, the paper mat devised by the Milk Producers Association in collaboration with Quality Travel of Truro. I slouched back to the hotel and watched a Tarzan movie.

In the early eighteenth century the often fog-bound but ice-free east coast of Nova Scotia was chosen by the French as the site of a fortress intended to protect their colony of New France. Louisburg was founded in 1713 and built in the 1720s and 1730s. It soon attracted a population of 2000 and became the largest trading centre in America after Philadelphia and Boston. Although it prospered, its defences were far from adequate, and it was frequently attacked by the British, who captured the fortress in 1745 and again in 1758. Two years later the British destroyed Louisburg, and for two hundred years the mists swirled over the few remaining ruins and the weed-packed foundations. Then in 1961, it was decided to excavate Louisburg and reconstruct it. The project began as a means of reemploying local workers who had lost their livelihoods as Cape Breton sunk ever deeper into a bog of economic depression. It is now fashionable to berate such schemes for failing to provide 'real jobs', but reconstructed Louisburg looked enduring enough to me. The work was not undertaken lightly. Unemployed miners were retrained as masons and carpenters; ten historians were assigned to work on the voluminous documentary evidence; over a million artifacts were dug up; original materials, where they survived beneath the earth, were reused; carpentry and ironwork were designed to reproduce not just a vague eighteenth century style, but the very designs that would have been used at Louisburg in the year 1744.

Louisburg, then, is a serious place, but I approached it warily. I recalled my visits to Williamsburg in Virginia, another historical reconstruction which, although worthwhile and enjoyably instructive, was clearly doctored and prettified for yer average tourist. I feared the worst as I arrived at the Louisburg Visitor Reception Centre through a thick fog that was undoubtedly authentic Cape Breton weather, but even on this July morning it was damp and cold enough to numb my fingers and chill my toes, which I need for walking.

From the Reception Centre a free bus takes visitors to a fisherman's cottage by the shore. Since the site is administered by a federal agency, Parks Canada, all commentaries are given in French as well as English. I stepped into the cottage and sped towards a blazing log fire. As at Williamsburg, the building was occupied by men and women in eighteenth century costume going about their daily tasks – salting cod, of course, and long tongues of the creamy white fish flesh were being laid out on racks. The food on the table, the remains of a hurried breakfast, was only half-eaten, and the beds were unmade. This seemed admirable in its naturalism, for 1744 surely had its fair share of slobs. After I'd warmed my hands at the fire, I walked down a muddy lane to the Dauphin Gate, where I was challenged by a sentry, in French. Where was I from? he demanded to know, pointing his blunderbuss at my kneecaps. 'Londres,' I said proudly, knowing how to handle loutish frogs, and glared at him. He glared back and told me I was free to 'visit' the town, but would have to leave at the end of the day. Nothing would induce me to stay, I replied, and he let me pass.

Only about one fifth of Louisburg has been reconstructed, though most of the foundations have been uncovered, and are accessible to visitors. What makes Louisburg so brilliantly successful is that every attempt has been made to reconstruct it as a community and not just as a collection of old buildings. The fiction of Louisburg is that it affects to carry on its business as though a summer day in 1744 were infinitely repeatable. In some of the gardens vegetables and herbs are grown – with difficulty, given the rare appearances of the sun – and children, attired in long skirts and breeches, were playing skittles and *boules* in the streets. This they did whether there were onlookers or not. It was not only the houses and offices – from the lavish governor's residence within the magnificent citadel to more lowly cottages – that had been reconstructed, but also such subsidiary buildings as icehouses and lime kilns. I also enjoyed the untidiness of the place. The streets were rough and the grassy verges unkempt; an authentic touch I was relieved to find absent was the custom of emptying slops into the gutter. In one house, kitchen maids were preparing to cook omelettes over an open fire in long-handled iron pans; while one woman beat the eggs, another reached up to pluck from the rafters some bunches of herbs that were hanging there. As the clock chimed at noon, some of the skittle-playing children I'd seen earlier came running in, sat down at the long wooden table in front of the fire, and devoured those omelettes.

Their appetite put me in mind of my own. It had been awakened by the aroma of fresh loaves piled up at the bakery, but the smallest size for sale there was a pound and a half of wholemeal, an invitation to an attack of eighteenth century indigestion. There are two inns side by side at Louisburg, and I chose the marginally grander of the two, the Epée Royale. The food was basic but good: vegetable soup and heavy white bread, grilled trout with ample fresh vegetables, apple tart served with cheese. Wine was served in large goblets, the napkins, of rough linen, were the size of a hand towel, and the crockery and cutlery were heavy and crude. At the next table sat a party of Ukrainians, probably from one of the prairie provinces, an inauthentic note, though doubtless an Englishman would have been an even more rare sight in eighteenth century Louisburg.

While I was enjoying my lunch, the fog rolled out to sea and the unveiled sun was beaming down on Louisburg. The transformation was complete, for not only did the crisp dance of light and shade enliven the streetscape, but the mercury had done a sprint up the thermometer. By a bridge I came across a group of children and their minder, all authentically dressed, playing a precursor of the game of Pooh Sticks. During the more tedious moments of the game, they told me that their clothing, like the houses, had been built up from the foundations. Every item was hand-made: even buttonholes had been hand-stitched and spectacles rimmed in eighteenth century style. This almost fanatical insistence on authenticity rules Louisburg. In the guardhouse I found account books open on the commanding officer's desk. A recently used quill had been tossed alongside them, and fresh black ink gleamed in the well of the desk. In the officers' quarters the glassware on the dining table was heavy and green-tinted because of its lead content; while the governor, to judge from his table, only drank from the finest crystal; and at more lowly houses, there was no glassware at all, but only pewter goblets. The 'inhabitants' of the houses will tell you exactly who used to live in them, from what part of France they came, their social standing, how many children they spawned, the occupations they pursued. This is not a fictional planting of ghosts, but historical data that emerged from exhaustive documentary study.

Those who supervised the rebuilding of Louisburg had an understanding not only of the niceties of historical reconstruction but a recognition that the energies of even the most enthralled tourist are limited. And so there are, along almost every street, houses that have an eighteenth century exterior but a decidedly twentieth century interior, containing exhibits and displays (including original watercolours of the eighteenth century settlement) and, most considerately of all, small lounges where foot-weary visitors can put their feet up for ten minutes while leafing through books and magazines.

As I was strolling back towards the drawbridge, I saw a squad of scruffy soldiers stomping along in front of me. They marched towards the cannon mounted on a small demi-bastion that juts into the sea near the entrance to the fortress. These guns are fired twice a day, and I stayed to watch. Under the eye of their lieutenant, the soldiers rammed the powder down the cannon and then touched the trailing fuse with a lighted taper. Nothing happened. Six times they attempted to ignite the fuse, and five times they stood there shrugging their shoulders. Eventually, after about ten minutes, the soldiers blocked their ears and there was a boom which seemed to throw a punch at my chest as a 26-pound cannonball was lobbed out to sea.

No wonder the French lost Louisburg.

During the ride back to Sydney my taxi driver muttered sourly about the new Conservative government in Ottawa, though he conceded that the Liberals had run up huge deficits: 'The Liberals were $34 billion in the red. That's a lot of hay.'

The driver was in the mood for money, for we were only hours away from the lottery draw. Most provincial governments encourage their citizens to squander their hard-earned money by gambling away a portion of it each week or month. Whenever a draw failed to produce a winner, the jackpot was increased, and that night it stood at the handsome sum of $15.6 million. Did the driver have a ticket? Yes, he did, and more than one. And what, I asked him, would he do if he won?

'I'd get a new roof on the house, and new siding, you should see the old one we got, I'd make sure my kids were secure, not give them a fortune but make sure they'd never go without, and I'd give some money to Israel.' Israel? I glanced at the driver. It did indeed seem I'd chanced upon one of the few local residents who was not only not of Scottish descent, but Jewish to boot. But he hadn't finished with his list. 'And I'd take this job, and I'd shove it up their ass. Sideways.'

The sun was shining on Sydney as it had shone on Louisburg, so I asked the driver to drop me off not at my hotel but at Wentworth Park, an agreeable patch of grass and water not far from downtown. As I put my feet up on a bench and opened a book, I heard the strident wails of car horns being elbowed, a sound that heralds the passage of a wedding party. The cars pulled up along the opposite side of the small lake, and I hurried over to pay my respects. Legs swathed in pink chiffon swung out from the back seats of cars as a platoon of young women in full-length gowns sought to make graceful exits from Hyundais and Mazdas. There were six or more, all identically dressed in ripples of pink. They were aided to a vertical position by young men in white tails, white shoes, and shiny cummerbunds. What was going on? Was this a group wedding to be refereed by the Bhagwan Shree Rajneesh or Reverend Sun Myung Moon? 'Are you *all* getting married today?' I asked them. No, no, they assured me. Only one of them was the bride, the rest were bridesmaids. And with that the Cartlands-in-waiting scurried down the path to the water's edge, where a photographer stood ready to capture the fleeting moment for ever.

As I stood watching this pretty sight, I heard in the distance the blaring of more horns, and minutes later another motorcade rounded the bend and came to a halt. This time the brides were in pale blue chiffon, with matching bands around their white hats; their menfolk wore grey suits and cummerbunds and were being throttled by wing collars. This second wedding party had successfully upstaged the first by tying a beribboned facsimile of a multi-tiered wedding cake to the roof of the leading car. The gals in blue now trooped down to the lake, where a second photographer was on duty. I had by now abandoned the first party for the new arrivals, who clearly came from a higher stratum of local society than the others. The paterfamilias bore a strong resemblance to Sam the Eagle, and standing alongside him was Aunt Darleen, dressed in the uniform of what a seven-year-old friend of mine habitually calls the Starvation Army; Darleen was as stout as the unexpurgated Hymns Ancient and Modern.

Just as the flashbulbs began to fly, wedding party No. 3 pulled up (pink again for the ladies, but black tuxedos and pink ties and cummerbunds for the fellas), followed minutes later by No. 4. This last bunch was my favourite. The girls were in yellow, an original choice, and their smiling escorts wore ties and cummerbunds that were either yellow or a daring tartan of yellow, black, and red; this, they insisted to me, represented Clan Macleod. I have tactfully remained silent about the three preceding brides, but No. 4 was genuinely pretty, and so were her svelte bridesmaids, who were stylishly dressed in gowns that didn't look like rejects from an origami class. The side was let down, however, by Aunt Beryl, who was squat, which no one can hold against her, and who chose – and this we must hold her responsible for – to wear a powder blue tunic miniskirt; she was also the only relative on display that afternoon – and it seemed that all Sydney was on view – to wear a matching sweatband through her hair.

It had been Barbara Crosbie who had remarked to me that the prevailing view of Cape Bretoners was that they are 'Newfoundlanders with their brains blown out', and I was beginning to understand what she meant. I tiptoed away from this orgy of commemoration that would fill the photographers' windows of Sydney for weeks to come. That evening there was a mighty

35

thunderstorm – a cosmic rebuke to the sun for daring to shine earlier that day – and as I sat in my hotel room watching on TV the racing results in French, I mused that the huge slaps of noise were amplifications of sundering hymens in motel rooms all around Sydney. Either that, or a round of applause, echoing my own, for the good people of Sydney who had so charmingly honoured my visit to their struggling community by sacrificing so many of their choicest virgins on the same day.

3

Loyalist Smokes

It was tempting to stay in Nova Scotia all summer long, since the season is regarded as an extended ceilidh. On George Street in Sydney I found the headquarters of the Gaelic Society of Cape Breton, and it's said that there are more Gaelic speakers here than in Scotland. The range of festivities was overwhelming. There was the annual Scotsburn porkchop barbecue accompanied by a pipe band, and New Glasgow's Festival of the Tartans, with Highland dancing and piping and drumming, and Chester's Municipal Old Home Week. If I lingered for just one more week I could attend the orgiastic Pioneer Participation Days at New Ross, with its luridly advertised 'hands-on activities of pioneer origin for the entire family'.

Instead I moved east and north into New Brunswick. I had a train reservation for early on Sunday morning, and presented myself well in time at Sydney station. The train had arrived, but Via Rail officials were busily herding passengers away from it and into a waiting bus. Explanations were garbled, but it gradually became clear that there was a shortage of carriages, and passengers going to Truro and beyond were required to take a bus instead. I was quite pleased about this. I had wanted to drive the Cabot Trail, a panoramic road that follows the rugged northern Cape Breton coastline for 185 miles, but weather forecasts had been gloomy and I saw little point in repeating some of my Newfoundland experiences of motoring for hours through mist and rain. The road to Truro passed just south of the Cabot Trail, and I hoped for glimpses of the coastline.

Not so some of the other passengers. One especially irate gentleman announced that he refused to travel by bus, which he loathed. This didn't bother the rail officials, who doubtless felt that if he chose to spend the rest of the day waiting for a non-existent train to Truro he was at liberty to do so. It was a lovely journey; the sun actually shone. West of Sydney the road takes a leap over the Great Bras d'Or, a fjord that burrows inland to a large lake. We passed Baddeck, where Alexander Graham Bell once lived, and then came to Whycocomagh, which, Googoo's Micmac Basket Shop reminded us, is on an Indian reservation. As we sped through these little towns, I couldn't help feeling I was journeying down a checklist. This was to prove the most intractable aspect of my visit to Canada. Even in the Maritimes, which compared to western and northern Canada are densely inhabited, a flying visit was an exercise in frustration. A Cape Breton fishing village is a way of life, a confrontation with the elements, not a tourist attraction.

The bus shuddered through the quiet Sunday streets of Truro and parked along the very platform of the railway station, compounding Via Rail's humiliation by arriving there well before the scheduled though non-existent train. The sun was shining merrily, so while my fellow passengers crowded into the waiting room and fed the Coke machine, I perched on a luggage trolley on the platform and ate an excellent lunch of bread and cheese and some sturdy Hungarian wine I'd unearthed in Sydney. The connecting train arrived on schedule and I settled in to a window seat and let the landscape roll by. Strawberry farms gave way to endless spruce forests, and at some point we slipped across the border into New Brunswick. Gradually the vegetation began to change again. Deciduous trees waved a paler green among the sombre spruce, and occasional meadows and farmhouses broke through the woodlands. The timing of our arrival in Saint John couldn't have been bettered. Twice a day the muscled waters from the Bay of Fundy rush up the Saint John River, which, of course, is attempting to flow into the bay. The tide wins, and the result is the aquatic mayhem of the 'reversing falls', which I was able to glimpse as the train trundled across the bridge. There wasn't time to leave the train and dart into town to buy a bagful of dulce, a brown stringy seaweed that is a speciality of New Brunswick. It wasn't until I arrived in Ottawa months later that an acquaintance gave me the opportunity to taste some. It was even more revolting, more salty and chewy than any maritime horror devised by the Japanese.

It was thoroughly dark by the time the train reached the provincial capital of Fredericton. Strictly speaking, it didn't reach Fredericton at all, for the station is twenty miles outside the town. Fortunately a bone-shaking bus was there to meet the train and convey a handful of passengers into the town.

New Brunswick is the most genteel of the Maritime provinces. It was the destination for 14,000 Empire Loyalists who fled the rebellious United States in 1783. There were to be times during my visit when it seemed that the battles of two centuries ago were still being fought. Unlike the other Maritime provinces, New Brunswick has a substantial French contingent; about one third of the population of 700,000 is, to use the jargon term employed throughout Canada, Francophone. All transactions made under the aegis of the federal government may be conducted in either of the two official Canadian languages, English or French. In a post office or Air Canada office or law court, for instance, service must be provided in both languages. The provinces, however, have greater freedom to make their own rules as to which language or languages should be employed. Québec, notoriously, enacted Bill 101 after the Parti Québécois won power in 1976; that law not only makes French the official language of the province, but, in the early stages of the legislation, prohibited advertising in English within the province. New Brunswick, however, is the only Canadian province that is officially bilingual, an admirable development. For it seemed absurd that the presence within a single great country of two major linguistic groups should be a source of strife, rather than a resource to be treasured. New Brunswick, where admittedly the two linguistic groups are more evenly balanced than in any other province, has taken this positive step to encourage both languages, and hence both cultures, to flourish side by side.

The other great resource of New Brunswick is the presence (from time to time) of Richard Hatfield, who has been its premier for over fifteen years. Because of the federal structure of Canada, each province has its own miniature parliamentary democracy, complete with a legislative assembly, and a government led by a prime minister, though the term premier is more commonly used. Provincial premiers are powerful figures in their own right. The political sport of the provinces is to defame the federal government in Ottawa, which is always perceived as encroaching on provincial powers enshrined in the articles of Confederation. As in the United States, where 'states' rights' are often at loggerheads with federal powers, there is continuous argument about where the boundaries lie between the jurisdictions of each governmental authority. Canadian provinces have greater autonomy than the states south of the border, if only because Confederation has given the provinces ownership of their natural resources, and hence an economic power that can be considerable indeed.

New Brunswick, with an economy based on farming and lumber and fishing rather than large-scale manufacturing or mining or oil, has little clout within the federal system. Premier Hatfield has, however, done all any one man could do to prevent his province from being ignored. A bachelor of taste and style, he has long been known for his somewhat cavalier approach to his duties. A fondness for lengthy visits to European capitals and other playgrounds far from his own shores has long been noted. The story goes that when Hatfield was asked how he would explain to his constituents why he so rarely favoured them with his presence, he replied: 'I was elected to run New Brunswick. No one said I had to *live* there.'

The controversy surrounding Premier Hatfield has, however, less to do with his prime ministerial style than with his personal habits. While he was accompanying Her Majesty the Queen on a leg of a state visit, the Royal Canadian Mounted Police unexpectedly discovered in his baggage a small quantity of marijuana. This, instead of delighting the Canadian people, shocked them profoundly. To think that one of their leaders might be up to the same hanky-panky as millions of other Canadians! Hatfield stoutly denied that he indulged in the weed, insisted that the incriminating smokes had been planted, and intimated that some members of the police force were out to get him. The matter was put in the hands of the legal authorities, and in January 1985 Richard Hatfield was tried and acquitted.

But the fun wasn't over. Early in 1985 two youths revealed to reporters that back in 1981 Richard Hatfield had invited some students back to his house after attending a party. Then, alleged the youths, the premier of New Brunswick offered his guests some choice cocaine. For many weeks Hatfield refused to make any comment on this story, presumably thinking that to do so would dignify it with the ontological possibility of its being true. Inevitably such haughty silence was increasingly regarded as somehow incriminating, and eventually he denied the whole story with the utmost vehemence.

It was a tricky issue. A man who frequented Truman Capote's lively parties on Long Island was certainly vulnerable to attacks of this kind. Hatfield stuck to his guns, but his troubles were not over. His difficulties were compounded by questions about his large expenses claims and the disclosure that he used a government plane to fly to Toronto to consult his lawyers. He was regarded more and more as a political liability, and was under pressure, even from his own party, to resign. Shortly after my arrival in Fredericton, Richard Hatfield was scheduled to go into a political huddle with his 'caucus', his fellow Tories in the legislative assembly. The meeting, to be held over three days in a remote logging camp deep in the New Brunswick forests, was unlikely to be particularly relaxing for Hatfield, so I decided to contact him as soon as possible.

Once I had installed myself at the Elms Tourist Home, I dug out my address book and scribbled down the phone numbers I needed. It was 10.30 on a Sunday night, but it seemed unlikely that the fun-loving premier would have donned his nightcap by now. After only a few rings, a voice answered, a female voice. I was taken aback. Had I stumbled across some fresh turpitude?

'May I speak to Mr Hatfield?'

'Mr Hatfield?'

'Mr Richard Hatfield? This is the premier's residence?'

'No, it is not,' replied a very firm voice. 'What made you suppose it was?'

'I was given his number in London, but clearly it's the wrong number. I am very sorry to have disturbed you at this late hour.'

'That's quite all right. You'll find Mr Hatfield's number in the phone directory. And if you can't reach him, you can always leave a note at his residence, which is quite close to Waterloo Row.'

'You've been most kind. Thank you again.'

The correct number was indeed in the phone book, but there was no reply. I decided to contact another citizen of Fredericton. Miss Louise Hill was, I'd been told, a pillar of the community, the former librarian to the legislative assembly, the daughter of a general, and, like many Frederictonians, a staunch Empire Loyalist.

'May I speak to Miss Hill?'

'This is Miss Hill.'

There was something familiar about that voice. Then I realized I was speaking to the same lady whom I had suspected of larking about with Mr Hatfield. I had inadvertently scribbled down the same number twice. She was extremely gracious about the matter despite the late hour, even amused at having been mistaken for a playmate of the premier's. She was, after all, in her mid-eighties. She invited me to tea the next day.

Fredericton has found the perfect formula for gentility. There is no industry to speak of in this capital, and there is none of the maritime clutter of grimy Saint John further down the river. The capital is the home of the legislature, of a university founded in 1785, a school of forestry, and an army garrison. Here Julia Beckwith wrote the first Canadian novel, *St Ursula's Convent*. And here Oscar Wilde lectured to the citizenry in the Opera House kernelled within the City Hall. Nowadays Fredericton is home to brigades of civil servants, relatively well paid and used to the comforts of life. The town makes the most of its river front, while the broad residential streets saunter inland, allowing ample space in which to display the splendid elm trees for which Fredericton is deservedly famous. The citizens of this stylish little capital are understandably vexed by the claim to superiority staked by Saint John on the grounds that the first Loyalist families to arrive in the province settled there and only came upriver to Fredericton in search of greater safety. Saint John is the larger town, but Fredericton is the provincial capital, which settles the matter.

As in every city hall of substance in Canada, local art is well represented in the council chamber – in this instance by ghastly tapestries that honour Fredericton's two hundredth birthday. They were interpreted for me by an extremely pretty girl dressed, for some reason, as Marie Antoinette. Her silks and brocades, she told me, weighed a ton, and tiny pearls of sweat glistened on her tall neck. The tour was given, of course, in both official languages, and her soft English sentences were followed immediately by her own translations into what could only with charity be called French. The Francophones in my party kept turning to each other in puzzlement as Marie Antoinette garbled yet another sentence. Over at the well-preserved Military Compound near the river, there was no such problem, as the only visitors were — wait for it – Anglophone. I was intrigued to learn that during the last century wives had lived in the same barrack dormitory as the soldiers, up to sixteen to a room. If a soldier died, his widow had to marry another soldier within twenty-four hours or face eviction. This seemed to establish many a precedent for wacky behaviour, and it helped to be able to place Richard Hatfield in this historical context. Beneath the cell block a trapdoor concealed a seven-foot-deep chamber known as the Black Hole, no doubt used to dispose of recalcitrant brides.

Fredericton is celebrated for its Victorian architecture. There's certainly no shortage of it, but it is nearly all hideous. The town is at least coherent, and has been left relatively unspoiled. Its pomposities, as well as its charms, are intact. I was impressed, however, by Wilmot United Church, a startling white Gothic edifice enlivened with black trim, while the piers inside are painted baby blue and brown. The church steeple originally consisted of a wooden hand pointing upwards to the heavens, but the structure became unsound; it was taken down and is now displayed in the church hall. These signposts to the hereafter are not uncommon in Canada, and there's another famous example in the Newfoundland outport of Twillingate. Further along Queen Street a Victorian mansion has been transformed into the National Exhibition Centre, and upstairs I found the local Sports Hall of Fame (Temple de Renommé Sportif). Loyalist sentiments were manifested throughout the town. Near the Legislative Assembly Building a tree has been planted by the Imperial Order of the Daughters of Empire, and an old people's home in town is run by the International Order of the King's Daughters and Sons, which makes it the world's most exclusive geriatric ward. Many shop windows displayed Union Jacks propped up against a portrait of the Queen, as though she were running for mayor that year.

Almost as well known as Richard Hatfield and the Queen is local lad Max Beaverbrook, who inflicted the *Daily Express* on the British public for decades. He never forgot his native town, though, and innumerable public buildings, including the principal hotel and the art gallery, bear his name. From a statue in Officers Square his unlovely features survey the town like an animated raisin. Beyond the art gallery, which contains many good English canvases as well as the world's largest collection of Cornelius Krieghoff paintings, stands Christ Church Cathedral. Presided over by Archbishop Nutter, Christ Church claims to be the 'first entirely new' cathedral foundation in British North America, whatever that means. The present structure was completed in 1853 and bears a remarkable resemblance to Snettisham church in Norfolk; and so it should, for it was modelled on Snettisham. Separated from their native towns by thousands of miles, settlers clearly felt urged to replicate at least their names – Stratford, London, Kensington – and sometimes their architecture.

Shortly before lunchtime I returned to the Elms Tourist Home. There was, as I had come to expect in such establishments, a directive pinned up in each room. 'It is a home away from home,' it began promisingly, but then the tone became more menacing: ' . . . a place that guests may like or dislike but should not try to change' – as though guests had to be deterred from their customary urges to rearrange the furniture and uproot the herbaceous borders. A more ominous pronouncement followed: 'ATTENTION. This is not a licensed establishment. Any tangible evidence of an alcoholic beverage and the guest will be asked to leave immediately.' I have to come clean about this: I still had an ample supply of Hungarian red, not to mention a hip flask of Scotch for those difficult moments when the morale needs particular encouragement. Evidence there was, and since the bottles were actually on top of my dressing table, it was undeniably tangible. I addressed myself to the problem by diminishing it, and poured myself a glass of the red. At that moment my landlady, who had a good prose style if a mean-minded temperament, knocked on my door.

'It's nearly lunchtime, Mr Brook, and I'd like to do your room.'

'I'll be out in two minutes.' I was in imminent danger of being flung out onto the street. I could hide the bottles, but two glasses were polluted by grape and malt and there was no sink in my room. Cautiously, I opened the door. Carry Nation had retreated downstairs. A swift reconnaissance established that the doors to some other rooms had been left open, pending occupation by fresh tenants. I tucked bottles and glasses under my arm and sped into a neighbouring room, where I deposited them under the bed; at the same time I cunningly substituted the clean glasses from the empty room for those I had concealed. The switch completed, I ambled down the stairs and informed Cotton Mather that she was welcome to do her worst. Although I was taking a modest pleasure in this farcical duplicity, it still seemed a silly way for a partly grown man to have to behave merely to preserve his right to enjoy an aperitif. I recalled that William Gass, in his book *On Being Blue*, records the following curse: 'May your cock continue life as a Canadian.' It had always baffled me until I came to Fredericton. Now it was beginning to make sense.

I walked back into town to take tea with Miss Hill. Waterloo Row follows the curve of the Saint John River. Every few minutes a jogger would totter along the paths that line the landscaped riverbank overlooked by the large indifferent houses. I soon came to Miss Hill's, which, while commodious, was less palatial than many of its neighbours, and rang the bell. After a short pause the door slowly opened and I found myself staring into a front parlour. Was the door being opened by an invisible hand? I looked down and about a foot below my chin I saw some strands of grey hair.

Not an aged poodle, but my hostess, who was bent almost double by some arthritic ailment. This made the initial social niceties more of a hurdle than usual, but some pleasantries about cocaine cleared the air as she waved me in. As she installed herself in a chair I noticed how her deformed body fitted the angular form of the furniture perfectly, so that when seated Miss Hill gave the appearance of being bolt upright and unimpaired by any rigidity of the joints.

While she busied herself in the kitchen preparing our tea, I took the opportunity to snoop. The house's woeful gloominess was enclosed and intensified by sombre panelling. Miss Hill had already spoken to me of 'Daddy' – General Hill to you and me – and his portraits were everywhere; on a landing a glass case exhibited his medals. His name recurred frequently in her conversation; she was devoted to his memory, which she guarded fiercely.

The second passion of her life was equally well displayed. A small pile of large books pressed down on a coffee table; from the cover of each beamed the familiar features of various stars of the current production of the British Royal Family. Back issues of a magazine called *Monarchy Canada* lay flung on a desk. In Fredericton the Loyalists are still loyal. Many decades ago, Miss Hill found herself rowing across a lake in the company of a military acquaintance of her father's. The officer made an ungallant reference to King George III, alluding, it is said, to his affliction with syphilis; Miss Hill responded by whacking the officer with an oar. Fearful of a similar fate, I resolved to be respectful.

'Didn't the Queen visit Fredericton not too long ago?' I asked politely, feigning interest.

'Yes, indeed. And more recently Prince Andrew was here. I organized a tea party here on Waterloo Row and just before he was due to drive by we all gathered on the porch. But all we saw was a black limousine moving at high speed, and half an hour later the same black limousine came in the opposite direction, again at high speed. But never mind. We had a delicious tea. I regret to say I had no greater success when the Queen was here. Together with some of my United Empire Loyalist friends, I stood on the street waving my Union Jack, but Her Majesty was looking the other way when her car drove past. Of course I was invited to the official luncheon – delicious food – but as you can tell, my eyes aren't what they used to be, and from the distance I mistook the Queen for Richard Hatfield's niece.'

This was my cue to change the subject. What did she think of the Premier's alleged activities? Did she think it likely that he smoked marijuana?

'Well, my dear, I really couldn't say, but it would certainly explain some of his recent speeches.'

I had only intended to stay for half an hour or so, not wishing to tire the old lady, but she had other plans. She thought it would be useful for me to meet an economic development officer for New Brunswick, and so had invited him and his family to join us at five o'clock. We would then have high tea. The Price family arrived punctually, and the tea tray was replaced by old crystal and a bottle of Dubonnet, which we all polished off. At about six o'clock we sat down to eat.

Miss Hill pushed a loaded plate towards me. 'Have some of my bread. I baked it yesterday. It contains no milk, no eggs, no butter, no nice things at all. Doctor's orders. It's all nonsense, of course.'

I mentioned that I hadn't heard much French spoken in the streets of Fredericton; it still seemed very much a town of British descendants. That, I was told, is because most of the French-speaking Acadians live further north. Acadians had been the original settlers in this area in the 1680s and again in the 1730s; they had been expelled by the British in 1759, though many returned thirty years later. People who don't live in the province often assume that the Acadians and the Québeckers are the same people, but they have little in common: they come from a different part of France and speak different dialects, and their histories within Canada are distinct.

'Acadians were farmers,' explained Miss Hill, 'ill educated, square pegs in round holes.' She must have caught my look of surprise in hearing this slightly patronizing definition, for she continued: 'But so were we all. Why else come to live in north America? There had to be something wrong with you – usually your religion or your politics. The Loyalists and the Acadians have always got on well together in New Brunswick. Until recently, that is, when the Québec people came in and stirred things up.'

'Come, come, Louise,' murmured Mrs Price, but Miss Hill was not to be stopped.

'And then Trudeau foisted that metric business on us, and the French language.'

Mrs Price changed the subject. It happened that both ladies were active members of the local historical society. Indeed, Miss Hill was the author of an important study of old Fredericton. She and Mrs Price were soon arguing about where the very first legislative assemblies had taken place when the town was founded. Miss Hill had demonstrated, nay proved, that the prevailing theories were wrong, and that documentary evidence had been misinterpreted. While we, her audience, munched carrot cake and sipped our tea, she regaled us with the story of how she had come across yellowing pages that established – and so forth. Her frame may have been crippled, but her mind wasn't, and she lectured us with admirable ferocity and erudition. Unwilling to interrupt the oration, Mrs Price slid a hand across the table and reached for the tea pot.

' . . . that foolish article is entirely wrong since the inn could never have been used for such a purpose before 1790 . . .' Out of the corner of her eye she spotted Mrs Price's manoeuvre, but didn't even pause for breath: ' . . . oh, thank you for pouring, my dear. I have to talk.'

The next day I travelled up the lovely valley of the broad Saint John River. Every village seemed to contain an equal number of houses and churches, whether United, Baptist, or Anglican, and all these structures were much the same size. Wooded slopes dipped down to the river banks, and flower-filled meadows shone as brightly as the flowing water. At Hartland we passed but did not cross the world's longest covered bridge; almost 400 yards long, it is far more spectacular than anything along these lines found in New England. In front of some of the houses in these small prosperous villages fluttered Union Jacks. Though a commonplace sight in this part of New Brunswick, it still struck me as odd. It was touching that British descendants, who were inspired to come here because of their loyalty to the Crown (and their detestation of a fledgling democracy in the Thirteen Colonies), were keen to recall their roots. But had I been a non-British Canadian – such as one of the third of the population of New Brunswick of French descent – I might have felt offended at seeing the flag of another nation flying in almost every village. It seemed a startling case of arrested political development to have failed, even after two centuries, to adopt the flag of the nation one inhabits, although it is true that the Union Jack used to be the flag of Canada too. I was beginning to understand how it might be possible for many Canadians not to feel at home within their own country.

Later that afternoon I arrived in Edmundston. No Union Jacks here. This is an Acadian town, kept alive if malodorous by the presence of large paper and pulp mills. For 85 percent of the inhabitants, French-Canadian is the language, as exemplified by the following shop sign: *Finition de Vos Photos en 1 Hr.* Local whimsy has it that Edmundston is the capital of the fictitious Republic of Madawaska, which is inhabited by a people known as Brayons. I had arrived here during the annual Fête des Brayons, which proved a desultory affair. The festival was featuring local and Québécois musical groups, as well as l'Orchestre Bavarois Hans Stumpf and Marie-Lise et Les Country Boys. Posters announced the imminent Plus Beau Bébé Brayon contest and a pool tournament. I was keen to join in the festivities, but the principal attraction that evening was a dance for the over-fifties. Everybody must have been at home fastening their corsets before the dance, for loudspeakers attached to lampposts blared such *chansons* as 'Leader of the Pack', 'Peggy Sue', and 'Tutti Frutti' into streets that were almost entirely deserted.

The whole town, and its absurd festival, was clearly a fraud, an elaborate movie set for a surrealist screenplay, *L'Année Dernière à Edmundston*, and before I could be hired as an extra I eagerly boarded the bus to Québec.

Part Three

Quebec

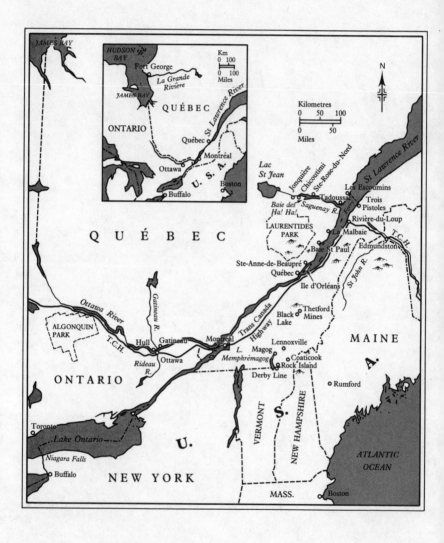

4

Unconsummated Divorce

When, fifteen years ago, I lived in Boston, I would occasionally drive up through Maine to Québec City for a long weekend. Boston was a congenial city but an American one, and I missed Europe. I missed the texture of old stone and the scrawled *plat du jour* on a menu, and I could find both of those in Québec. On returning to the city after a long absence my former affection welled up once again. Not that Québec is an especially attractive city, despite its splendid site high over the St Lawrence River. With its grey stone and raucous climate, it reminds me of Old Aberdeen – only physically, I hasten to add, for the atmosphere of Québec City is almost hedonistic, and no one could say that about Aberdeen. Within its partially reconstructed walls, the old city covers a small area, and the bulk of the municipality spreads out through a string of modern suburbs such as Ste Foy.

Québec City is no Paris, and that is its very charm. It is unequivocally provincial. With its ancient university, its churches and convents, its hotels and restaurants, it is urban, but not cosmopolitan. It is, however, European, with that density of habitation that packs together public buildings and churches, boutiques and convents, into a thickly jumbled profusion of squares and streets, alleys and terraces. To me the appeal of Québec City lies less in its superficial picturesque quality than in its austerity, and I dislike many of the attempts now being made to prettify the old town: the quaint signs, the colourful windowboxes, the heightening of antique architectural features. Streets such as St Anne that cater to the tourists – and admittedly do it well – are not half as expressive as, say, rue Sainte Famille. This lane descends a hill and is flanked on the right by a harsh authoritarian building that is part of Laval University. The structure is relatively recent – it dates from 1920 – but its uncompromising, unlovely bulk is closer to the grim Jansenist spirit of the town than the ardent but obsequious crowd-pleasing of many of the main streets. At the foot of rue Sainte Famille stands a row of cottages dating from the 1750s that bring some modest charm to the austere street. More characteristic of Québec as a whole are the tall stone townhouses, entered through raised doorways so that the ground-floor windows are often just above snooping level. On rue St Louis most tourists walk straight past the fine Maison Maillou, for with its navy blue shutters set against rough grey stone walls, the house does not call attention to itself, but it is very French and very handsome. The townhouse interiors are guarded not only by stern doorways, but by shutters that fold over double glazing that shields a layer of starched lace curtains. Block-faced old women still lift a corner of those curtains to peer out at the weather. This is a city of exteriors; the houses are not welcoming but excluding.

An ecclesiastical atmosphere permeates the city like incense, for although the Catholic Church has lost its former stranglehold, the old town still seems packed with nuns. The ancient seminary is as severe as the houses, though the bright whitewashed walls around the courtyard modify an austerity that would be oppressive were it not for the wealth of details that have accrued over the centuries. Most visitors rightly admire the great panoramas from the terraces overlooking the river and from the ancient citadel, but they are not what makes the town unique. Québec, unlike a modern city, exalts the idiosyncratic. A chimneystack or a doorway or a previously unnoticed alley keeps one's interest alive, and though the city is small, it never seems to pall. There are still quiet spots frequented only by cats and tourists who have put the guidebooks away and allowed themselves to stray. At the end of rue Mont Carmel, for instance, is a small park, scarcely more than a garden, but the view is fine and the mood sombre but tranquil, in contrast to its aura three centuries ago when a windmill supported a three-gun battery. The old fortifications of the city, which date from the late seventeenth century, have been more or less rebuilt, and it's possible to walk their length for about three miles.

The churches in this very ecclesiastical city are resplendent. The Anglican cathedral of 1804 has a magnificent interior, complete with box pews and wooden gallery; its broad but shallow apse is, like any English church of the same vintage, lined with memorial tablets. A few streets away stands, in complete contrast, Notre Dame de Québec. There has been a church on this site since the 1640s, though the present structure dates from 1925. The conservative citizens didn't adopt a modern idiom when the church was rebuilt, and the interior is resolutely baroque, with voluptuous gilt furnishings. Another rebuilt church is the equally sumptuous chapel of the Ursuline convent, adorned with a pulpit and reredos in luxurious black, white and gold. An elaborate screen divides the nuns' choir from the public area of the chapel. More grilles – how rigidly the laity was kept at bay! – fence off the founder's burial chapel. This is a historical spot, for Montcalm is buried here, and a notice sternly informs visitors, 'RESPECTUOUS CLOTHES REQUIRED'. Another contrast to Catholic elaboration is provided at St Andrew's Church of 1810, the oldest Presbyterian church in Canada, though the country has certainly made up for lost time since. Here, in contrast with the more stratified disposition of the Anglican Cathedral, an appropriately nonconformist note is sounded by having the pews curved so that the entire congregation can face the elevated pulpit behind the altar.

The provincial motto is *Je me souviens* (I remember), though a translation of 'I haven't forgotten' catches the hint of aggrieved menace I always detect in the words. Ironically, the motto was taken from a Loyalist poem. History was not kind to the people of Québec. The Frenchman Champlain was astute enough to nail this site as a future colonial centre in 1608, and the settlement grew rapidly. Bishop Laval, after whom the university is named, arrived in 1659 and initiated the unremitting ecclesiastical control that strangled Québec for three centuries. When, during the eighteenth century, Britain and France began to battle it out for control of the strategically crucial river, it was inevitable that Québec City would be much fought over. The decisive encounter took place in 1759. The British general James Wolfe began to besiege the city in July. Late on 12 September the British forces crept up on to the Plains of Abraham, the broady grassy plateau adjoining the present-day citadel. The following day the French commander Montcalm led his troops into battle against the encroaching besiegers. For Wolfe as well as Montcalm it was a fatal encounter, and the outcome was a rout of the French forces. This was the end of New France, and the beginning of the French-Canadian mentality enshrined in the motto *Je me souviens*.

Although the battle heralded the beginning of the end of French rule, it certainly wasn't the end of French influence. To this day Québec City remains resolutely French in language and culture. Its half million inhabitants are, unlike the population of Montréal, overwhelmingly of French descent. As Montréal became increasingly important as a cultural and commercial centre within Canada, the influence of Québec City began to diminish. Montréal had to participate, at least commercially, in the life of the rest of North America, leaving Québec free to retreat into the certainties of French-Canadian culture, an ethos dominated by the Church. As recently as thirty years ago the province was, notoriously, a society ruled by demagogues in league with the power of the Church; the *curé* and the *notaire*, as the only educated citizens of innumerable small towns and villages, exercised a powerful, and usually reactionary, influence. Education rarely proved intellectually liberating, since it reiterated the largely authoritarian values current when the province was originally colonized. In the 1960s, with what became known as the Quiet Revolution, these traditional cultural arbiters rapidly lost influence, and within a decade or so Québec had become more outward-looking, more sophisticated, more liberal. The schools and universities no longer supplied a constant stream of small-town priests, doctors and lawyers, but began to educate scientists and engineers as well. Churchgoing is no longer ubiquitous, and, most astonishing of all, the birthrate is decreasing for the first time. The Quiet Revolution also brought political changes. The province gained the confidence to assert its identity within the larger Canadian confederation, even though it chose to do so by insisting on the irreconcilable differences between its culture and that of the predominantly English culture that enveloped it. Political separatism gathered force and in 1968 the Parti Québécois was founded. Just eight years later, to the astonishment not only of the rest of Canada but of the Parti's own leaders, it was elected into office, and for nine years the province was ruled by a party that officially espoused separatism.

Some would argue that it's a sign of the PQ's triumph that sovereignty is no longer considered important among French Québécois. In office, the PQ leader René Lévesque diluted the principle of separatism to the less clearly defined one of 'sovereignty-association', and his successor in 1985, Pierre-Marc Johnson, was even less convincing in his allegiance to the once cardinal principle of separatism. Sovereignty-association was always a mystifying concept, since it proposed an autonomous nation that freely delegated some of its powers to another nation. As Graham Fraser summarized Lévesque's position in his book on the PQ: 'He was proposing a country that would have a seat at the

54

United Nations – but not its own money; would collect all its own taxes, but not be able to control interest rates; pass all its own laws, but be unable to control the foreign-exchange value of the dollar.' Or in the cogent words of a joke doing the rounds in the late 1970s: 'Quebeckers want an independent Quebec – in a strong Canada.' Mordecai Richler has made the same point more wittily: 'They wanted out of this marriage of convenience that is called Canada. Mind you, they wanted out with a favorable property settlement. A little understanding, a lot of alimony.' Still, the electorate seemed content to have a government moving in a vaguely defined direction even though its ultimate destination was uncertain. Nine years in power came to an end in December 1985, when the Liberals swamped the PQ in the provincial elections, and no fewer than eighteen ministers lost their seats, as did, with delicious irony, the Liberal leader Robert Bourassa.

Québécois worry about their identity almost as much as other Canadians do, though with less justification. French Canada is instantly identifiable as a place apart. Glancing through the visitors' book at Louisburg, I easily identified the French-Canadian signatories, because their handwriting differs from that of their British-Canadian compatriots. It would surely be impossible to distinguish between the handwriting of Americans or Germans from different parts of their respective countries, but here in Canada this minor cultural indicator signified the almost total cultural separation of French Canadians. There are other such indicators. French Canadians seem, and I say this on the basis of observations in crowded cafés rather than on statistical evidence, to be far heavier smokers than their compatriots outside the province. René Lévesque, himself a chain smoker, seems to epitomize the Québécois male. In France the president, whether the patrician Giscard or the high-minded socialist Mitterand, invariably projects an air of superiority, as though, for his period of office, he represents France itself. Lévesque is short, dishevelled, a tribune of the people rather than a patrician; he could have walked straight off the set of an old René Clair film. Consciously or not, he represents a France that no longer exists. But this exaggeratedly Gallic type, downtrodden but feisty, still exists in Québec, and if he doesn't, people would like him to. It is striking that the flag of Québec incorporates four *fleurs-du-lis*. Ah very French, you think, until you recall that the *fleur-du-lis* is a symbol of a royalist France that has been defunct for almost two centuries, despite the occasional Napoleonic intervention. (British Canada's parallel anachronism is the annual observance of Queen Victoria's birthday on 24 May, decades after Britain has forgotten all about it.) Québec, then, is French, but it is not France; it is Canadian, but it is not Canada.

The events that brought about the downfall of French Québec are most easily recalled at the citadel, positioned on a formidably fortified hill on the edge of the old town. The ramparts that surround it include outer walls spacious enough to enclose a tennis court. Before touring the citadel, which was built in the 1820s and is still in use, visitors are compelled to attend the Changing of the Guard. The soldiers' uniforms are essentially British in design: red coats and bearskin hats. But all commands are issued in French, which I found culturally dislocating. An excellent band wandered about the parade ground, and the pounding of the drums and the growl of the brass reverberated thunderously off the barrack walls. One soldier gripped a leash attached to a goat with gilded horns, and at various times during the long ceremony, the goat was tugged around the parade ground and, despite the splendour of its outfit, did not seem to be enjoying itself. How unsoldierly these French-Canadians were! While at ease, they grinned and smirked, mostly in the direction of teenage girls in tight shorts. The drills were of a high standard, but there was no sense of military preparedness, and without any doubt a platoon of halberdiers could have taken the citadel that morning with a minimum of casualties. Myself, I'd have had that guard changed and back at work in half the time. Almost without exception, the soldiers were moustachioed. Moustaches are common in Québec, even among men, but here they seemed almost part of the uniform. When I questioned a soldier about this urgent matter, he confirmed my observation but couldn't explain it. During the tedious moments on the parade ground, I could at least admire the views: of the Château Frontenac, which like most buildings named Château in Canada turns out to be a luxurious Canadian Pacific hotel, and, in another direction, of the typically undistinguished Hilton tower. The best view of all unfurls itself from the Prince of Wales bastion, which overlooks the St Lawrence and the Plains of Abraham, now a park.

Back in the city, the most popular panorama is enjoyed from the Terrasse Dufferin, a boardwalk that carpets the clifftop in front of the Château Frontenac. The spot is overlooked by a statue of Champlain, who is depicted as stamping his foot with impatience

('Merde! Vaincu encore'), though more probably he was just feeling the cold. While the bulky Frontenac looks splendid from a distance, a closer view reveals it as pastiche, and brings into focus the dull caramel brick of which it is built. Steep flights of steps lead down from the Terrasse to the lower town, for old Québec thrived at two levels, the lower of which huddles around the port. During the nineteenth century the Lower Town, which architecturally must have equalled the Upper, became a slum. In recent years it has been renovated at a cost of over $30 million. Without the efforts of the restorers, there's little doubt that the entire area would have been razed and replaced by container warehouses and car parks, so it seems churlish to carp at what has been done here. But I'll carp anyway, for the restoration struck me as extreme, and lacking in the sensitivity displayed at Louisburg. In the Lower Town features not deemed 'authentic' – post seventeenth and eighteenth century, in other words – were simply removed. Extra storeys built on to older houses in later decades were dismantled, and new 'authentic' roofs have taken their place. Brand-new dormer windows and rearranged fenestration contort the ramshackle old structures into pattern-book shape. Old buildings and their accretions eventually become stylistically coherent, with occasional exceptions. By ignoring this principle, the restorers of the Lower Town have preserved the letter and throttled the spirit. As a tourist attraction it works well, for some of the old mansions have been converted into excellent small museums; and the Place Royale, the ancient square surrounded by former merchants' houses in the heart of the Lower Town and the very spot where in 1608 Champlain founded French North America, is always crowded. Notre Dame des Victoires, founded here in 1688 and rebuilt in the same style in 1759, is the most charming of Québec's churches, with its cream and gold interior and the castlelike construction of the High Altar. By wandering down some of less tampered-with streets, such as rue St Pierre and rue St Paul, towards the Vieux Port, I filtered through my mind a better sense of what the old Lower Town must have been like, say, a century ago. The old houses along these streets have been less fanatically restored than those around the Place Royale. Small restaurants, chic and high-priced, as well as design and crafts boutiques, keep the lights burning, more, I suspect, in anticipation of a steady influx of lucre than in response to a present demand. Even more off the tourist beat are the streets beyond the fortifications that slope down to the Lower Town. Here, along Olivier, Richelieu and

D'Aiguillon are tucked-in houses and artisans' cottages, vestiges of old Québec that lie midway between the walled city and the sprawling suburbs.

Québec reserves its greatest charm for night-time. The terraces of cafés and bars are crowded with people sipping an aperitif or a brandy. The vigorous rooflines of Château Frontenac and some of the large public buildings are floodlit. Down in the Lower Town a string quartet had found a vacant corner and was sending a divertimento by Mozart spinning into the night. In the Upper Town, near the central Place d'Armes, musicians – playing a mouth organ, a variety of banjo, and a clackety castanet tapped against the thigh – sang out fast and lively Québécois songs, and passersby joined in the choruses. In front of the musicians an old man, his white hair spilling out from beneath a well-chewed panama, danced a stately jig. From the Terrasse Dufferin, the lights of the town of Levis, on the opposite bank of the St Lawrence, twinkled brightly, and I could see the fat little ferry chugging its way across the river.

After that steady diet of cod and chips in the Maritimes, the cuisine could only improve. In Québec, however, even the restaurants that trawl for tourists are good, and the inexpensive set lunch at Aux Vieux Canadiens, a charming cottage dating from 1677 in the centre of town, included cabbage soup, *darne de saumon en cidre*, and maple sugar cake. Soups – of leek and barley and pea – were good everywhere, and so was the fish. To some tastes, Québecois cooking, which often relies on thick soups, meat pies, and maple sugar desserts, is oppressively heavy, but I enjoyed it. I've enjoyed it even more in winter, when the cold stimulates a craving for dishes that provide nourishment rather than finesse. Not that Québec City is the place to find good regional cooking. Apart from Aux Vieux Canadiens and a handful of other similar restaurants, most establishments offer more classical French cooking, as well as the usual profusion of pizzas and kebabs. To find authentic Québecois cooking, not to mention authentic Québecois, I was directed towards the hinterland.

5

Frrwe

Although soutanes rarely swish through the streets of Québec City any longer, the Catholic message is still proclaimed loud and clear at Ste Anne-de-Beaupré, a neo-Romanesque basilica about fifteen miles downstream from the city. It's a building of enormous confidence, raised on a commanding scale, its height and breadth plastered with mosaics and galleries. The faithful stuff their petitions into boxes for forwarding to the saint, but are spared the trouble of lighting drippy wax candles; those at the basilica are oil-fed. An even more impressive manifestation of the Church in the age of cost-benefit analysis is the presence within the basilica of a pier encircled by a dozen or so statues of Ste Anne, thus enabling as many devout as there are statues to make their supplications simultaneously.

The immense shrine was built in the early 1930s to replace a more modest pilgrimage church when the crowds, who have been flocking here since the seventeenth century, grew too great to be accommodated. The old church can still be visited, and nearby a reproduction of the Santa Scala in Rome has been constructed. I saw two ladies arrive, rosaries a-jingle, and begin their ascent together on their knees. The lady in the purple was definitely moving at a faster pace, and I wondered whether greater devotion was shown by taking the stairs slowly, so as to maximize the discomfort, or whether a brisk climb showed an even more commendable fervour. Below the Santa Scala is the Grotte de l'Agonie – yes, more agony – with hideous statuary forming the appropriate gut-wrenching tableaux. A day at Ste Anne-de-Beaupré can be a day out for all the family, for adjoining the mighty basilica is a museum, a seminary, a cyclorama (whatever that is), and a shop peddling religious souvenirs. These are reasonably salubrious manifestations of religious enthusiasm, but a more bizarre instance of old-style Catholic looniness was being enacted on the streets of Montréal, where two brothers called Blondin were on the fiftieth day of a hunger strike designed to induce the Pope to reveal the third secret disclosed to three Portuguese children at Fatima by the Virgin Mary in 1917. And at Ste-Marthe-sur-le-Lac, 6000 worshippers, including many terminally ill people, would shortly be gazing at a statute of the Virgin whose eyes were said to drip blood. They were not rewarded with the incarnadine flow, for, according to the statue's owner, Jean-Guy Beauregard, it only weeps when he's alone with it.

Leaving the supplicants to get on with their beseechings, I backtracked to the Montmorency Falls, a wall of water that tumbles from high cliffs down to the river. The Québécois quite rightly point out that these falls, 274 feet high, clock up 80 feet more than the market leader at Niagara, and are the highest in eastern Canada. A nearby bridge vaults the St Lawrence and lands on the Ile d'Orléans. I first came to the island fifteen years ago and instantly succumbed to its charm. The shape of a plump reefer, the island is about eighteen miles long; at its widest, about three miles across. It too was originally settled in the seventeenth century, and though little remains from that time, the island still has, in many places, an essentially eighteenth-century appearance. It is my practice, on occasion, to use outdated guidebooks when I'm sightseeing. The contrast between the up-to-date evidence of my eyes and the printed descriptions of a half-century ago can be stimulating. Or not, as the case may be. This habit of mine is an exercise in the history of taste, an excuse to grieve for the ravages of time, and, to be sure, an affectation. When I first came to the Ile d'Orléans in 1971, I used an excellent guidebook dating from the 1930s. It mentioned the excellent local cheese. In the village of St Pierre, according to the guidebook, stands a red and white farmhouse where the farmer's wife occasionally sells some of her fine cheeses. I found the house without difficulty, the door was opened by the lady described in her youth thirty-five years earlier, and she took me down to the cellars and showed me a small stacked pile of yellow cheeses. I bought one. When ripened and ready to eat two months later, it proved quite delicious.

Fifteen years later it seemed unlikely that I could pull the same trick again. An old man was digging in the vegetable garden along one side of the house, and I approached him. Alas, he told me, his wife had died some years ago, and though he still very occasionally made the cheese I recalled, he had none available at the moment. As we talked, I looked past his stubbly cheeks towards the mainland. The garden sloped towards the river, and there was a view onto the gentle hills of the north shore. It was not dramatic, but it was wonderfully harmonious: layers of landscape sandwiched between sky and river, and illuminated by the morning sunshine.

Before leaving St Pierre I went to look at the church. Its austere stone exterior of 1720 didn't prepare me for the refinements within. The lovely cream and gold interior, furnished with box pews and gilt altars, is in a neo-classical style, adorned with pilasters and cartouches more appropriate for a ballroom. For some reason the village authorities have decided to enhance the beauty of the church by installing a video box that blares into the echoing space. I found all six island churches worth a visit. That at Ste Famille is a mid-eighteenth century building with a decorative scheme similar to that of St Pierre, only grander, with pot-bellied side galleries and a two-storeyed west gallery. More recent alterations show a lapse in taste and sensitivity, for the bad large paintings on the walls sprawl coarsely against the elegance of the earlier decorations. The size and opulence of these churches reflect the settled affluence of the island, as does the domestic architecture. The Ile d'Orléans is dotted with farmhouses similar to the one where I'd called earlier in the day. They are simple white buildings, often high-roofed and trimmed with scarlet or green paint; alongside them stand large dignified barns painted to the same scheme. Some of the old manors, including one built in 1680, have been converted into restaurants. So has the lovely Moulin de St Laurent, an old water mill of 1635; here the menu features *escalope de veau au kiwi* and minstrels entertain the diners who drive out from the city. Near the pretty village of St Jean stands the Manoir Mauvide of 1734, imposing in its relation to the other more modest houses of the village, yet still restrained and provincial in its Norman design, with plain shuttered windows and a tall roof. The front wall, facing the river, still bears the dents of British cannonballs fired during the siege of 1759.

From St Jean a gravel road crosses the island to Ste Famille through a rippling deck of orchards, fields and copses, past banks of wild flowers and rushes and cows dreaming in the meadows. This is fertile land, and although working farmers are gradually being replaced by retired couples and second-home owners from the cities, you can still buy local strawberries, raspberries, and maple sugar products from roadside stands. Until 1935 the island was accessible only by water, but the bridge inevitably kicked it into the twentieth century. These changes were noticeable to me even after an absence of fifteen years. There are more new houses, and the old manors and barns are now flourishing businesses, restaurants or art galleries. It was summer now, of course, and the islanders, cashing in on the considerable tourist trade, were at their most demonstrative. Fifteen years ago I had been here in the depth of winter, when the doors were closed and the manors shuttered behind snowbanks, and nothing was stirring. While the lovely island was still delighting me now, it had moved me then, and it no longer did.

I returned to the mainland and crossed the Laurentides Park, 5600 square miles of heavily wooded hills and lakes. I soon wearied of ridge after ridge of conifers. Where Québec City and the Ile d'Orléans had beguiled me with the density of their habitation, their human scale – localities you could rummage around in – the Laurentides seemed a bland emptiness in which humans, unless in pursuit of fish and game, had little place. I drove off the main road to a small lake, one of 1500 in the park, where I picnicked. At the water's edge tadpoles flipflopped through the shallows, and the lake was fringed by clumps of marigolds and daisies, and I was plagued by small acupuncturing bugs.

I stopped at Chicoutimi, close to Lac St Jean, because this part of the province is almost entirely French; the English language is not a useful skill around the shores of Lac St Jean. Of the seventeenth-century trading post and the settlement founded on its site by Peter Macleod in 1842 in defiance of the Hudson's Bay Company monopoly, nothing survives. The only old part of Chicoutimi is around the harbour, and that's scheduled to be torn down. A new commercial harbour is being built a few miles downstream; the present harbour will be restricted to pleasure craft in the future, and the old docks will become a park.

I spent half a day with a former CBC journalist, a native of the town. There was nothing about Chicoutimi that Robert didn't admire and love. He showed me its schools, its parks and bridges, the newspaper offices and CBC studios, the disused paper mill that was being converted into an exhibition hall and theatre, the sites of yet unbuilt offices. The region derives its prosperity from the three large aluminium plants that employ 8000 people. The plant at Jonquière, a few miles west of Chicoutimi, was built in 1928, and no fewer than fifty smokestacks snub the surrounding forests as they clamber into the sky. It looked more like the Ruhr valley than rural Québec. It won't be there much longer, for there are plans to replace it with a modern plant at Chicoutimi that won't assert its function so forcefully. Industrialization at Lac St Jean has been facilitated by the deep ship channel gouged by the Saguenay River; near its banks stand paper mills, a large military base, a Union Carbide plant (which must do wonders for the residents' peace of mind), and two power stations.

We dined at a pleasant downtown restaurant, so I could sample more Québécois cooking in the form of pea soup, which many English Canadians dismiss with ignorant derision, *chaussons au boeuf* (a kind of meat pasty), and rich *tarte au sucre blanc*. Over our meal, we talked about Québec's controversial language law, commonly known as Bill 101. While the federal government, under Trudeau, and New Brunswick, alone among the provinces, had moved towards official bilingualism, the PQ walked the opposite way. It enacted legislation declaring French the official language of the province; henceforth all official and commercial transactions would have to be conducted in French and only in French. Bilingualism was the highway to assimilation and thus to the eventual destruction of French Canadian culture. In some instances this law was taken to extremes, and some shop signs not in French resulted in prosecutions. A 'Merry Christmas' sign in a Hull jewellery shop nearly landed the owner with a $1000 fine. A centuries-old injustice was being replaced by a brand-new variant. The law required companies with over fifty employees to conduct all their internal communications in French, even when all fifty were Anglophone. Bill 101 set in motion the 'francization' of all topographical names. Only when the repatriation of Canada's constitution from Britain by Trudeau led to the adoption of a nationwide Charter of Rights in November 1981 were some of the provisions of Bill 101 superseded by federal law. To the polyglot residents of some of the Montréal inner suburbs, where groceries are bought in Greek or Portuguese more often than either French or English, Bill 101 was an absurdity. It also occurred to immigrants that the displacement of English would negate the reasons why they emigrated in the first place. They hadn't come to Canada to exchange one provincialism for another, and wanted their children to grow up speaking English. This was close to the central objection to Bill 101: Québec was not, and never would be, an independent nation, and to pull the English tongue out by the roots would merely further the cultural and economic isolation of an already marginal corner of the world. Paranoia had become enshrined in law.

Robert defended the law. 'Anglos in Québec have rights that no French Canadians outside this province have. Go to Ontario and see what rights the hundreds of thousands of Francophones there have to speak their own language and maintain their own culture!' This was true. Ontario had never made any significant concessions to its numerous French-speaking inhabitants. If Francophones in Ontario were required to conform to the majority culture, then it was not unreasonable for the less than 20% of the population of Québec that was not Francophone to come to terms with the fact that they were, linguistically, in a minority, though they had been behaving for decades as though it weren't so. Tales are legion of Montréalers going into shops and offices in the city where they were born, and being refused service if they couldn't speak English. Top positions in Montréal law firms and corporations were out of bounds to all but a handful of French Canadians. Bill 101 was a reaction to centuries of cultural humiliation at the hands of a powerful minority. Even so, Anglophones who move to Québec are entitled to send their children to schools where English is the first language – though this does not apply to the children of immigrants whose first language was not English.

'Let me tell you a story,' continued Robert. 'I was out with the CBC in Alberta, and one evening I ran into a friend from Québec. We went off for a meal, and naturally we spoke French together. A woman came over to us from another table and said to us: "When you're here, you talk white, you understand?" "What is white, madame?" I asked her. "English, of course." "In that case, madame, I speak super-white – because I at least have the intelligence to have learnt two languages while you can only manage one."'

Exactly how Bill 101 would put a stop to such humiliations never became clear to me. In my experience, the law itself encouraged retaliatory idiocies. As I was riding the night bus from New Brunswick to Québec City, the driver made some announcements in French that I couldn't follow. I dozed off, only to be shaken awake by the driver at 2 a.m. at Rivière-du-Loup. In acceptable English he told me he would not be stopping in Québec City after all and I should change buses immediately. Fortunately he'd remembered that I was going to Québec City, otherwise I would have ended up somewhere else at dawn. The problem could have been averted had he made his announcements in both languages, as is the practice on the federally run trains and ferries.

It wasn't that the bus driver couldn't speak English; it's that he decided not to, which, under Québec law, he was perfectly entitled to do. But it seemed, to say the least, a daft way to provide a bus service.

I always spoke French in Québec; the hard part was understanding what was being said in reply. Québecois French bears the same relation to Parisian French that scrambled eggs have to raw ones. The vocabulary differs too in innumerable ways. The Québécois say *breuvage*, where the French would say *boisson*, and *tabagie* instead of *tabac*. The accent supposedly derives from Normandy and Brittany, from which most Québécois emigrated centuries ago, though to my ears the flattened vowels more closely resemble the dialects of the Midi. *Flan* is pronounced *fla'*, and *froid* emerges as *frrwe*. Under such circumstances, it is surely reasonable for bus carriers, whose customers inevitably include people from outside the province, to make sure important announcements (such as 'We've changed our mind – this bus isn't going where you think – change at the next stop') are understood. (In Anthony Burgess's *Earthly Powers*, the narrator attends a film festival: 'Next morning we watched the Quebec entry, *Et Patati et Patata*. The French jurors protested that they could understand neither the Canadian French dialogue nor the English subtitles. I raged at them and said: Christ, it's only eighteenth-century Norman.')

Yet it is not hard to understand Québécois hostility to the English language. There has been a sizeable Anglophone community in Québec, especially in Montréal, for centuries, and large segments of that community never troubled to learn the language spoken by 80% of the people, and, as mentioned earlier, would routinely refuse to communicate with French Canadians who failed to speak English. Some days later in Montréal, I got to know a young banker, who in background and upbringing was typical of well-heeled Anglophone Québec. Yet he defended Bill 101, pointing out that if 20% of the inhabitants refused to learn the language spoken by 80% of the population, they should go and live somewhere else – as, indeed, many had done. He himself was fluent in both languages, and had no sympathy for smug Anglophone parents who kept their children ignorant of French. Now, indeed, it had become *de rigueur* in sophisticated circles to be bilingual, and parents in Toronto and even Vancouver, thousands of miles from the nearest acute accent, told me they send their children to French schools. One of Shannie Duff's daughters had also spoken fluent French, even though you're as likely to hear Russian as French spoken in the streets of St John's.

The next morning, a beautiful warm Sunday, I took a cruise down the Saguenay River in the *Marjolaine II*. With the exception of three women from Toronto and Halifax who had come up for the weekend from Québec City, where they were taking a French 'immersion course' at Laval, the forty other passengers were all French Canadian. The men were mostly of squarish build, like Viking chessmen; their lined and weathered faces, which were also shaped like fists, shifted cautiously beneath brushes of close-cropped grey hair. The French Canadian women of Montréal are the best dressed in Canada, but their sartorial influence hadn't reached Lac St Jean, and most of the women on board were as alluring as nylon sheets. A ten-year-old girl with pretty features and buck teeth was clearly retarded, and her communications were restricted to repetitions of 'Papa!' and randomly timed high-pitched yeeps. One of the crew, a burly factotum with a large round face that beamed with good nature, removed a ship's badge from his lapel and pinned it to the girl's, and her pleasure was warm and instantaneous for a few moments until her mind walked off the edge once again.

From the water downtown Chicoutimi was strikingly ugly. Its older buildings resembled those of most early twentieth century American cities – square crewcut brick boxes, unrelated to each other, commercial blocks hard to distinguish from residential ones. There were no leaps of roofline or variations in colouring, let alone any notion that the placing of parts affects the perception of the whole. The view was redeemed, as so often in Québec towns, by the towers of the cathedral and the abundance of trees. The boat moved slowly downstream over water that was brown-black and so placid that only the broad wake of the boat disturbed the smoothness by rippling it into a supple plasticity that churned the reflected sky into an impression of shattering glass. We passed the broad Baie des Ha! Ha! where ships dock to serve the nearby aluminium and paper mills.

We approached Cap Trinité, an immense granite cliff that rises 1400 feet in three tiers, from one of which a large statue of the Madonna, placed here in 1881, gazes out over the river. The *Marjolaine* cut its motor and over the loudspeaker came the melody of Gounod's 'Ave Maria'. Nobody sank to their knees in adoration, but we all stood uneasily on deck until the sickly sweet music played itself out. Fortunately there was no religious statuary on top of Cap Eternité, which is even taller than its neighbour. Glaciers had carved the immensely deep Saguenay fjord – almost a thousand feet deep in places – between these mighty granite walls for about a hundred miles, though few spots were as dramatic as these. At Baie Eternité the *Marjolaine* turned and chugged back fifteen miles to the hamlet of Ste Rose-du-Nord, a much touted beauty spot. Its riverside setting tucked between wooded hills is certainly attractive, but few details grabbed one's attention. The small Musée de la Nature was clearly an expensive waste of time, an attempt by local landlords to empty tourists' pockets of spare change, and the church is blandly modern; its furnishings made from heavily varnished driftwood showed a striking idea being ineptly executed. To appreciate fully the wonders of the twenty houses of Ste Rose, the cruise managers had allotted us two hours. I selected a hummock and read a book, then boarded a school bus that transported us back to Chicoutimi so bumpily it could have untied shoelaces without human intervention. I recovered my car and drove down the north bank of the Saguenay, along a road lined with pink willow herb, past sheltered lakes and pummelling rivers, to Tadoussac, where the Saguenay debouches into the St Lawrence. Beautifully situated, the village is dominated by the marina and the long low-slung resort hotel. Near the water stands another building that claims to be the oldest of its kind in North America, in this case the oldest wooden chapel, which opened for business in 1747. It's a charming red-roofed and wood-panelled building, very small, with a chandelier shaped like an inverted daddy-long-legs. Old missals are displayed in a glass case together with an image of Christ in his crib labelled 'Holly Child Lodging'.

An evening prowl took me past the Café des Fjords, a small restaurant with a large terrace. It was crowded, which was encouraging, and I was drawn in immediately by the sign *Fruits de mer à volonté*. After a mere *tarte au bleuets* for lunch, I was hungry and took generous samples from this buffet, which included soup, piles of lobster claws, greenery, fruit salad, apple tart, coffee. I spent the next two hours sitting out on the terrace sucking lobster meat from the spines. Small children were kept amused by a bubble machine that sent a steady stream of soapy bubbles wafting through the air, older ones poked at an open-air pool table, and the bearded *patron* whizzed about in a wheelchair as if it were a Harley Davidson, and chatted to his customers. After a short walk I returned to my hotel, where I spent the night being gently roasted, since my room was directly above the kitchens, and the window couldn't be opened more than an inch.

The broad green waters of the St Lawrence are crammed with algae and plankton and shrimps. Gourmet whales scorn plump ocean fish and instead flock here to scoop up great mouthfuls of the dandruff-sized stuff, and in the summer boats laden with tourists cruise out into the estuary to watch them at it. Beluga whales makes their most southerly appearance here. At the turn of the century there were an estimated 5000 of them in this area, but now only about 350 remain, and ecologists suspect that although beluga are a protected species, they are in danger of eventual extinction in the St Lawrence if the Saguenay River isn't cleaned up soon. The Alcan aluminium smelter at Jonquière is suspected of being the primary source of pollutants that poison a dozen or more whales each year. Fin whales, the second largest whales in the world, weighing in at between forty and sixty tons, and reaching seventy feet in length, also feed here, as do a few other species.

The next morning I walked to the quayside to board the *Lachance III*, a very flashy boat especially equipped for whale watching. It lunged towards the estuary and after about fifteen minutes some warm sunshine was unplugged as we hit banks of mist. The water grew choppy. A few miles from shore, the captain cut the engines and implored us to be utterly silent. Moments later a minke whale, long and black, came looping through the water, soon followed by a white beluga threading its way more playfully. Many of the tourists on board were more than casual sightseers, for they came equipped not only with multi-lensed cameras but with libraries of books about cetaceans. People compared notes on their luck in spotting the rarer species, and the guide said it had been four years since she had last seen a humpback whale in the St Lawrence. Blue whales had also been sighted. With my first glimpse of a minke, I had a conversion experience and the connoisseurship of my fellow passengers no longer seemed pretentious. The whales mesmerized me with their combination of size and grace. How elegantly these vast animals loped and looped through the dark green water! Is it too much to ask for human beings to forgo killing and eating creatures so refined and paradoxical in their nature? I suppose it is.

The boat chugged on for a while, until the captain cut the motor once again. The fog had thickened, and as the boat rocked in the damp chill silence, we leaned far over the rail and peered into the grey. Nothing. For minutes we stood silent and motionless. Then through the misty dankness came the most extraordinary sounds:

the peep-peep of belugas, the brief spouting of a minke, and longer harsher exhalations that turned out to be the blowing of two fin whales. It was maddening to know that these two mighty whales were within yards of the boat – not a common occurrence – and yet not visible to us. The smaller whales, the beluga and minke, came into view and began to tease us by swimming right up to the side of the boat, then plunging before surfacing again in an unexpected spot. They did this repeatedly, as though they knew we were trying to observe them and had resolved to indulge us and frustrate us at the same time. The fin whales continued to taunt us from behind the curtain of fog, swishing and rasping as they blew and blew.

Because the fog had blindfolded us, the captain offered all passengers a free trip on a future excursion. When at the quayside I attempted to take advantage of this kind offer, I discovered the afternoon cruises were fully booked, so that was that. Still, I was hooked. I wanted another crack at whale-watching – not to mention another crack at the seafood *à volonté* at the Café des Fjords that evening. I picnicked in a cemetery – always ideal for al fresco lunches. One is rarely disturbed – zombies don't go for cheese and fruit – and there are plenty of surfaces on which to prop victuals and glasses. After lunch I drove past the tall Tadoussac sand dunes and through a pretty landscape of lakes and farms to Les Escoumins. Here a ferry crosses to Trois Pistoles. Whales, surely, were just as likely to oblige the passengers on an inexpensive ferry as on a high-priced cruise. The fog had now cleared and I had a fine view of the river and of the charming little town of Trois Pistoles, with its pastel-coloured houses on stilts along the shore. As before, I saw dozens of belugas and a few minkes, but no larger whales. Three belugas came romping up to the boat, twisting and turning through the waves, and just as it seemed they were about to biff their snouts, they would plunge and surface a hundred yards on the other side.

It was back to the Café des Fjords for more claw-chewing that evening, and after a stroll down to the marina, I returned to my hotel, where I'd switched rooms. It made no difference. It was just as hot and airless. Moreover, the youth of Tadoussac chose the car park beneath my window as their social club. Their cheerful voices didn't disturb me as much as the constant revving of their mopeds. Eventually they dispersed to go and do their homework or rob a gas station, and their low-keyed racket was replaced by the roaring of the bus engines and air-conditioning systems, for the car park also served as the town bus station. At midnight the bus roared off to wake the dead of another village, and now the only sounds to vex me emanated from the television set turned up to maximum mindlessness in the nearby lounge. Personal investigation revealed a mound of fat disguised as a man drenched in beer – a self-inflicted shower, the empty cans surrounding him like a fairy ring suggested – who was dozing through a programme he wasn't watching. He protested not as I turned down the volume, since he was physically incapable of rising from his chair. I always sleep much better in cities than in the country. The country's so damn noisy.

6

Monsieur Tremblay, I Presume?

A century ago many prosperous North American industrialists and other rich folk fixed upon the county of Charlevoix as the landscape in which to fritter away their summers. Charlevoix, which stretches from the west bank of the Saguenay as far as Baie St Paul not far from Québec City, is a region of rolling hills and wooded headlands, of bays and coves, of farms and orchards. Logging, shipbuilding, and farming were once the principal occupations, and the settled quality of the landscape, partially cleared and inhabited since the early seventeenth century, is resplendent and satisfying. Sobering too, for almost everywhere the modest human intrusions are dwarfed by the grandeur of hills, forests, and the ocean-like river. The detail of the landscape is as beguiling as the sweep of it, well exemplified at Port-au-Persil, a hamlet tucked into the cleavage between very steep hills. It's a charming spot. Right by the water stand a small grey church and a handful of houses with verandahs on both floors; a knot of cows chomp away at a steep meadow, and the thickly wooded promontories on either side protect the village from the most inclement extremities of the weather. A stream rushes down a hillside and cascades into the sea, providing a focal point for the village as well as a gathering ground for children.

From the larger and more dispersed settlement of Cap-à-l'Aigle, there's a splendid view of La Malbaie, or Murray Bay, to give it its former name. The slopes around Malbaie – so named by Champlain when he ran aground here in 1608, suggesting he didn't much care for the spot – are speckled with the summer houses built here a century ago. From Cap-à-l'Aigle the headlands sweep around the bay. The novelist Laure Conan was born in Malbaie 140 years ago, and the local museum, stuffed with local handicrafts and rustic furnishings, is named after her. A more abysmal collection of badly made artifacts I have rarely seen. No doubt the crudity of the furnishings accurately mirrors the harshness of life on the farms of Charlevoix, but it almost seemed that poverty of

71

imagination, a lockjaw of the spirit, was being applauded here. The presentation of the displays suggested that visitors were to admire exhibits not just for their historical value but for their supposed merit. I recall particularly a grandfather clock made of a patchwork of woods and ineptly painted with a faded design. Why was the case made of a random collection of woods? Not, surely, because of a shortage of timber. Presumably, whoever made the object didn't give a damn what the end result looked like.

The contemporary handicrafts on view were, if anything, even more deplorable, because those who laboured so whimsically at fashioning them lacked the excuse of desperate poverty and cold fingers. Anno 1950 gave the world a cute carving of a little boy in a cap with a bunch of ducks. Bad enough, and worse that it should be rewarded with precious space in a museum. Far more interesting were two collections of photographs. Those by Jean Palardy dating from the 1930s depict a rural population remaining cheerful in the face of adversity, which mostly takes the form of snow. The other photographs, by an immigrant Hungarian, were taken forty years later, and show a stark landscape, hard peasant faces, and indications of an oppressive piety in the form of grossly overloaded altars crammed into corners of parlours. Palardy's images capture a culture secure in its shared values; the newcomer's eye was observing a culture in decay.

There was no permanent exhibition at the museum to suggest that Murray Bay was once among the most fashionable resorts in North America. Much of old Murray Bay is intact. Step outside and climb the hill. On either side of the Boulevard des Falaises that overlooks Malbaie are the summer houses of the rich. Given that these shores were frequented by the likes of American President Taft, I had expected to find houses on the scale of those at Newport, Rhode Island, where the so-called 'cottages' are palatial mansions, ostentatious pastiches of great European houses. Here above the St Lawrence, even the largest houses are built on a modest scale, roomy to be sure, but designed for comfort and relaxation rather than display. Their affectation is their self-conscious rusticity; large porches and steep gables and the use of gnarled logs as a building material indicate a longing for quaintness, for disorderly houses that resemble extended nurseries. Should you crave vulgar display, it is available in generous quantities a couple of miles away. The Manoir de Richelieu was built on a clifftop in 1899 (and rebuilt in 1928) – its name a further reminder that Québec still seems to yearn for the *ancien régime*, as though the province would like a King Louis of its own to counter the apparent omnipresence in Canada of the British Royal Family. The Manoir is an unashamedly grandiose resort hotel, a great grey pile surrounded by gardens and a golf course. It's a place for public vacationing, its atmosphere reminiscent of a British holiday camp. On the terrace overlooking the sea you may enjoy a preprandial drink served in a plastic cup and lunch may be taken in a cafeteria that offers such delicacies as *shortcake au banane*. The public rooms are imposing but are thoroughfares rather than corners of repose. You can take your children to the Manoir de Richelieu knowing that you can be sure of having them off your hands for hours at a time.

Despite the screech of its name, the next spot along the coast, Ste Irénée, is far more delectable, with its breezy open setting looking onto the usual wooded humps and scattered meadows. The road curls down to a long broad beach, which is unsavoury at low tide. Not that this matters much, since the water is too cold for most human beings to enjoy. There's a more secluded beach at Cape aux Oies, reached down a long steep dirt road. This beach is immense and, because of its relative isolation, uncrowded. With the wind romping through my hair I stood by the shore and looked out over the bleak broad rock-strewn mudflats. I grew more excited as I drove towards St Joseph-de-la-Rive, home of the Papeterie de St Gilles. Collectors of my work will no doubt be familiar with the articles I wrote twelve years ago on hand papermaking in the United States, a subject of absorbing interest to about four hundred people. Years ago in France I had chanced upon a crafts exhibition which included a demonstration of hand papermaking, and I astonished and delighted the crowd by rolling up my sleeves and producing a very creditable example of the papermaker's art. So I was looking forward to a fresh opportunity to show off at the only hand paper mill in Canada. Not a chance. As I walked in the door all I could hear was the thunder of cylinder presses. There was a papermaker at work, but in an inaccessible corner. In a display case were the products, certified as handmade, of the Papeterie – packets of six or eight sheets and envelopes priced absurdly at ten dollars. A couple of women sat in a corner, presumably counting their money. I wandered about, trying to look interested, but nobody paid me the slightest attention. Since I don't see the point of opening a workshop to the public if you aren't prepared to take any notice of the public, I walked out, noisily.

The Ile d'Orléans isn't the only large island plumped into the middle of the bottle-green St Lawrence. Near the artists' colony of Baie St Paul the Ile aux Coudres lies a mile or so offshore. Since there is no bridge linking mainland and island, I assumed, and was encouraged to do so by innumerable tourist brochures, that Coudres would be even more rooted in the past than Orléans. Not a bit of it. It was first discovered in 1535 by Cartier, who named the island after the hazelnut trees that proliferated here. One or two buildings survive from the seventeenth and eighteenth centuries, but the vast majority are less than a century old. The large church of St Pierre, in a debased neo-classical style, was built in 1885, and even the old 'historic' windmills, with one exception, date from the early years of this century. Unlike the Ile d'Orléans, Coudres is well stocked with resort hotels, and it was to one of these, La Roche Pleureuse, that I made my way at the close of the afternoon. None of these resort hotels is down on the beach – nobody is that anxious to swim in frigid waters off mudflats – and La Roche Pleureuse is situated among pleasant gardens on a hillock overlooking the river.

My fellow guests were entirely French Canadian. The food in the dining room that evening was hardly Québécois, but presented the usual hotel fare of simply prepared meat and fish. A waitress offered me the choice of entrecote, escalope, or poached salmon. Just as in Sydney, where I'd been served accessories, such as the salad and styrofoam rolls, that are standard dinner-table equipment throughout the United States, so here too, in the heart of French Canada, I was served a baked potato wrapped in silver foil. That's a perfect'y acceptable way to cook potatoes, but it can hardly compare with the French ways of preparing them. It was another reminder, however trivial in itself, that Québec is not France. Canadians commonly observe that the Québécois are more receptive to influence from the United States than are Anglophone Canadians. Because sharing a language actually invites cultural penetration from below the 49th parallel, many Anglophone Canadians are defensive about what they regard as infiltration by a noisy and overwhelming culture from the United States.

Québécois, on the other hand, can't even understand the TV programmes and paperback books that flood north into Canada, so they cannot feel threatened by them. Where Anglophone Canadians concern themselves, quite understandably, with 'Canadian content' in broadcasting and with the problems of foreign (i.e. US) ownership of a large part of the Canadian economy, for Québécois the problem scarcely arises. In Québec, Canadian content is achieved simply by using the French language. Consequently, French Canadians can and do help themselves without guilt to whichever features of US culture they fancy. This was to become particularly noticeable closer to the border, and also in Montréal, where the current fad was to drink a carbonized liquid that to most Americans, whose tastebuds are amputated at an early age, passes for beer: Budweiser. Since Canadian lager-style beers such as Labatts and Molson, though far from wonderful, are a distinct improvement over their US counterparts, this perverse preference can only be put down to fashion and the subtle cajoling of the advertising industry. It defies credibility to maintain that anyone in Québec drinks Budweiser because they like it better than their home-brewed products.

It was dark by the time I finished dinner. I took a walk through the gardens, where I encountered a floodlit shuffleboard. Enjoying the warm fresh evening air, I sat on a bench and watched. After a few minutes a man in a cloth cap came up and asked me to join his team. This wasn't chumminess on his part, but need; one of his team members had been called away. I thanked Monsieur Tremblay (I don't know whether that was his name, but almost everyone in Charlevoix is called Tremblay) but pointed out that I'd never played shuffleboard in my life, and would not be an ornament to his team. He seemed completely unconcerned by this and recruited me despite my protests. He needed an extra player and I was the only spare body in the vicinity. I soon got the hang of the game and thwacked the flat discs with fair accuracy. Who said that the French and the English don't get on? My prowess won me the fleeting admiration of my new-found mates. Just as I was finding my true form, they all decided the game was over and my career as international shuffleboard ace ended abruptly. I lingered outside for a few minutes longer until a plague of moths like animated confetti began to trouble me. But back at the hotel, fresh entertainments were on offer.

A lounge had been converted into a temporary ballroom. A band triple-timed the occasional waltz, but most of the dancing was performed in groups. I am a victim of my generation, for whom dancing is ideally a free-form wriggle adumbrating an anticipated sexual act. Group dances do not appeal to me, though on a number of Burns nights I have contributed, most elegantly, to a few whirls of Strip the Willow, which is a Scottish dance and not a card game. Here, on the Ile aux Coudres, the local equivalent was something called Le Canard, which had all the grace of the waddling bird it is named after. It was, I regret to say, a variant of the wretched hokey-cokey, and my growing affection for Québécois culture was replaced by dismay. Arms flapped, bottoms wiggled, throats yapped. Four white-haired ladies I'd earlier mistaken for oatmeal-reared Nova Scotians were happily dancing with each other. Were these the same people who have given the world the *fête champêtre*, the Tuileries Gardens, La Grande Jatte? The answer to this question is of course – no. The forefathers of these people had left France decades before any of the above-mentioned pleasures, now seen as so quintessentially French in their refinement, were invented. Yet it was clear that everyone, whatever their age, was having a whale of a time. I walked out onto the terrace. I was the outsider, snooping on packaged holidaymakers at their revels. They had not thought twice about counting me in on the shuffleboard track, and no doubt would have made me equally welcome on the dance floor. I didn't belong, of course, and my taste for adventure and novelty certainly didn't run to Le Canard.

It became apparent to me, and not for the last time, that I hadn't begun to get the measure of this country and its people. Physically, the land, so vast, so raw, is still wide open. Unlike much of the uninhabited open space of the United States, almost all unoccupied land in Canada is owned by the crown. As public rather than private land, it is theoretically accessible; unfenced, unmarked, unpossessed. Yet at the same time the societies that have developed on those lands seem closed and inward to an astonishing degree, whether in the singularly uniform human stock of Newfoundland, or the Gaelic communities of Cape Breton, or the French Canadian towns of Québec. What unifying consciousness could there be among peoples who lead such disparate lives? No answer leapt to mind beyond a recognition of the sheer distance that separated these groups. Instead, I was confronted by what seemed to be a paradox: vast open spaces that nurtured ultra-provincial societies.

The next morning I left for Baie St Paul. This summer the renowned artists' colony was attempting an intriguing experiment. Twelve young painters, not all from Québec, had been invited to share the town's hockey arena, temporarily converted into a gigantic studio. For one month the twelve artists would

76

work in public, and visitors were welcome to observe them. When I looked in, there were only three painters at work. Not at work, exactly, for one of them, Nicholas Pitre, was clad only in green shorts and was doing his morning exercises. While he toned his body I chatted to him, curious to know whether working in public exacerbated the artists' competitiveness. Fluency had little to do with ability, but in this public arena fluency and nonchalance seemed to have the psychological edge. He was blandly dismissive of my theory. 'We all accept we're doing different things. You'll find competition in the United States, not in Québec.'

This struck me as coy, as if he seriously expected me to believe that the meaner emotions somehow evaporated in French Canada. It was too early in this month of public painting to judge the quality of the painters' work, so I went to the public gallery next door to inspect what their predecessors had achieved. The overblown, overwrought paintings on view were discouraging. If there is no such thing as competitiveness in Québec, as Pitre had airily suggested, then there is less incentive to produce work of high and exacting quality. But then I hadn't believed him, and so one would have to advance another, less accommodating, theory to explain such proud mediocrity. So-called artists' colonies surely substitute for healthy competitiveness a common currency of complacency, an instant granting of artistic status by virtue of the artist's mere presence. I was glad to leave art and return to the original.

7

Along the Border

Fifteen years ago, when I first drove from New England to Québec City, I took the road through northern Maine into the southerly part of Québec known as the Eastern Townships. Large tracts of northern Maine were, and are, wilderness. Most of this land is owned by timber companies, and large areas of forest are inaccessible except along roads maintained by and for the use of those companies. I used to find it an uncomfortable landscape: those seemingly endless coniferous forests, with only occasional bald spots formed by lakes, ponds, and rivers. There were no towns, and few villages. In season hunters and fishermen unlock their camps and lakeside cottages, but in winter it was a desolate place. I assumed that Québec would be much the same, since I knew Canada to be more thickly forested and more thinly populated even than New England.

Soon after crossing the border I was astonished by the complete transformation of the landscape. Instead of rolling wooded hills, there was a broad river valley, thickly settled and intensely farmed. Every few miles along this valley of the Chaudière I would come to a small town grouped around a church. Not only was this pattern of settlement completely unexpected, but its social organization was quite different too. The villages of Maine dribble out along the road, haphazard, formless, with farm equipment dealers and gas stations mixed in among the houses and schools. Here in Québec, there was a European neatness to the villages, with the houses gathered tightly around the church, like piglets at teat. The tall churches formed the radiant nucleus of the village as their bright aluminium roofs and steeples caught the sun – when it shone – and glinted and flashed against the sky. The land had been occupied and settled as Maine had never been. I had taken long country walks in central Maine and frequently stumbled over the foundations of houses long decayed. Clearly there had been many areas of Maine where, in the last century, cultivation had been attempted and then abandoned. A farmer near Rumford once told me that as a boy he had known many farms along his valley; now his was the only one left. In the Chaudière valley, in contrast, much of the forest had been cleared and the silhouettes of tractors still glided along the crests of the hills. The fields flowed in strips down the hillsides so that each farmer could have access to the river. With light industry contributing its smokestacks and detritus to the landscape, the Chaudière valley was far from lovely, but it was a satisfying landscape precisely because it was so thoroughly settled. Wilderness makes me uncomfortable. I can marvel at it, but its defining emptiness unsettles me, and I prefer to see signs, however discreet, of human habitation and human care.

Now, fifteen years later, the valley seemed more industrialized than before, and the little towns and villages had grown and sprawled. The older houses still grabbed for the church in the old way, but on the fringes of each village were identical careless agglomerations of service shops, gas stations, workshops, each with their car park and storage lots. They were ugly in the American way; primacy had been given to the needs of cars and their users. A mid-twentieth century preoccupation had been imposed upon nineteenth-century settlements. The farms were still there, though, and the summery air was pungent with the rich ripe smell of fertilizer.

Other parts of the Townships are more heavily industrialized. It was here, indeed, that the mixed blessing of the snowmobile was invented. At Thetford Mines, to the west, is a lunar landscape of asbestos mines. The first mine opened in 1878; today there are five open pits and two that are underground. The open-pit mines are an extraordinary sight: some of them are miles across and, guarded by mountainous slag heaps, appear almost as deep as they are wide. Within the pits stand multi-storey buildings, puny beneath the broad grey cliffs of the mine. Near the settlement of Black Lake immense grey-green humps of tailings elbow the horizon out of the field of vision. The expanses look as drab and unproductive as a lava field, as though the subterranean asbestos had bubbled up and overflowed, covering fields and lakes with dense grey powder. This unprepossessing but vast natural resource used to be American-owned, which long irked the Parti Québécois, especially since almost the entire production was shipped abroad to be processed. After years of negotiation, the Québec government managed to acquire a major share in the ownership of the mines from the American General Dynamics Corporation.

This propaganda victory – restoring the control of natural resources to Canadians – was promptly rewarded by a worldwide slump in asbestos prices.

Meandering through this corner of the province, I couldn't help recalling some of my earlier visits, and I was suddenly overcome by the impulse to make the journey in reverse. I had once owned a farm in Maine. I hadn't laid eyes on the place since 1972 and wondered whether it was still standing. I pointed the car in the direction of the United States and put my foot down. As I sped through those dark depressing forests beyond the border, I saw a moose dipping its Bugatti nose into a lake. During the countless weekends I'd spent in Maine keeping an eye out for the wildlife, I had never laid eyes on a single moose. Now, on a lightning trip, I whizzed straight past one. Nature can be so irritating.

Shortly before dusk I came to West Peru. Down a pretty valley towards Mount Katahdin lay the property I had once owned. The boxy gabled farmhouse was still girdled by its rickety porch, and at least one of the huge barns was standing. Seated on the porch was a tall man with a ponytail. I parked the car and walked towards him. Hounds leapt towards me, but he called them off.

'You don't know me,' I began, 'but . . .'

'I know who you are,' he replied. 'I bought this house from you.'

Yes, it was the same aged hippie who'd bought the place thirteen years earlier. He invited me in to look round, but I declined. I didn't want to see the changes he had made.

I hadn't been a popular presence in the valley, and the house had been vandalized more than once. There'd been some understandable resentment of me as an outsider buying a second home. The valley was, if the truth be told, a rural slum, of the kind so common throughout the United States, where families live in conditions approaching squalor while surrounded by material goods. Many of my neighbours lived in houses scarcely better than shacks, but the rutted driveways were usually blocked by snowmobiles and cars. Many of these families were of French-Canadian origin, and some were first-generation immigrants. I wondered whether they ever regretted the move. Although I observed less squalor, or less visible squalor, now than fifteen years ago, much of the village, especially near my former farm, still looked like a rat's nest, and I hadn't seen anything this tawdry in Canada. Rural Canadians exhibit a British neatness of fences and flowerbeds; not for them the custom of living surrounded by your junk. I left West Peru with my fit of nostalgia satisfied. I had never belonged there and was right to have left when I did. I crossed back into Canada just south of Coaticook, where I found a motel that was more welcoming than the suspicious glances of my former neighbours.

This corner of the Eastern Townships has pockets of English settlement. Most Québécois of British descent who don't live in Montréal live around here. The small university town of Lennox-ville is conspicuously English, though it is now relegated to suburban status on the edge of French-Canadian Sherbrooke. I drove west to Magog, a resort on the northern shore of Lake Memphremagog, a snaking body of water that slithers south of the border into Vermont. The outskirts of Magog looked more like Los Angeles than Québec; every worst feature of American urban sprawl had been adopted but not adapted. Perhaps the Québécois, anxious not only to assert their independence but to show the world how confidently they could swagger towards the end of the twentieth century, had rushed to embrace the most unlovely values of modern America. No, that explanation struck me as too specious. More likely, the outskirts of Magog, like those of just about every large town in Canada, simply demonstrated how clinging has been the economic embrace of Canada by the United States.

Magog has a pleasant esplanade, where I sat for a while watching holidaymakers messing about in boats. Then I drove down the west shore to the monastery of St Benoit-au-Lac, a foundation celebrated not only for great monkish deeds but for its costly blue cheese. The stepped design of the thickly built monastic buildings suggested a joint Carolingian and Saxon inspiration. The interior, with its ungainly yellow bricks and multi-coloured tiles, was especially hideous. I hurried to the chapel to hear the Gregorian chant sung at Mass, but arrived just as it was ending. Keen to console the flesh for the sorrows of the spirit, I headed for the abbey shop to buy some of the famous cheese. A sign declared that it was closed from 11 until 2, which seemed decidedly eccentric. For a moment I thought I was back in England, where tourists are punished for venturing forth on a Sunday by finding that most pubs don't serve food on holidays.

Ambling down a long sombre corridor, I saw two visitors hurrying towards a tall monk. A middle-aged man in shorts asked the black-robed monk whether he would mind being photographed with his wife. Once outside St Peter's in Rome I had been exchanging theological conundrums with Cardinal Hume when a group of clerics and nuns rushed up to ask me to photograph them while they nudged the scarlet. This monk, however, was young and very giggly, and scarcely seemed quite in that league. Nevertheless he willingly agreed to this Japanese deviation, and the wee wife, who only came up to his waist, stationed herself beside the holy man and they both beamed. Deprived of my lunchtime cheese, I took myself off to Bolton Centre, shopped, then found the local cemetery, where I picnicked in the company of innumerable Clarks, Peabodys, and Longfellows.

On the opposite shore I visited Georgeville, an old Loyalist settlement that exhibited an enchanting dignity reminiscent of better known New England villages: stately white clapboard houses, built in the mid-nineteenth century and half concealed by rows of tall maples, faced each other across the one street. Only a house whimsically named 'The Wee Hoose' detracted from the dignity. A lane led down to the shore. From here I could glimpse the tower of St Benoit rising above the wooded slopes opposite. Children, spending the summer here, bathed from the jetties, while their older siblings raced about in small dinghies. In the window of the general store had been posted the day camp schedule, which effectively undermined whatever education the children had by then acquired. One notice offered 'Congradulations!' to participants in the Lake Swim; these felicitations even extended to Alan Gustafson, who only made it 'quarter of the way'. Despite his humiliation, Alan was still included on the 'trip to monastry'.

I drove south until I came to Beebe Plain. Its museum contained the usual collections of textiles, furnishings, and old spectacles, but also a remarkable number of top hats, a wedding gown of 1951, and a mould of J. D. McFayden's hand. Artless old photographs gave an impression of social life in the village almost a century ago. A few miles further on I came to the border town of Rock Island where I decided to waste the time of the editor of the *Stanstead Journal*, a weekly published here since 1845. I asked her whether many of the English-speaking residents of the Townships had moved out over the last ten years. She told me that many had left in 1976, but not just English-speaking residents. 'It was a case of bad government, not French government,' she added. The demographic balance hadn't changed much in recent years, and the two communities were equally represented in the Townships. She demonstrated for me the accents of that other prominent local

community, the United States, to show how distinct the Townships accent is from that of Vermont, even though the two groups
enjoy close proximity and frequent contact. As a rather forceful
gesture of good will, a local worthy had long ago built the town
library so that the building actually straddles the border. A line
across the floor marks the boundary, and it is also visible on the
floor above, which contains a most delightful 400-seat opera
house, a replica of an old Boston theatre. In the summer plays are
still performed here. The library itself is used by both communities, Rock Island and Derby Line, Vermont. A civilized place, its
periodicals room is furnished with wicker armchairs and a sofa, of
which I took advantage.

The next day I went to see the novelist Mordecai Richler, whose
summer house overlooks Lake Memphremagog. Loud classical
music was booming out from the windows, so my progress up the
driveway was not heard by my host, though a large dog came to
greet me. I've had enough flesh taken out of me by friendly-
seeming hounds, and wasn't going to be double-crossed by this
one. Since, however, he was blocking my access to the front door, I
couldn't ring the bell. I tried yelling, and this racket, conjoined
with that made by the dog, eventually attracted Richler's attention. Like many very funny men, Richler has a lugubrious
manner. His gloomy eyes, resting above capacious pouches and
below tousled greying hair, appraised me mournfully. The novelist was wearing loose overlarge clothes that contributed to his
dishevelled appearance, even shabbier than my own, and in
marked contrast to that of his tall elegant wife. Richler had
recently collected some essays about politics and culture in
Québec under the half-ironic title of *Home Sweet Home*. His
assessment was sombre, and he had inveighed against the excesses
of the Parti Québécois. The picture he painted of his province was
affectionate but pained, as though it had never quite matched his
high expectations. The only sentimentality in the book was
reserved for sports.

Over the last year the fortunes of Québec had seemed to be
reviving. The much remarked upon flight of Anglophones was
over and some were beginning to return to Montréal. Over lunch I
asked Richler whether he now took a less gloomy view. He didn't.
He certainly applauded some of the social democratic measures
introduced by the PQ, such as electoral reform, laws protecting
green belts, and insurance reform. 'But now that independence

has been dropped as an aim, the only thing that drives them is an urge to fight Ottawa, which is exactly what every other province likes to do. Québécois are full of self-pity, always complaining about the raw deal they've had from Ottawa, but the truth is that the West got screwed more than Québec. The PQ's days have to be numbered, because without the independence issue, the party is like a train without an engine.' He still wasn't too happy about the language laws although they had been modified. 'When Bill 101 was first passed, the desire to eliminate every trace of the English language from the province became vengeful. And the danger for the French Canadians is one of ghettoization.'

The main deck of Richler's house, which is perched on a steep slope above the lake, contains a spacious living room and an even more spacious room containing the pool table. By lying on it, you could enjoy a sumptuous view of water and woods and sky. In *The Apprenticeship of Duddy Kravitz* the hero's aspiration is to own a patch of lake and woods north of Montréal, to stake a claim in the wilderness. I don't wish to imply that Richler is to be confused with his creation, but it seemed odd to see such an essentially urban writer taking his ease in so restful a spot. The Townships seemed like an enclave, a reservation inhabited by people far removed from the raucous streets of downtown Montréal. The contrast between the Chaudière valley and Maine had been complete, but there was less discernible difference between the Townships and northern New England. The dignified little towns with their broad streets, handsome wooden houses, and mellow trees, seemed alike on both sides of the border. So did the pace of life, and the culture, the sports and the television, the uses to which the land was put. Yet the historic memories of the two peoples were poles apart. The Townships were settled by Loyalists and by French Canadians. Their history, and the values embodied in that history, persisted; it was an orderly region, with no hint of the revolutionary, prosperous and settled, even complacent. The influx of summer visitors from Montréal, and the presence of many summer cottages, ruffled the tone but did little to alter the face the Townships present to the world.

Later that afternoon I was at North Hatley, a high-toned resort village on the shores of Lake Massawippi. The first men to build their summer houses here were not businessmen from Montréal, as one might have expected, but Southerners from the United States, who felt uneasy taking their holidays in the north of their own country in the years immediately following the Civil War.

Instead they came north into Canada and by 1900 the private houses were supplemented by about fifteen hotels. Many of those inns have now vanished, but have been replaced by formerly private homes, such as Hovey Manor, which was originally owned by a captain of industry from Georgia. The house is modelled on Mount Vernon, perhaps not the most tactful of architectural models to adopt for your Canadian residence. Down the road is the Auberge Hatley, a distinctive four-gabled house of 1903 now owned by the dapper Robert Gagnon. I needed to catch my breath on arrival, and collapsed beneath a parasol by the garden pool. An iced Campari was brought to me from the outdoor bar and I settled down for half an hour to do nothing more strenuous than enjoy the view of the lake.

As the sun sank, I rose, and went indoors to eat a most sumptuous meal: there were memorable ravioli filled with snails and served in a light garlic broth, lamb stuffed with its own minced kidneys and herbs, and a platter of no fewer than seven desserts. Although no more than half an hour's drive from the US border, the culinary delights of Auberge Hatley – not to mention the comfort of its accommodations – remain unknown to most Vermonters. According to Gagnon, 80% of his clientele are Québécois, but an increasing number of Americans from south of the border are beginning to discover the inn. Once word spreads of M. Gagnon's *terrine au chocolat*, the process is sure to accelerate. It would have been pleasant to linger in the lounges at Auberge Hatley, but I was expected in Montréal that evening, and there was a long drive ahead of me. The roads were empty of traffic but not of insect life, and an entire bestiary flattened itself against my windscreen and headlights as I pressed steadily through the balmy August night.

8

Naked City

In my short-trouser years my best friend came from Montréal. His father exchanged cash for erudition on a British television quiz show, but the entire family was Canadian. So was his nanny, previously his mother's nanny, who affected to be severe in the best Scottish-Canadian manner, but was in truth kindly and humorous beneath it. Christopher, whose disposable pocket-money income eclipsed mine and whose upbringing had been less orderly than my own, helped push me into swaggering adolescence. At the age of thirteen he was a heavy smoker, swore skilfully, took me to amusement arcades to burn a couple of shillings, used a Leica when I was still twirling a Brownie, and talked knowingly about girls at a time when I knew none. He was handsome and confident, and I moved rather in his shadow. He was a boy of strong opinions, all of which he voiced regularly. Although most of his closest friends were Jewish, he was not above the occasional anti-Semitic jibe, unthinkingly based on received opinion more than personal experience. He was virulently anti-Catholic, a prejudice fuelled and bolstered by the redoubtable nanny, who riveted me with terrible tales of how Catholic mothers perish in childbirth in order that their newborn infants shall live. And so forth.

When Christopher was fourteen, he returned to Canada and four years went by before we met again, this time in his native city. The Montréal he showed me was an English Montréal. At no time was I aware that he or anyone in his family had more than a rudimentary knowledge of the French language. Christopher had matured with all his prejudices intact. He took me to St Joseph's Oratory not to pray or admire but to pour scorn on Catholic credulousness. At the time I thought little of it, but revisiting the city after a gap of twenty years, it was not difficult to appreciate why French-Canadian nationalism had triumphed so decisively a decade ago. I don't think it ever occurred to Christopher, or to tens of thousands of other British-Canadian Montrealers, that their attitude was arrogant; they took it as given that they belonged to an educated elite, and that French Canadians, whatever their numerical status, didn't count for much and were somehow ineligible for full human consideration by virtue of their barbaric religion, incomprehensible dialect and insular culture.

The Montréal of his youth has certainly been modified, but it was essentially French even then and language laws and other recent developments have only altered the city in its degree of Frenchness. The English-speaking citizens may have controlled the economic life of the province, but they had never been able to dominate the tone of the city. Yet I was surprised, having heard so many tales of executive flight, to find how intact the English quarters of Montréal still are. Twenty years ago the inner suburb of Westmount was exclusively English-speaking; now French is heard on its steep streets and from behind the high fences of its grand houses. You'll still find here some of the few remaining road signs in Québec that say STOP instead of ARRET, and on Greene Street you can have tea at the Café Oxford, buy your clothes at Carriage Trade, order a catered meal from By George, and stop at the Avenue Bookshop to tickle the chin of Orwell the marmalade cat. On the same street I watched a dignified old lady parking a Jaguar which sported the following bumper sticker: LET ME TELL YOU ABOUT MY GRANDCHILD-REN. I ran after her, imploring her to satisfy my curiosity, but the old tease wouldn't tell me a thing, not even whether they were legitimate.

A few blocks away, on Lansdowne, a condominium develop-ment is dangled before the moneyed public in a manner that suggested the matter-of-fact Canadians, when pushed, can ex-hibit as much vulgarity as any coven of copywriters in the United States: 'In search of excellence? Finally. A luxury con-dominium that delivers your personal statement. Success. Un-matched anywhere in the city. Le 200 Lansdowne in Westmount. Beyond elite.' The British style still gasps along at some of the old clubs in downtown Montréal on and near Sherbrooke Street; here all the rituals of London clubland have been embalmed in their North American setting. Perhaps there are French-Canadian members, but I heard no French spoken during the enjoyable claret-drenched evening I spent at the University Club, and I imagine that any Francophone Québécois would with some justification fail to see what purpose could possibly be served by joining such an institution.

Even though the walls between French and English have crumbled in recent years, Montréal is still a city of enclaves. Mordecai Richler's novels portray the Jewish quarters of the city that existed in his childhood. Of that thickly populated district little remains, for many Jews prospered sufficiently to allow them to move to more sedate suburbs, but their place has been taken by other, more recent arrivals. One Saturday morning I drove up the Avenue du Parc, with its string of Greek restaurants, and then east along Laurier; these blocks along Laurier used to be unprepossessing, but now they are being smartened up, and bright shopfronts dazzle among less colourful façades. I turned up Boulevard St Laurent, which everyone in the city calls the Main, through what's left of the Jewish quarter, and soon found myself in the Italian quarter.

From rue Mozart, where I parked, it was just a few paces to the Marché du Nord, which resembles a display of prize fruits and vegetables suddenly invaded by the general public. There were huge sooty black plums the size of tennis balls, green and yellow watermelons stacked beneath the stalls, bulbs of garlic plaited on their stalks, a smell of ripe canteloupes mugging occasional whiffs of greeny mint, peppers enthusiastically marked DOLCI DOLCI DOLCI!, bunches of basil hanging from chains suspended between the concrete pillars of the market square, a battalion of honeys, baby Italian aubergines erupting from green stalks with the texture of aged skin, green and yellow haricot beans, buckets of lumpish broad beans going cheap, scrubbed potatoes, fresh corn skinned back to reveal pale yellow grains ('*très sucré!*'), riotous spinach curling in on itself ('Bueno, bueno,' murmured a woman approvingly as she fingered the leaves), white radishes like mandrake roots, pale green 'white' *zucchini*, lizardy sage, two-foot-long wispy dill, orange *zucchini* blossoms destined to frolic with glistening wet cos lettuces in salads. And weaving their way between the crowded stalls were West Indians in straining shorts and hair curlers, determined Italians with shopping baskets that bulged as capaciously as their paunches, thoughtful chin-stroking invaders from Westmount, burly French Canadians with packs of Craven A tucked beneath the shoulder straps of their white T-shirts. Officialdom's attempt to force a metric system on Canada was in disarray here for, though some stalls had signs scrawled in kilos as well, almost all gave equal prominence to the old system. The Mulroney government had given the nod to relaxations of enforced metrication, and in large cities and conservative rural townships alike, kilos and metres began to be displaced by the archaic yet familiar mysteries of pounds and yards.

The European profusion of the Marché du Nord was in vibrant contrast to the decorum of the Atwater Market, situated closer to the English-speaking districts on the other side of the city. Earlier that morning produce had been stacked onto the stalls with a bricklayer's precision, as though the goods were too lovely and precious to be sold or even fingered by jowly matrons feeling their way towards a ratatouille. Fruit and vegetables were scrubbed so as to extinguish any associations with such lowly elements as earth and compost. If the northern Montréal market was a marvellous mélange of Paris, Naples, and Lisbon, Atwater was more American in style; its teeth had been capped and there were no grey hairs.

From the Marché du Nord, I drove down St Denis past small brick apartment buildings; outside staircases like aircraft ramps led up to balconied first floors. A street sign baffled me, not because it was in French, but because it was in no known language. It declared: ADVANCED GREEN WHEN FLASHING. I asked around, but no one was able to translate it. Below Laurier, the boulevard changed from subdued inner suburb to raunchier city strip, jammed with French, Vietnamese, and Greek restaurants, the occasional Club Erotique, and a bar on every block. I turned off St Denis at rue Roy, took a deep breath, and plunged into Waldman's. Mayhem! Expensive leather shoes slithered on floors that were sluiced down every few minutes, sometimes deliberately, at other times by accident whenever plump lobsters were hauled protesting from two-tiered pools. Piles of salt cod filled spare corners. I elbowed my way to the fresh fish counter. There were huge cherrystone clams that could barely be contained in the palm of a hand, long reddish fillets of baby shark, huge slabs of pike with skin like adders, plump wriggling carp, and piles of deep pink red snappers reclining on hillocks of chipped ice.

No two customers spoke the same language; communication thrived on gesture and yell, growl and grab. Jews favoured the carp, Chinese ordered the most suspect spiny-finned and puff-headed species, Italians, *fritto misto* in mind, went for small whole fish, and a handful of Indian women in *saris* dithered elegantly over the counter. The crowds at Waldman's were not foodies out to test the latest recipe from a chic magazine. The shoppers here revelled in food, and recognized its worth and quality; meals and their preparation were pivotal occupations that gave form and substance to the most drab and unpromising of days. Those whose primary concern was filling their stomachs speedily headed for the frozen-food bins, which contained not only slabs of unidentifiable fillet and finger hacked and stomped into brickettes by Newfoundland fish packers, but such improbabilities as *coquilles de homard*, turtle meat, and *escargots en brioche*.

The pleasures of stuffing yourself with food were first elevated to the art of gastronomy in nineteenth-century Paris. The Canadian equivalent of bourgeois prosperity founded on the pursuit of trade and commerce had its roots in Vieux Montréal. When Christopher had taken me there two decades ago at the midnight hour, it had been dark and sinister; bulky massive warehouses and commercial buildings glowered over deserted streets. Here and there dim yellow lights indicated that a restaurant or bar was still open, but for the most part the old town was still and forbidding. It's sombre still, for the heavy grey stone buildings continue to overshadow the narrow lanes, but there are places among the network of austere commercial streets that reveal now, as they must have done a century ago, the grandeur of Vieux Montréal. Where the Lower Town of Québec City is archly quaint in its recreation of bustling seventeenth century small businesses and maritime trading offices, Vieux Montréal affirms the solidity and ambition of nineteenth century commercialism. True, there are older churches and seminaries from the seventeenth century, together with eighteenth century houses such as the Château Ramezay, but the mighty commercial buildings mostly date from a period of Victorian prosperity. As the city moved to preserve its most ancient quarter, new uses had to be found for these imposing buildings, and inevitably restaurants and studios and loft flats were carved out of spaces once taken up by winches and ledgers and bales.

Many sneer at such prosperous middle-class invasions of once dilapidated downtown areas, but I applaud adaptations that allow old districts to be preserved without being fossilized. Vieux Montréal still feels alive, and its character has not been violated by the injection of new blood along the long handsome streets such as St Paul. Vieux Montréal succeeds where the Lower Town of Québec City fails because there has been no programmatic zeal to remove 'unhistorical' later accretions. The essentially nineteenth century character of the old town, with its mighty church and massive municipal buildings – even the City Hall of 1926 resembles a French Renaissance extravaganza more typical of the previous century – is intact. While the Lower Town of Québec City has been recreated essentially as a tourist attraction – admittedly a successful one – Vieux Montréal remains integral to the city that has grown around it.

Québec City is irretrievably provincial, which is in large part its charm. Vieux Montréal, on the evidence of its architecture, always aspired to greater things. The scale is altogether more grandiose, reflecting Montréal's standing in the mid-nineteeth century as a colonial capital and a major centre of communications and finance. Take the neo-Gothic church of Notre Dame that dominates the spacious Place d'Armes. Here the fervour of institutional Catholicism blends happily with civic pride. Lavishly ornamented with wood carvings and gold leaf and polychrome decoration, there is little echo here of the Jansenism and cloistered piety of the Québec City churches (a severity that can, however, be conveniently recaptured at the austere seminary of 1685 adjoining the church); the spirit here is closer to the proud splendour of Italian baroque, where the worldly is used, with varying degrees of success, as a vehicle for the spiritual. The nave and the double-decker galleries overlooking it were built to seat 3000, a remarkable number when one recalls that when the church was built in the 1820s the population of Montréal was no more than 15,000.

The Place d'Armes is not the only spot where the urban pride of old Montréal lives on. A few hundred yards to the east are two more squares, named after Cartier and Vauquelin; both are spacious and invigorating, since even on hot days a breeze often wafts up from the St Lawrence. (It was Cartier who first came to what was then the Indian village of Hochelaga in 1535, though the Europeans didn't settle here until a century later, when Montréal proved a well situated base for the French fur trade.) Shoppers and visitors congregate here, and there's always somebody around who has unpacked a guitar at the base of Canada's version of Nelson's Column and is strumming tunelessly to the accompaniment of cigarette or marijuana smoke, while tourists enjoy an overpriced ice cream or beer at a café before ambling down to the rue Bonsecours and its famous sailors' church. Fewer tourists stroll as far west as the loveliest spot in Vieux Montréal, and indeed one of the most enchanting groups of buildings in Canada: the Youville Stables. A gate leads into a beautiful courtyard overlooked by dignified early nineteenth century buildings, their walls awash with ivy; stately gravel paths flow across the lawns and tubs packed with flowers provide a welcome burst of colour amidst the restraint of grey stone and clipped green lawn.

Vieux Montréal is a triumph of the urban and the urbane, basking in the self-confidence of a major city, rather than the busy inward-looking diffidence of provincial Québec City. A century ago, of course, nobody lived in this wholly commercial district, and rich merchants and bankers built their homes a mile or so away on the flanks of the mountain that forms the assertive focal point of the city. Few of the mansions of downtown Montréal have survived, but Westmount is reasonably intact. Its social composition may have altered but not its stolid, supremely comfortable suburban character. From the City Hall the streets rise steeply up the side of Mount Royal, while closer to Summit Park the roads curl and zigzag as they snuggle against the crown of the hill. From the lookout close to the top, there are fine views onto city, river and bridges, and the distant mountain of St Hilaire. Some of the largest houses stand close to the summit; the favourite form of ostentation here is represented by houses that resemble Elizabethan-style borstals, imposing and broad but unwelcoming behind their high gates. On the steepest slopes some houses are built on stilts, giving the newer among them a fleeting resemblance to the perilously sited houses of the Hollywood canyons. What did seem surprising was the absence of large estates. Even the grandest houses had been built on small lots, so that mansions stood side by side like a row of dowagers at a court reception. It was clear from the grouping of some recently built houses that many property owners fortunate enough to possess an acre or two around their mansion had sold off most of the land to developers, who had promptly erected three or four more houses. Thus privacy was traded for loot.

While the British Montrealers looked down on their city from the side of the mountain facing the river, the prosperous French community looked north from its buttocks, on which they built their own suburb of Outremont, almost as lavish as Westmount and arguably more stylish. As in Westmount, its residents have immediate access to the splendid hilltop park designed by Olmsted, whose other masterpiece of landscape design is Central Park in New York. The claims of Outremont to sophistication were severely dented while I was in Montréal by a new by-law forbidding the wearing of bathing suits in the city park; convicted offenders faced a $300 fine or sixty days in jail. This dotty example of municipal nannying raised all manner of interesting questions, such as whether it was permissible to omit to wear a swimming costume – or anything else – in the park, or whether a bra might be substituted for a bikini top without fear of prosecution, and so forth. For a city as devoted to pleasure as Montréal, it was a preposterous bit of backsliding, handing whole belts of cartridges to those who still snipe at the French-Canadian community as meagre-minded and priest-ridden. It was one of those contradictions that made Montréal, at the very least, interesting.

Another was the seemingly irremovable presence of Mayor Drapeau, an old-style city boss who ran Montréal as though it were his personal domain. From 1954 to 1986 he presided over one municipal disaster after another without the slightest damage to his political reputation. His most notorious failure was the building of the Olympic Stadium and indeed the entire staging of the Olympic Games in 1976, which had left Montréal stupendously in debt, despite Drapeau's insistence that the project was bound to make a profit. One of these years, when the city has finally paid off its debt, its rulers may get round to putting a roof on the stadium. The roof arrived five years after the Games ended, but has yet to be unpacked. Drapeau, who steamrollered his way through countless such situations by sheer force of personality, became an institution, a cartoon sketch typifying one aspect of the French-Canadian character just as the weary yet passionate chain-smoking Lévesque typifies another. The Olympic disaster would have ruined most political careers, but Drapeau survived longer than most, if only because Montréal seemed willing to tolerate his political lapses for the pleasure of having aboard an authentic rascal whom it was hard to approve of but equally hard to dislike. Moreover, Expo 1967 brought the city to the attention of the world, and its island sites survive as one of Canada's great gardens and pleasure grounds. None of this can have harmed Drapeau's reputation. In November 1986, however, the long reign came to an end, when Drapeau's civic machine was annihilated at the polls by a reformist movement. The new mayor, Jean Doré, campaigned for more open government, and 67% of voters agreed with him. Adieu, Jean Drapeau.

I paid my respects to another Montréal institution, Brother André. On a hillside near Outremont stands the vast basilica of St Joseph, like a trim and streamlined Sacré Coeur, rising above the oratory that this good-hearted priest founded. He was born in 1845 and with, it is said, the aid of St Joseph (former carpenter and eclipsed husband of the Virgin Mary who has since made good as the patron of a good death and of the month of March) he effected various cures that established his reputation as a healer. He founded the modest oratory in 1904, and it has swollen into a major North American shrine that attracts over 2 million visitors each year. The original chapel still stands, though overshadowed by the mighty Renaissance-style basilica that was begun in 1924 but only completed in 1967, thirty years after André's death. Above the original chapel is the spartan room where he lived. It contains two beds, one for himself, and the other for any sick pilgrim in sudden need of a place to rest. The room's contents – the oil stove on which he cooked his meals, a small basin, religious paintings and statuettes – are as spare as the man himself, whose life was so singlemindedly dedicated to the spiritual.

The crypt church at the foot of the basilica was packed with the faithful, and I had to worm my way through the crowd to the votive chapel, the lofty chamber that Christopher had shown me in 1965 as an illustration of Papist superstition. The chapel is still jammed with its formidable collection of crutches and surgical boots, barnacling the walls and pillars between the side chapels. Beneath a statue of St Joseph 3500 lamps are available to pilgrims wishing to implore his aid. Close by is Brother André's tomb, at which visitors are requested to sign a petition urging his canonization. In 1982 André came close when the Pope beatified him, and I dare say the family of saints is already polishing up a spare halo.

Shrines may be designed to wrest miraculous cures from obliging saints, but they are also required to process pilgrims with speed and efficiency. To this end an escalator hums up to the oratory museum, which contains the usual memorabilia as well as a reconstruction of André's office. Especially thrilling is the actual hospital room in which the potential saint died. When the room was scheduled for redecoration, the nuns who ran the hospital donated it, complete with original furniture and linen, to the oratory. The only thing missing from the room is the corpse. Well, not entirely, for André's heart was plucked out and is kept in the museum, thus offering pilgrims yet another opportunity for fervent prayer. I wonder whether the pious priest would have been entirely happy with a cult of the personality as thoroughgoing as that once accorded to Lenin or Mao. The very ghoulishness of the museum seems related less to a spiritual contemplation of a holy man than to a primitive magical reliance on the supposed healing properties of relics. These morbid wallowings had inspired in Christopher feelings not far short of plain disgust, but my response lacked his fury. From the acorn of Brother André's simplicity had grown the mighty oak of the pretentious basilica, the green dome of which was loftier than that of St Paul's in London and soared 150 feet higher than the towers of Notre Dame in Paris. A cinema and another museum, this one dedicated to St Joseph (admission fee charged), a restaurant and hostel, traffic jams in the car park, and the immense concrete-piered movie-set vastness of the basilica itself, all this testified to the industriousness of the Church as institution rather than to the healing powers of a good man. No Catholic would presume to separate the man from the institution that nurtured him and that he desired to sustain, but to nonbelievers the contrast is inescapable and far from admirable. Religions discourage a sense of irony. Had I been in the mood that afternoon to offer up a prayer, it would have been to thank the divinity for my lack of faith in it.

'We've had an interesting summer,' said Mark, a burly rugger-playing banker – a new model, with brains. 'You should have been here in July, when Alcoholics Anonymous held their convention here. There were fifty thousand teetotalers on the streets, and for days you couldn't get a Seven Up for love or money. And following that, the next convention to hit town was the Jehovah's Witnesses.'

We were sitting in Mark's flat a few streets away from the McGill University campus. It was a warm evening and as we were downing a beer before setting out for a walk, we were joined by his friend Katya, a tall dark woman who had come to Montréal to perfect her French.

'Katya,' I mused. 'Are you from a Russian family?'

She nodded.

'You must be one of those crazies from British Columbia,' I said, jokingly, recalling that fervent members of a Russian religious sect known as the Dukhobors had settled in the Canadian west. The Orthodox clergy in Tsarist Russia had not had much time for the Dukhobors, an agrarian sect who adopted Tolstoy's pacifism; with the novelist's help they had emigrated to Canada, a case of jumping before they were pushed. To this day about 5000 continue to propound their eccentric theology (denying, for instance, the divinity of Christ, and proclaiming the metempsychosis of the soul) and to practise their quaint custom of running naked through the streets and burning down their property from time to time. (A few days earlier three Dukhobor women were arrested and later jailed for seven years and more for reverting to their ancient pastime of arson and burning down the Dukhobor Museum in Castlegar.)

My little jest didn't go down terribly well, since Katya was indeed from a Dukhobor family in Castlegar. She was also a smoker and I kept a close eye on her box of matches.

At first I was wary of Mark. I had loathed rugger at school, where I'd been forced at gunpoint to spend countless sopping Wednesday afternoons being kneed in the groin in the midst of a sweaty huddle known as a scrum. Fortunately Mark was no thug. Moreover, he told me with justifiable pride, he had sported a ponytail for months, concealing this mark of Cain beneath his shirt collar. I found the idea of a corporate banker in a ponytail pleasing and warmed to him at once.

His flat was near the Main, the central boulevard that divides Anglophone Montréal to the west from the Francophone territory to the east. We crossed it on Prince Arthur, a lane lined with outdoor cafés and frequented by street musicians collecting pennies from passing American tourists.

'Prince Arthur used to be a big centre for trashy art until the culture police came along and cleaned it up,' explained Mark. We followed Prince Arthur as far as Carré St Louis, Montréal's answer to Washington Square. Just south of the square, where St Denis crosses Sherbrooke, Mark showed me what he correctly described as 'the world's largest statue of a man having a shit'. St Denis itself is the city's most enjoyable street, packed with bars and restaurants, trendy boutiques, and pointless little shops selling non-items such as balloons. Dope was being peddled by classic dope peddlers, with their shifty eyes and hunched shoulders and straggling locks creamy with grease. St Denis is in the French part of the city, but Mark pointed out that the social topography of Montréal had grown more subtle in recent years.

'Twenty years ago, when I was a kid, the English community, walking east from Westmount, would come to St Urbain, then to Clark, and then to the Main, and the next place after Main was Europe. Nobody ever went into French East Montréal. There was no need. That's changed. Now the trendy thing for Anglos to do is to hang out on St Denis. Of course it works both ways, and clued-up French kids walk west to Crescent and hang out there at the bars and night clubs. They probably wouldn't be seen dead in a French restaurant on St Denis.'

Our meanderings took us down to Ste Catherine, where we played Spot the Transvestite. This led to fierce disputes that could only be resolved in one way, and that was not what any of us had in mind. So, cherishing our illusions, we marched north again and stopped for another round of beers on St Denis before ending up at one of the lively Greek restaurants that have been cloned along Duluth. I preferred these crowded unpredictable streets to the much touted but distinctly bland right-angled efficiencies of Montréal's immense subterranean complexes. In January, it's true, I had been grateful for the shelter and for the easy access to hundreds of shops and restaurants, not to mention railway and subway stations, hotels, cinemas, and office blocks. When mountains of slush made the streets almost impassable, I'd been as thankful as everyone else for the artifice of the underground city. While blizzards howled, I'd sat comfortably in the multi-tiered, escalatored atrium of the Complexe Desjardins eating ice cream and watching, don't ask why, a demonstration of fencing. But a shopping mall, even one with corridors seven miles long and an abundance of free entertainment, remains a shopping mall, and I would burrow my way out to the less arid environment of the open street whenever the weather lifted its snowy skirts. Now, in the summer, subterranean Montréal was as alluring as an airport terminal compared to the theatre of the streets.

I remarked to Mark and Katya that Montréal had an atmosphere I hadn't encountered in other parts of Canada. Canadians are notoriously law-abiding; as has often been pointed out, the Loyalists and their descendants opted for a monarchical and hierarchical form of parliamentary government rather than the more unpredictable, opportunist, democratic system favoured south of the border. In the small towns of the Maritime provinces, hardly a soul had jay-walked, not, it seemed, merely because it was frowned upon but because crossing a street against the light hadn't even occurred to the majority of the population as a possible course of action. None of this applied in Montréal, where jay-walking simply wasn't, couldn't be, an issue, and where the drivers screeched round corners and flung their vehicles forward from traffic lights as though they had taken driving lessons in Rome.

Mark agreed. 'People here are hedonists, they like to live on the edge, and they certainly aren't particularly law-abiding. Ten years ago everybody in every café was arguing nonstop, usually about politics. These days they're still arguing, though less often about politics. Montrealers are volatile; our idea of fun is finding a new restaurant. The women, and I'm talking about the French-Canadian women here, are the most beautiful in Canada – don't you agree? –'

'No question about it.'

' – and they're also the best dressed. People here care about style, about the impression they're making. It's an essentially European attitude, which is why Montréal has the best ambience of any Canadian city. It's good and relaxed, and there isn't too much respect for the law. Did you know that Montréal is the armed bank robbery capital of the world?'

After some treacly Greek pastries, we returned to St Urbain to a coffee house called Santropol. My idea of a place for coffee is anywhere that provides you with a seat and a mug. But Santropol wanted its customers to enjoy a greater sense of occasion. A twenty-minute wait for a table built up suspense. My espresso arrived with a garnish of sliced honeydew, engaging but quite unnecessary. If I want melon with my coffee, I'm quite capable of asking for it, and the chocolate cheesecake we ordered (with three forks) had fruit salad to keep it company. The calories slowed us down for a while, and as we pondered the wisdom of devouring cheesecake on top of baklava, I remarked that Montréal certainly didn't appear to be the depressed, floundering city I'd heard about.

There had, said Mark, indeed been a slump here in the 1970s. Anglophone families, one out of seven, had left the city in droves, but not only because of the PQ's election victory. The process had begun some time before, when the economy had begun shifting westward to British Columbia and Alberta, which was beginning to enjoy its astounding oil boom. But the election of Lévesque had appeared to doom the provincial economy if only because outside investment dried up. In 1978 the huge Sun Life company moved its headquarters to Toronto, on the grounds that Bill 101 inhibited recruitment of suitably competent people to conduct an operation that was not restricted to the province of Québec. Moreover, the exodus of corporations and their executives to Toronto and points further west caused a 30% drop in property prices in one year and led to a serious decline in tax revenues. Taxes, indeed, had been another reason why many people had moved away. Roughly speaking, taxes in Québec are almost 15% higher than they are in, say, Ontario, though those on low salaries are not at a similar disadvantage and housing costs are lower in Québec. But higher rates of taxation for the reasonably well paid not only prompted executives to move elsewhere, but hindered Québec corporations in their attempts to recruit from outside the province. In addition, the interventionist policies of the social-democratic PQ swelled the ranks of the provincial civil service; Québec under the PQ had four times as many public employees per capita as California. With a civil service payroll swallowing about half the provincial budget, it wasn't surprising that many better-off residents resented the squandering, as they saw it, of half their tax revenues on a local bureaucracy. Had it not been for massive Keynesian projects such as the hydroelectric installations up at James Bay, the damage to the local economy might have been far more devastating.

But this has all changed. The PQ no longer proclaims its belief in sovereignty as a political option, and by 1985 only 4% of Québécois claimed to favour separatism. Whatever the rhetoric, Québec is going to remain part of the federal structure of Canada, and now this is beyond doubt, the province, and Montréal, are no longer shunned. The city is resuming its importance as a financial centre, the stock market is doing well, new businesses are sprouting, and the property market is showing signs of life again. Montréal may have been wounded by corporate flight, but the province as a whole was not greatly affected, for it had never been a major centre of corporate activity. The battle of principle has been won: French Canadians have restored the primacy of their language within their own province, and they need no longer feel unwelcome in their own land. Their sense of grievance has dissipated. Montréal can once again be an open and receptive city, cosmopolitan and international.

Mark was not unhappy with the way things had worked out. Although from a well-entrenched and prosperous British Canadian family, he had had a good deal of sympathy with the PQ and thought it perfectly reasonable that French should be the first language of the province. He and other Anglophones in his office spoke French as a matter of course during their working day. 'Only one thing angered me. It was when Lévesque declared that Pierre Trudeau wasn't a true Québécois because his mother was Anglophone. That enraged me. I was born in Montréal General Hospital, my family's been here for generations, I'm completely bilingual, and who was Lévesque to say I wasn't Québécois? What time is it?'

'Midnight.'

'You know what I feel like? A swim.'

'Now?'

'Sure. I know a place twenty minutes from here where we can swim at one of the most beautiful places in the world. Am I right, Katya? Isn't it one of the most beautiful places in the world?'

She nodded. It was still warm, and Mark's suggestion was appealing. We returned to his flat to collect some towels and then drove towards the river, crossing over the narrow Royal Victoria Bridge, which has a surface of metal grates that supposedly deter ice from forming. They also don't allow tyres to get a good grip, and the car appeared to be slithering wildly, giving the impression that we were about to crash into approaching vehicles. I was timing Mark – he had promised paradise in twenty minutes – and all I could see was drab suburbia. 'We're almost there,' he said, turning down yet another street lined with uniform houses. I continued to mock until we turned in at a gate and down an ill-lit driveway.

'Is this it?'

'Yes. Welcome to St Bruno.' A provincial park of 2000 acres, St Bruno had belonged to Mark's family. It was opened to the public a few years ago but the family still retains a few feudal rights. Some of his relatives still live on the estate, and only members of the family may use the lake. Mooning by the lake shore was a mansion where his great aunt still lived. Mark cut the car lights as we approached it since he didn't want to wake his sleeping relatives. The path to the jetty took us straight past one of the bedroom windows, and Katya and I crept like cat burglars through the undergrowth, following the glow of Mark's cigarette. A minute later we emerged at the lakeside and walked out onto the jetty.

'Well, am I right?'

It was, beyond question, beautiful. There was a full moon and the placid surface of the lake rippled creamily in the soft light, while behind the shore opposite the slopes of Mont St Bruno were outlined against the glittering sky. We undressed rapidly and dived into the water, scattering ducks in all directions. We swam out to a raft, then back to a jetty for a cigarette, then out to the raft again. It seemed indeed extraordinary that we were only twenty minutes away from a city of three million people; there was no sound apart from our own splashings in the water and the whoop of waterfowl. Some nights, Mark told us, you could hear the cries of loons on the lake. St Bruno was magical because it was so utterly unexpected. Nor did the presence of a naked and shapely young woman detract from the pleasure of the moment. Skinny-dipping, of course, poses no problems to anyone with a good Dukhobor upbringing. Yet our nocturnal bathe was a sensuous rather than a sensual indulgence, and only when Katya hauled herself out of the water and onto the jetty and the glistening water shimmered down her long body did I question the distinction.

Swimming rights in a once private lake seemed, on first thoughts, a curious privilege to treasure, but after five minutes of immersion in those still, warm, black waters I could fully see why Mark valued the place so highly, and thought nothing of driving out here in the middle of the night to bathe and revel in a corner of Canada that, in an ancestral sense that had to be rare and private and uncommunicable, was part of who he was.

9

Non Compris

Canada plucks its wealth from the elements themselves. Fresh water, for instance. Canada owns a sizable proportion of the world's supply of this basic commodity, and is presently considering a scheme to build a ninety-mile dam across Hudson's Bay to create a colossal reservoir that can be marketed, principally to the United States, at a healthy profit. This scheme has been kicking around for years and has recently been revived; whether it is likely to succeed or even get off the ground few will predict, other than those who have a vested interest in the outcome. The investment in such a scheme would be colossal, but then Canadian governments, whether federal or provincial, have always had a fondness for such projects; hence the profusion of crown corporations across the economic face of the country.

Québec has not been slow to exploit its other great liquid resource: hydroelectric power. The most ambitious project of this kind was undertaken at James Bay, the southeastern corner of Hudson's Bay, about 700 miles north of Montréal (or 1000 miles by road). Through this barren area of stunted spruce and lakes that seem to occupy as much space as the land flows La Grande Rivière. Dams have been dotted along its 500-mile length, and the largest project of all, known as LG2, has been constructed close to the Bay. It was the Liberal Party that urged these mammoth projects on the province; in the early 1970s, the Parti Québécois thought hydroelectric power old-fashioned and proposed a policy of building nuclear reactors.

Hydro Québec, the crown corporation that runs these projects, understandably boasts of its achievements, but is rather more reticent about the enormous difficulties encountered in their construction. At one point 18,000 workers were involved; five airports were built as well as 1000 miles of roads. The difficulties were compounded by the wretched working conditions encountered in the cold and remote north; there were problems with union contracts, and horrific tales of wastage and sabotage – one

102

union official smashed all the generators at LG2 and caused $35 million worth of damage and a seven-week closure, since without electricity the site could not function. Moreover, the 8000 Cree Indians and Inuit who lived near James Bay persuaded a court to shut the construction site down for another week until Hydro Québec agreed to negotiate an expensive land claims settlement, finally reached in 1975 and incorporating not only protection for the Indians and their way of life but a degree of self-management. In all, the constructions at James Bay have cost $15 billion.

The controversies have been supplanted in the public mind by the indisputable commercial success of the project, though there is still bitterness within Canada about the prices charged for power from James Bay. Prince Edward Island and Newfoundland both pay Hydro Québec more for their electricity than does New England, and there have been howls of protest that a foreign nation should be able to purchase energy at a cost lower than that demanded from fellow provinces. Close contact from the start with American bankers fuelled suspicions that, whatever the benefits to Canada, the principal beneficiaries of the James Bay project would be the Americans, with their insatiable appetite for cheap energy. On the other hand, Hydro Québec is not a charitable organization; it follows the standard business practice of negotiating the best deals it possibly can, and the harsh truth is that Newfoundland negotiated a lousy contract for itself. Although Hydro Québec has been retrenching in recent years, it still accounts for about a fifth of all economic activity in Québec. By the early 1980s it was the most profitable corporation in Canada. It remains central to Québec's economic performance, not to mention its self-image as technologically advanced and pioneering. Hydro Québec has almost 20,000 employees and annual sales of about $3.5 billion, which have to be offset against huge interest payments on the loans that financed James Bay. The corporation cannot rest on its laurels, and works furiously to sell its considerable surplus production; it also sells its expertise to Third World nations. The trump card that Hydro Québec holds is that hydroelectric power, at a third of the price of nuclear-generated power, remains a bargain.

At 5.30 one morning I crept out of the house where I was staying. An overgrown youth in shorts, toiling up the Westmount slopes as I descended, stared at me with distinct hostility. True, I had affixed a paper tissue to my chin to stanch a shaving cut, but I didn't look any more weird than he did. Glowering, we slid by each other. At the bus stop on St James I joined a group of people on their way to work, mostly French-Canadian security men and Anglophone airport officials in polyester pantsuits. They all clutched lunch boxes. At the airport I joined 135 James Bay workers flying out to begin their week's shift. Employees work eight days at the site, then have six days off, a popular division of work and leisure that allows them to spend reasonable stretches of time with their families. The same plane would return from LG2 to Montréal that afternoon bearing a complementary batch of workers whose shift was over.

From the plane I had an excellent view through limpid air down onto nothingness. The land was swashed a blotchy khaki-green, darker where jack pine and black spruce rose above the scrub and stood like sentries along the banks of meandering streams and rivers. Below me a single and utterly empty road wound between the peat bogs so beloved of mosquitoes. The only bumps on the landscape were mounds and hillocks of granite the colour of elephant hide; occasional flecks of quartz and mica flickered over the grey. Eventually there were signs of man's determined reshaping of the landscape: rows of pylons trod across the muskeg, earthworks gashed the scanty topsoil, and storage tanks were ranged like thimbles along the horizon.

The airport terminal consisted of a single smoke-filled room that gradually emptied as the newly arrived workers filed onto buses. Besides myself, there were half a dozen other visitors to the site that day, all French Canadian. Our guide led us onto a bus for the twenty-minute drive to Centrale. Here at headquarters we were shown scale models of various components of the complex and sat through the usual doggedly informative video. Not that the information was uninteresting. The very scale of the project guaranteed that. It had taken fourteen years to construct LG2, and entire rivers in the La Grande basin had been diverted so as to increase the rate of flow of their waters. The basin as a whole is the size of England, or, in American terms, the area of New England. An immense dam two miles long and almost 500 feet high and dike walls banked with enormous boulders create the reservoir from which the water falls 450 feet to the underground turbines. Because of the sheer pressure of the water, the flow must be directed from the turbines into a surge chamber, where its force can be dissipated before being returned to the river a mile away. Such was the scale of the construction that Hydro Québec had to replant ten million flowers and trees, not simply for their decorative value and to provide a habitat for local wildlife but to ensure that the meagre topsoil isn't exposed and blown away. Inuit who live north of La Grande near Ungava Bay are less convinced by Hydro Québec's concern for the environment. In 1984 the engineers released water from an over-full reservoir not through spillways but into the Caniapiscau River, a decision that resulted in the drowning of 10,000 caribou at Limestone Falls.

From Centrale we were driven past the dam to a lookout tower. From here there was a good view onto the spillway, ten vast steps hewn from the rock, each 440 feet across and dropping 30 feet to the step below. This extraordinary staircase is used only during the spring runoff, when it becomes necessary to drain off a few trillion cubic feet of excess meltwater gathering in the reservoir. Springtime also brings other problems, for when the ice breaks up, its shiftings often deracinate the trees that still stand along the bed of the reservoir, which soon becomes littered with floating tree trunks that can damage the turbines. These trees have to be culled from the reservoir, then burnt, since they have no commercial value.

For lunch our party returned to Centrale, where we ate with everybody else in the cafeteria. The food was plentiful and good. Smartly dressed executives and stewardesses from the daily flight mingled with burly bearded workers and technicians. A giant of a man seated opposite me wore a badge certifying him as a member of the Association des Pères Noëls du Province du Québec. After forty minutes our tour resumed. The guide distributed hardhats, which we donned before driving a thousand yards into the rockface towards the turbine rooms. We entered an immense hall 600 yards in length. At various points along the hall, steps led down to the sixteen turbines; their unceasing activity provoked a constant tremor. We rattled down a stairwell to a lower range of galleries and then into the turbine room itself. Piranesi would have had a field day down here. The guide chattered on, no doubt providing all manner of enlightening information, but the roar of the turbines blotted out every word. The noise was, if anything, even greater in the surge chamber, a hellish place with the roaring waters in constant and turbulent motion, throwing up a spray so misty I couldn't see the other end of the chamber, which was a third of a mile away from where I was standing. The mighty subterranean chamber is hewn from granite, and its rough walls – no point in wallpapering a room like this – highlighted the savagery of the place. I half expected to meet Alberich or Gollum scurrying towards me. Next time I am asked to direct a film version of *Rheingold*, I'll choose this place for location shots of Nibelheim.

After this exposure to brute force we were pacified by the smooth working of computer technology at the communications centre, which controls and monitors all the La Grande hydro plants as well as the complex cable network that disperses the newly created power throughout the province and beyond. The entire network is duplicated, so as to ensure there is no interruption to supply should one network break down. This was the last stage of our tour and by three in the afternoon we were on our way back to the airport. The other guests were all smiles as they took leave of our excellent guide. I, however, was too angry even to shake his hand.

Let me explain. The guide, quite reasonably since I was the only member of the group who wasn't a French Canadian, spoke in French. I can usually converse adequately in French, but there were two complicating factors in this case. First, much of the information was technical. Secondly, the guide spoke Québécois, not French, which meant I had to translate his accent as well as his words. As we were driving in from the airport, the guide, who had been explaining some of the difficulties encountered by the construction crew, paused and said, '*Compris?*' To which I said, No. He rapidly summarized what he'd said, I thanked him, and then he continued with his French commentary. At Centrale he rattled through his explanations of how the plant worked – even the French Canadians had some difficulty following this – but my failure to comprehend was so total that I took him aside and asked for a summary in English. He obliged, extremely rapidly, and then told me that it wouldn't be practical to translate everything he said and that I would just have to ask him specific questions at appropriate times. This proved equally impractical, given the speed of the tour. By the time we were leaving the turbine room, for instance, he was beginning to explain what was going on in the surge chamber.

I understood his problem, but he didn't seem to understand mine. There were times in the day – on the bus or over lunch – when he could have made an effort to see whether I was gathering the kind of information I needed. He did not do so. I felt as though I had been served an excellent meal while gagged. When I failed to shake his hand, he followed me into the airport. I should have

QUEBEC

asked him more questions, he said. I explained that had been
impractical. He then did his best to make amends and offered to
answer any questions I might have, but by the end of this long day
my curiosity was fading.

It was, in its way, an instructive note on which to end a visit to
Québec, for it had brought me face to face with the vexed
language issue. The guide spoke perfectly adequate English, not
fluent but slightly better than my French. He was right to give
priority to the rest of the visitors, but his refusal to do more than
the absolute minimum to ensure that I understood what I was
seeing was aggressive and counterproductive. I had not flown 2000
miles that day to be bored and frustrated.

Some weeks later I was talking to an official from Manitoba
Hydro who told me that foreign bureaucrats, negotiating deals
with Canadian hydroelectric companies, often hesitated to deal
with Hydro Québec, despite the corporation's undoubted exper-
tise, because they found it too laborious to work in French.
Officials from India, for instance, had found it wearisome and
time-wasting to have to employ teams of translators to work on
contracts and agreements. This story may be an exaggeration – I
have no direct evidence to support it – but after my own
experience at LG2 I am tempted to believe it.

It was not entirely the guide's fault. All my dealings with Hydro
Québec officials in Montréal had been in French and they
supposed that I would be able to understand the French explanations. This was flattering but unrealistic. Given the
difficulty of the situation, all I expected was that the guide would
try to meet me halfway so as to ensure that my day was not
wasted. This he failed to do. His nationalistic pride came into
collision with my need to gather information. Was I being, as he
undoubtedly thought, a typically arrogant Anglophone? I maintained that I was a foreign visitor with a job to do, and it was his
job to do his best under the circumstances to help me. I nursed my
rage all the way back to Montréal, and all the way out of the
province as I left for a brief trip to New York the next day.

Part Four

Ontario

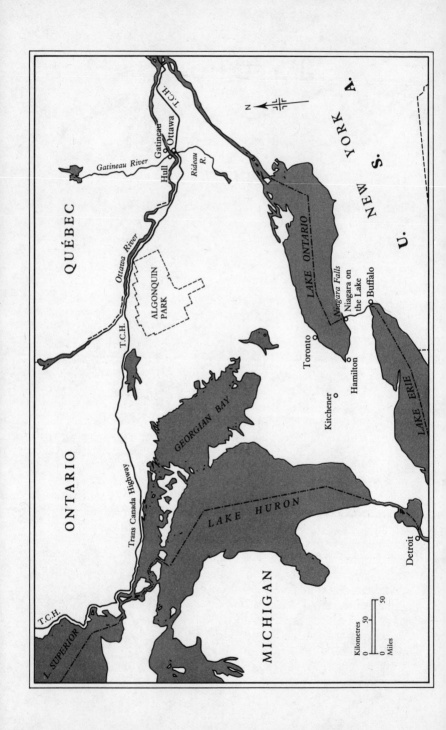

10

Toronto Il Buono

That brief visit to New York was designed to open up some space between Montréal and Toronto, to separate the cities by more than a flight. It may seem odd to choose to refresh the spirit in an even larger city, but it was the familiarity of Manhattan that I needed. I could put away my notebook, stop asking questions, neglect to be attentive. My few days in New York provided instances of a quality Canadian cities sacrifice in exchange for their orderly good nature—theatricality. No sooner had I arrived in Manhattan than I phoned a journalist friend. 'My God,' he gasped, 'what are you doing here at the end of August? You must be crazy. I've been advising all my friends to abandon ship. It's ninety-five degrees out there, there's no water in the city, they've taken all the air-conditioned subway cars out of service, and everyone is dying of AIDS. I'm leaving for California myself tomorrow. You'd better come right over and have dinner.'

Which I did. Canadians make me smile, but New Yorkers, with their calculated hysteria constantly buffeted against the magnificent absurdity of their environment, convey a sense of excitement that I find wonderfully stimulating – in short doses. I rediscovered their diffident sense of hilarity even in such an unpromising spot as a bus heading for New Jersey. On boarding at the Port Authority bus terminal, I offered the driver some dollar bills. He eyed me with a suspicion that was disconcertingly unctuous. With super-politeness, he observed that it was customary on this line to purchase tickets at the ticket office before boarding. I apologized profusely, pointing out that I was from out of town and didn't know the ropes.

'I realize that,' he said smoothly, nodding like a saddened priest in the confessional. 'I'm only telling you so that next time you won't make the same mistake. I hope,' he added, in tones expressing profound concern, 'I hope you don't think I'm *scolding* you?'

'Oh no, not at all. I'll be sure to remember next time. Sorry about the mistake.'

'That's quite all right. Now you just come right on board and make yourself at home. . . .'

When all passengers had boarded, the driver picked up his microphone and addressed us. It was the day after the New York State lottery jackpot had stood at $41 million – and been won. 'Imagine yourself,' soothed the driver, 'lying in a hammock, sea breezes wafting by your head. Soon you'll have cooled down after the excitement of not winning $41 million. When you're relaxed and ready, I'd like to inform you that this is the 143 bus and to remind you that smoking is permitted only at the rear of the bus. I have nothing further to add.'

Bus drivers who charm their passengers with one-man shows are rare in any city, but this kind of zaniness is not out of place in New York. In Toronto it would be inconceivable. There the drivers would prove to be, most of them, courteous and helpful, but lacking any whiff of eccentricity. True, what we mostly require from bus drivers is an ability to drive a bus rather than a compulsion to entertain, but what I enjoyed about the 143 bus driver was the unexpectedness of his behaviour. In Toronto, the unexpected doesn't happen. The city is safe and reliable, and utterly predictable. It may seem invidious continually to compare and contrast styles and behaviour found in the United States with their counterparts in Canada, but it is impossible not to do so. Because so much of Canada's culture, in the broadest sense, is avidly imported from the United States, a comparison of the two countries is positively invited. Moreover I could sharpen my focus on Canada by occasionally slipping across the border for a brief immersion in the United States, and then return. By juggling the two nations, I was trying to dispel the common notion that the United States is somehow the Real Thing of which Canada is a pale imitation. On this occasion I slunk into Ontario from Buffalo on board a bus. At the border we queued behind two other buses, both marked Gigbusters Inc. and occupied by hairy men in shorts who appeared not to have slept in a week. Formalities completed, the Toronto bus sped along the highway loyally named the Queen Elizabeth Way. It was not a thrilling ride, though it might have livened up had the bus taken the Sodom Road exit instead of hurtling straight past it. Behind me a baby screamed for an hour as though his teeth were being pulled, while his mother uselessly murmured, 'Good boy, good boy,' in defiance of all the evidence.

The financial hub of Toronto rises just behind the lakefront, where gleaming silver skyscrapers huddle together, their shiny newness a reminder of how recently Toronto has made the leap from Hogtown to international city. Here and there the wall of towers parts to reveal older buildings still in use such as the St Lawrence Market, Union Station and the Royal York Hotel, asserting themselves through breadth rather than height. The harbourfront development, with its Hilton, its restaurants, its pleasure boats, occupies the lakeside area beyond the Gardiner Expressway, which applies a tourniquet to the base of Toronto along the shore of Lake Ontario. About two miles north is another clutch of tall buildings, mostly elegant apartment blocks and hotels along or near Bloor Street. Toronto, unlike hilly Montréal, has to work hard to make its impression. For the most part it is a flat city laid out on an unadventurous grid system and topographically charmless, despite the wooded ravines cut by the rivers Humber and Don. Yonge, the main street running north from the lakeside, is a mess. There is no old commercial section remotely equivalent to Vieux Montréal, nor many traces of the European styles or influences that mark Québec. Britain hasn't embossed Ontario in the same way that French culture has been stamped on Québec. A handful of British commercial interests are entrenched here – branches of Boots, W. H. Smith, Marks & Spencer – and newsagents display copies of a magazine called *Britannia*, with its explanatory subtitle, 'Keeping in Touch with the British Way of Life', exemplified, in the issue then on sale, by video tapes of *Coronation Street*.

Yet the triumph of Toronto is to have risen above all its natural disadvantages, above all its reputation. Mark had only been stating the obvious, though stating it well, and with that air of superiority adopted by all Montrealers when they contemplate the rival city, when he pronounced: 'No one could ever mistake Toronto for Manila. The place just revels in its blandness. Toronto's greatest source of pride is that it's clean and that it works. If someone finds a gum wrapper on the subway platform, they phone their alderman to complain.' These prim virtues of safety and orderliness can of course be negative ones, tugging in their wake a dullness as all-encompassing as that mockingly invoked by Alexander Pope: 'All my commands are easy, short and full: My Sons! be proud, be selfish, and be dull.' Before the Second World War Toronto was a quintessentially Protestant city. Hundreds of hard-pewed kirks had tipped their congregations into Toronto, establishing its stern Presbyterian tones. It was Orange in its politico-religious colouring, and happily discriminated against any groups that differed from itself: blacks, Jews, and Catholics were among the obvious targets. Not only private clubs but hotels discriminated freely. Pleasure was ungodly and cinemas were closed on Sundays. That is mostly a thing of the past, and Toronto today is an open city.

Nonetheless it retains a certain smug propriety inherited from the not so distant days when it was a banking city, ultra-respectable, stuffy, self-righteous. Buying liquor still requires a trip to the provincial Liquor Control Board stores, a monopoly with a very limited range of wines and other drinks. The system has improved marginally since the days when you had to sign for each purchase. It is absurd that throughout Canada no independent liquor stores are permitted. Consequently, prices are high and choice is poor. Yet some provinces, such as Québec, actually lose money on their liquor stores, including those in central Montréal. It takes genius of a peculiar sort to operate a state monopoly at a thumping loss. Québec has been trying to 'privatize' its liquor stores, but there were so many restrictions attached to the sale that no one would touch them. Perhaps eventually the Canadians will treat their citizens as adults.

The transformation of Toronto was wrought by three waves of immigration. In the 1960s many draft-dodgers from the United States chose Toronto as their destination. Many of its new inhabitants were not only radical in their politics, but, as energetic new residents of a country more tolerant than their own, only too pleased for an opportunity to pump new blood into municipal politics. Their influence persists, and city politics have been lively and enlightened. 1960s radicals have now become city fathers. Then in the mid-1970s disillusioned Anglophones drifted into Toronto from Montréal, many in the wake of their employers. The more cosmopolitan Montrealers soon lent their own cultural sophistication to their new home. And the third wave of immigration, from outside North America, continues, shrinking the Anglo-Saxon population of Canada's largest city to about half the total. Toronto has for some time been, astonishingly, the largest Italian city outside Italy, with roughly half a million Italian residents and two Italian-language newspapers. There are also substantial Greek, Ukrainian, Portuguese and Chinese communities. Canada, with relatively liberal immigration policies, has not been slow to open its doors to suitably motivated people from the world over. There are West Indians and Dutch and Pakistanis and mainland Chinese, all bringing with them their culture and, as

Torontonians gratefully acknowledge, their food. After New York, Toronto must have the greatest concentration of restaurants of any North American city.

Although Canada does maintain control over immigration, I detected none of the fear of continued immigration that sours most European countries. Admittedly Canada has more room to expand than most. Mark told me he was convinced that for, say, the next two or three years Canada should simply usher in anyone who wanted to come here. He foresaw no difficulty in absorbing the few million new arrivals, since Canada is in his view underpopulated; indeed, all those new bodies and new skills and ideas would probably give a tremendous boost to the economy. Certainly the government seems to be leaning, ever so cautiously, in that direction, and the quota of 115,000 immigrants for 1986 represents a 30 percent increase on that for the previous year, though a decline since 1974, when almost a quarter of a million immigrants arrived. Moreover the chairman of the Commons immigration committee has urged an increase to 300,000 by 1990. Canada accepts about 20,000 refugees a year, including many who have been turned away by other countries. The swift arrival of immigrants in cities such as Toronto and Vancouver can lead to problems. Some, following the lead of French Canadians, have begun to demand their own schools, which many regard as divisive. Although racism is not unknown in Canada, the public rhetoric is anti-racist and it seems thoroughly accepted that Canada is, after all, a nation of immigrants. However, preference is given to immigrants who bring with them capital and other resources that will be invested in Canada.

Toronto is an obvious destination for immigrants; a fifth of all Canadian manufacturing industry is located in and around the city, and it has attracted the headquarters of most large Canadian corporations. One arrival from England told me: 'The energy of Canada comes from its immigrants. People born here take their way of life and standard of living for granted. We immigrants have to work for it.' Toronto, then, is diverse, in a continual state of flux, and culturally lively. With over forty theatre companies, it has long eclipsed other Canadian cities as a theatrical centre, and houses more art galleries than any other North American city with, again, the inevitable exception of New York. These changes have all taken place during the past twenty years, yet the reputation of Toronto as prim and smug – Toronto the Good – has stuck. The justification for that smugness is that Toronto is wonderfully habitable. Public transportation is excellent and dependable; city services function efficiently. There is, Torontonians boast, little racial tension and no rioting in their city, though the more honest of them will add that there have been sufficient checks on black immigration to ensure that ghettoes were never formed in the first place; consequently the white population has never felt remotely threatened by their new black neighbours. If Toronto had the same proportion of black citizens as, say, Detroit or Chicago, the story might be very different. The city is a middle-class paradise, and in that sense atypical of the rest of the country, which is an agglomeration of smaller communities heavily dependent on the exploitation of local resources and hence more vulnerable to fluctuations in the economy than Toronto, a white-collar city with a diversified industrial base.

Toronto may be lively, but it is not flamboyant. Not even the transplantation of exotic species from Europe and Asia, bearing highly marketable recipes for dim sum, pirogi, palascinta, bacalhao, rice'n peas, and osso buco, has been able to alter more than the façades of the city. There are Chinese shop signs in Toronto but the city remains staunchly, righteously, generously Anglo-Saxon, not given to demonstration or vulgarity or flashy self-display. It esteems its multiculturalism as the icing on the cake, the shine on its brogues, but its deepest concerns lie within itself. The biggest issue in the city, according to a local politician, is the Dome stadium: will future Torontonians be able to watch baseball with a roof over their heads? That's what gets them excited.

I had visited the city twice before, once in the middle of winter, when I took a room at a downtown hotel that was safe but seedy. The lower two floors were filled by bars patronized by small-time businessmen and small-time politicians. I learnt a good deal about the mores of the city during the two days I spent there. Waiting to use the pay phone in the lobby, I overheard an acutely embarrassed and extremely drunk man explaining to a relative why he wasn't going back to his wife that evening – or ever. The shambles of his explication and the heavy reliance on swearing seemed sucked up from a thick subsoil of stony despair. After ten minutes of increasing incoherence, the poor man gave up and shuffled back to the bar, where his mates had thoughtfully provided a further two rounds of rye for him during his absence.

On returning to my room I heard sounds from the adjacent room that seemed prompted by the ardour of the sexual act. A brief study made through the keyhole – the two rooms shared a connecting door – confirmed my supposition. A pair of long legs, for that was all that was visible of one body, were splayed beneath two brawny legs and pumpkin-sized buttocks. The climax achieved, he rolled off and she came into view. He was fifty and fat, and when he wasn't pile-driving the woman, was working his way through a case of beer. She was about thirty, quite attractive in a rangy way. In his high petulant voice the lover was complaining garrulously about injustices at the office. Her familiarity with the cast led me to deduce that she was a sympathetic secretary that he was able to bang after stressful board meetings. I was shocked, of course. To think that this kind of thing was going on in Toronto! And I was further shocked that so unappetizing a man was able to win the favours of a tolerably attractive young woman. Did not even lust and ambition owe some dues to taste?

Tut-tutting all the way from the keyhole I went out to dinner. Where two or more Chinese are gathered together, they open a restaurant. There must be a few hundred Chinese restaurants in Toronto, many of them conveniently bunched just west of the downtown area along Dundas and Spadina Streets. This used to be the old Jewish quarter of Kensington but it is now a Chinatown that rivals New York's in extent, overflowing not only with restaurants but with groceries, travel agents, ginseng importers, and pharmacies. Many of the best restaurants line Spadina, though their decor rarely rises above the minimum standards laid down for prison refectories. At the Great Wall, I tucked into a large steamed crab doused in a black bean sauce. It would have been sensible to have followed the lead of the fat fornicator at the hotel and taken off my clothes. There is no way to crack open and devour a steamed crab without spattering juices all over oneself, one's neighbours, the floor, the ceiling. After twenty minutes the deed was done. The succulent crab, reduced to sharp-edged shards, now resembled an exploded grenade, and a huge pile of paper napkins testified to the messiness of the struggle.

I walked back to the hotel via Yonge Street. The stretches south of Bloor are blotchy developments of offices and shops, utterly characterless. About halfway between Bloor and the lakeside lies Toronto's half-hearted red light district. The vice is tame enough: a few strip joints, one or two pornographic magazine outlets feebly disguised as paperback shops, and a single sex cinema, which, weary of its primary mission, was instead advertising films with 'frightening scenes, brutal violence'. Instead of wholesome vice, these few blocks of Yonge offered tawdry commercialism: 'sound warehouses', record shops, and, during the day, street stalls selling cheap sunglasses and tacky costume jewellery. Hamburger hovels and other fast food outlets fanned their revolting aromas into the street, where leather-jacketed youths ineffectually leered at passersby in a politely unsavoury manner. Further south is the huge Eaton Centre, a three-level glass-vaulted shopping complex, linked by a covered bridge to another department store. It was cold out, but I could walk for about half a mile alongside Yonge without having to leave the shelter of these shopping arcades. Apart from those who, like myself, were walking from one end to the other, there were a fair number of people, mostly kids, who were simply hanging out by the benches and tubs of trees. It was no secret in Toronto the Good that the less populous corners of the Eaton Centre were choice spots for whoring and drug-pushing. Eventually, after re-emerging into the cold air and weaving my way between glass skyscrapers, one per bank, I reached my hotel. My amorous neighbours had gone, and my sleep was undisturbed.

The next morning I moved to a bed and breakfast place run by a kindly and mild granny of a man; he was thirtyish, had worried eyes and five o'clock shadow. The oak floors of the rooms had been sanded and polished, and pretty chintzes were draped over the windows and beds; scented soaps and pot-pourris sweetened every room. It was like inhabiting a doll's house designed by Laura Ashley. The owner fussed endlessly. I would stagger in late at night to be confronted by his requests to know what delicacies would please me most at breakfast. At eight I would descend to the kitchen and join the other guests – mostly retired ladies from Vermont waiting for their husbands to breathe their last in Toronto's excellent hospitals – while Millicent put on his apron and whisked the batter for the French toast and quizzed us about the day to come. I'm not up to small talk at dawn, least of all detailed discussions of medical diagnoses (all bleak), and after two days of chintzes and reports of barium meals, I moved out and taxied through the snowy streets to Cabbagetown.

In a British city, Cabbagetown, despite its intriguing name, would be unremarkable. In London it would blend quite satisfactorily into a gentrified Streatham or Willesden, though the houses have marginally more charm than their British equivalents. This district, a mile or so east of downtown, is composed of tall narrow gabled houses, many of them with intricately carved wooden balconies perched within the gables; here and there are faint echoes of an Art Nouveau style. Down Parliament Street are quaint cafés and shops with names like For Pet's Sake. In a quiet cul-de-sac east of Parliament Street lives Barrie, warm-hearted and impulsive, who on the basis of a tenuous introduction invited me to move my luggage from Mrs Tiggy-Winkle's to her house. When I arrived, she scratched her head for a moment, then went upstairs, exiled a child from his room and installed me in his place. At first I felt embarrassed to be causing such dislocation in her household, but I soon realized that chaos was the natural order chez Barrie and my presence would scarcely be noticed. Barrie's own room was being occupied at that time by a candidate for the provincial assembly elections; the kitchen doubled as an extension of her campaign headquarters. Barrie herself slept in whichever empty room she found herself in at midnight.

Cabbagetown had changed around her. When she first moved here, the area was a shabby, run-down near slum, full of seedy boarding houses. As the new professionals began to throng into Toronto from the United States and Montréal, many of them, being dutifully countercultural, shunned the tedium of suburban life, and moved into decaying inner suburbs such as Cabbagetown. Ten years later it had become, somewhat to Barrie's alarm, positively chic. The biographer Phyllis Grosskurth lived down the road, and the Czech novelist Joseph Skvorecky was a neighbour. Literati and illuminati of various kinds, not to mention a world champion figure skater, dotted Cabbagetown's pleasant modest streets. Like an Advent calendar, you could open almost any window and espy something intriguing within. From a slum, Cabbagetown had become a neighbourhood, complete with its own residents' association and historical society.

No sooner had I moved my stuff into the room that had been appropriated on my behalf, than Barrie offered me a 'true Canadian experience – if you can stand it'. This turned out to be an opportunity to watch her twelve-year-old son Jamie play hockey. To her astonishment, I agreed at once. She tried to talk me out of it but failed. So we piled into her car, Jamie half-buried under pads and sticks and helmets in the back seat. On reaching Parliament Street we turned up towards a huge housing complex.

'This is Regent Park, the largest public housing project in the whole of Canada,' said Barrie. 'And can you believe it's actually safe? It's just the same as the rest of Toronto: clean, decent, cautious, boring, and safe. I once knew a guy running for the council and he was canvassing one of the blocks in Regent Park. Quite a task, with twelve thousand people living there. Anyway, he called on a voter and identified her accent as Trinidadian. He knew the island well and during their chat he mentioned to the woman that what he really missed were good rotis. It so happened that she was baking a batch of them at the time, so she obligingly fetched him one, which he wrapped in a napkin and put in his coat pocket. The next floor up he knocked on a door – another Trinidadian woman. They talked for a while, and then he asked her if there was anything she missed now that she'd come to Canada. "Oh yes," she replied, "I'd kill for a good roti." Triumphantly, the politician produced a roti from his pocket and handed it to her – still warm! That's the way to win elections.'

We were now dodging through winding streets past substantial stone and brick houses. 'This is Rosedale,' rasped Barrie, with a hint of disapproval. The houses, some of brick, others of stone, their rooflines gabled, their porches peaked, their gardens stacked with large-leaved shrubs, combined to form a collective character not at all reminiscent of the grand but uncluttered neo-colonial mansion suburbs of Highland Park in Dallas or Comuta, New Jersey. Instead they resembled a minimally distorted mirror image of Haslemere or Sunningdale, firmly British in its plushness, monitored quirkiness, and unshakable solidity. 'Old money. See how the roads wind, even though there's no reason why they should? That was to keep public transport out of here.'

'But I can see a bus directly ahead of us.'

'Yeh, the buses run here now. They're only used by the domestic staff, of course.'

Not far from Rosedale was the La Salle High School hockey rink, where Jamie's team, the Toronto Stingers, was to play that evening. The Toronto hockey league has a whole hierarchy of teams, depending on the age of the players. There are Adams and Bantams and Peewees, among others, and Jamie was a Peewee. The Toronto Stingers Peewees, Barrie and Jamie assured me, was the worst team in the whole city; 293 goals had been scored against the team that season, and the Stingers themselves had only managed to score 21.

Hockey is of course no laughing matter in Canada. It is played and followed with the utmost earnestness, and the rules and regulations governing not only the playing of the game but the structure of the leagues are as arcane and unyielding as anything dreamt up by the Curia. A gifted player will rapidly climb the hierarchical ladder and be recruited by one of the good teams. His parents will pay heavily for the privilege in the form of fees, and should the budding genius miss a game, his contract will specify fines to be paid – again by the parents. Should a player be sent into the penalty box or be cited for misconduct, the misdemeanour goes into his record – for life. Nobody seems to object to this grim regime. It's part of the way of life, like church bells in Italy. The kids, or those I met, were taking an enthusiastic but relaxed attitude to the game, unlike their parents, who behaved as if the outcome were equivalent to victory at Waterloo.

The man next to me, wrapped in a lumberjack's jacket and with a visored cap jutting out over his broad brow, kept up a monologue of encouragement to his team: 'Keep working, keep working, way to go! Hurry up, let her go you guys, let's wake up, let's work on it, let her go – oh my God, get up! That's a boy, stab him, get him, don't hesitate – move, shoot, hustle Paul hustle. . . . Talk about luck. . . . All the way, let's move, let's move, shoot the bloody thing.' At this point the referee, not for the first time, made a decision of which this particular parent did not approve. Paul's dad jumped up and down in rage. Loudly he McEnroed: 'Get outa the way, was that not a body check? If that wasn't a body check I need my eyes examined.' He turned to me and pointed at the referee. 'How did he get away with it?' 'Beats me,' I replied sympathetically. He babbled on: 'Jeez, the *other* team doesn't do anything, *they* don't touch anybody, oh no! Okay, ref, you won't be back next year – hey, he finally got a penalty – how the hell did that happen?'

Barrie, whose style was more sophisticated but whose voice was the vocal equivalent of paint stripper, kept up her own barrage of comments and yells, though she occasionally turned to me and shrugged, as if apologizing both for her misplaced enthusiasm and for the Stingers' appalling play. All the kids in Jamie's team were tiny – a dwarfs' squad – and the opposing team, the East Enders, was, on average, twice their size. As they raced onto the ice, towering over the Stingers, Barrie turned to me with a worried look: 'Puberty well under way there.' After a break, the Stingers pounded onto the ice, manfully brandishing their sticks, but the team was one short. After a moment's confusion, while someone taught the coach to count, another Peewee Stinger was dispatched onto the rink and promptly fell flat on his face. This was more than Barrie could stand, and she rose to her feet, yelling: 'C'mon boy, you can't skate on your stomach.' Every five minutes or so a Peewee would fall, or be felled by a giant East Ender, writhe in agony, and then be escorted off the ice to the cheers of his team-mates and the banging of their sticks.

'I wish I knew more about the game,' I said to Barrie during a break. 'Apart from having to get the puck into the goal, I don't understand much about it.'

'It's simple,' she explained. 'The main principle of the game is to skin 'em alive and eat 'em raw. How you do it is up to you.'

'Sounds dangerous for these twelve-year-olds.'

'Not as dangerous as for parents sitting in the bleachers. Last year a friend was sitting next to me at a pro game, and a puck came flying towards him. Next thing he knew all his teeth were jangling about in his mouth. That was just tough luck on him. It's written on your ticket in Latin: It's not our responsibility. So keep your eye on that puck.'

There was a tremendous cheer some minutes later when the Stingers almost scored. Barrie was screaming and yelling with her fifty-horsepower lungs as strenuously as the rest of the parents.

'Why all the fuss?' I wanted to know. 'They didn't score, did they?'

'Listen,' she growled. 'We Stingers supporters, we treat a shot at goal as the same thing as a goal.'

The Stingers lost 9–1.

I was grateful for Barrie's tour, but Toronto is no sightseers' paradise. It's a practical city, designed for making money and for spending it in stores or restaurants. It has a well laid out university, divided between various colleges, and good museums and concert halls. It is not a city of nooks and crannies; the peaked houses of Cabbagetown and the inhabited islands just offshore provide the closest thing to charm that Toronto has to offer. It is characteristic of Toronto that the boutiques of Yorkville, a former junkies' hangout yuppied to a higher social plane, should have become a tourist attraction. Not far away, the flamboyant entrepreneur Ed Mirvish has taken over a whole block of houses on Markham Street and turned it into Mirvish Village, a row of boutiques and galleries and bookshops, by painting the houses in bright colours, placing tubs filled with flowers on the pavement, prettifying the surroundings in every conceivable way. Nor is the result disagreeable, which is more than can be said for Honest Ed's, Mirvish's emporium on Bloor, its façade aswirl with eye-catching fairy lights and display windows filled with laudatory press cuttings, while its interior is simply a no-frills, no-decor discount house. It opens at noon, but by eleven there is already a queue lining up, or squatting, on the pavement outside, mostly Chinese and West Indian women in pursuit of some astonishing bargain. Opposite Honest Ed's was a cinema (now moved elsewhere) showing pornographic films; exemplifying the prissiness that characterizes Toronto at its worst, the cinema excused its existence with a sign piously murmuring that the establishment was 'devoted to exploring new areas of thought and emotional stimulation'. Thought?

A more engaging form of commerce flourishes near the waterfront at the St Lawrence Market. On Saturday mornings farmers from the hinterland – otherwise known as prosperous Southern Ontario – cart their wares into Toronto and sell them here. St Lawrence differed from Montréal's Marché du Nord in two respects: it offered far more than fruits and vegetables, and many of those thronging the market halls were clearly there for amusement as well as to stock their larders. Musicians – flautists, fiddlers, and accordion players – diverted the crowd as they sipped coffee and chewed on bagels or wedges of smoked ham. There was an astonishing variety of foodstuffs: exotica such as pirurutong (purple rice) from the Philippines, sweet white rice from Thailand, adzuki beans from Japan, goat's milk soup with oatmeal. In London it is hard to find kasha; at St Lawrence Market a stall offered three varieties. Even though it was the middle of winter, I had no difficulty finding strawberries and papaya. Cheese shops offered Wensleydale, Finnish Emmenthal, Romanian feta, Swiss Raclette, French Morbier. Breads included a strange cheese bread, Russian rye loaves, halla, pitta, and, I need hardly add, Estonian pastries. I queued up at the smoked meat section, overlooked by a whole suckling pig and a row of pig's heads, to sample Macedonian sausages with leeks, chorizo, Mennonite smoked sausages, and morcillas. The range of foodstuffs available confirmed an important feature of Canadian life: immigrant groups are not required to integrate as thoroughly as they would be in the United States. Naturally, a degree of immersion in Canadian mores is crucial to the survival of immigrant groups, but it is assumed, even expected, that such groups will retain their customs, their foods, their clothes, and indeed flaunt them, so that other Canadians may borrow from them.

More formal dining is no problem in Toronto. Elegant and luxurious French restaurants such as Le Tour Normande and Scaramouche didn't differ much from good French restaurants in any major city, but the West Side Grill close to prosperous Rosedale had a very different character. It gave the game away by failing to have a name sign over the façade, evidently being so chic that its patrons didn't require such aids. Inside it was elegant in a cool way, with pristine linen and gentle colours. It was clearly modelled on similar establishments found in Manhattan; even the name had echoes of New York. And of course the Grill came complete with one of those tall fey waiters who suddenly appears at table-side, looks down on you to make sure he has successfully interrupted your conversation, and then drawls softly: 'Would you like to hear about our specials this evening? For starters we have devilled dormouse lightly braised in cream and kummel and served in a coulis of organically grown gooseberry and Seville oranges. . . .'

(The West Side Grill later completed its venture into anonymity by going belly-up and vanishing altogether.)

11

Keeping Canada Canadian

Although Brian Mulroney, when he became prime minister of Canada, was hailed by some as a politician poured from the same mould that gelatinized Ronald Reagan, his policies in office have merely consolidated the broad centrism of Canadian politics. The interventionism practised by Liberal governments has been modified, but not scuppered; Mulroney's conservatism may be genuine but it is not radical. While in Britain and the United States conservative governments have chipped away at, and in some instances removed entire chunks from, the social services structure, Canada's generous social programmes are not regarded as under serious threat from the new government. The Conservatives have however been more receptive to the idea of free trade, notably between Canada and the United States, than were the Liberals. *Prima facie*, it certainly seems absurd that there should be trade barriers between two large countries with an extended common border and so many common interests. Tariffs protect certain industries but also perpetuate inefficiences, and at considerable expense to the taxpayers.

In the summer of 1985 Ottawa announced that talks aimed at establishing a free trade agreement between the two countries would shortly begin. Their aim, government officials observed, was freer trade rather than some crystalline ideal of Free Trade. These developments are bitterly and vociferously opposed by certain Canadian nationalists, and I called on one of the ringleaders, Abraham Rotstein, professor of economics at the University of Toronto, to see what objections he could possibly raise to what seemed an eminently sensible move.

Rotstein began by telling me I had got the whole thing wrong. The objections to free trade had nothing to do with tariffs, he said, adding that by 1987 96% of all imports from the United States would enter at tariffs of 5% or less. Nor does Rotstein dispute that, since Canada conducts 76% of its business with the United States, a larger market is in principle preferable to a smaller one. The difficulty is that the United States is pressing for what American politicians call a 'level playing field'. They attribute many of their economic difficulties to subsidized imports, though Rotstein argues that the excessively high dollar is a far more important reason. The 'level playing field' would require Canada to dismantle its system of subsidies to bring it into line with American practice. Regional development programmes designed to assist specific industries would, argues Rotstein, be endangered. So too would the structure of Canada's lumber industry. Most forests are owned by the crown, and tracts are leased to lumber companies that pay a 'stumpage fee' according to the amount of timber felled. Because, argues the American lumber industry, these stumpage fees are lower than equivalent fees paid by US lumber companies, they constitute a hidden subsidy and should be brought into line with American practice. (This argument ignores the fact that while average stumpage fees in Canada are lower than the average American fees, the gap is still less than the variation in fees between some of the American states.)

Some American politicians also argue that Canada's Medicare system gives Canadian fishermen an unfair trading advantage. Because the United States lacks an adequate medical welfare system, American fishery companies have to contribute to their employees' medical insurance, which, it's alleged, puts them at a disadvantage. Although in the past it was established that social programmes were not equivalent to subsidies, and the International Trading Commission has ruled that the same is true of stumpage fees, the issue has been reopened by American congressmen who seek legislation that would simply redefine such programmes and fees as subsidies. Rotstein fears that, as a condition of concluding any free trade treaty, the Americans may demand that all hidden subsidies – including social programmes, regional development schemes, and research programmes – be dismantled. This would amount to a radical restructuring of Canadian society, and that, says Rotstein, is far too high a price to pay.

The nationalists are appalled by the extent to which the United States dominates the Canadian economy, and oppose any moves that would, in their eyes, consolidate that domination. In Ontario, which has the greatest concentration of Canadian industry, about 70% of companies are American-owned. Rotstein fears that Mulroney's insistence that, in the words of a Tory slogan, Canada is 'open for business' might well increase such ownership. This has implications for Canadian sovereignty too, for the United States obliges Canadian subsidiaries of US corporations to obey US commercial law rather than Canadian law. The United States is fond of trade embargoes, and requires Canadian companies under American ownership to observe them, even when the Canadian government refuses to subscribe to them. Moreover, American business regulation is obsessed with anti-trust laws; but Canada's size, argues Rotstein, means that in certain industries a concentration of manufacturing rather than competition between individual companies may be necessary for their survival. Furthermore, major trade unions, like major industries, are often no more than branches of American unions, and orders are more likely to come from Detroit or Pittsburgh than from Toronto or Ottawa. Free trade, then, is seen not so much as a tinkering with economic systems of exchange, but as a threat to Canada's political independence.

Cultural independence too, what's left of it, would also be increasingly threatened. Rotstein recognizes that the United States will always dominate Canadian culture. 'But it's a question of degree. We'd just like the occasional Canadian paperback or feature film shown in our cinemas. We'd like an occasional alternative to what the United States sends over the border. All we're asking for is a modest Canadian presence in our cultural life.'

I mentioned to Rotstein that in certain spheres it seemed to me that the American domination of Canadian life was close to total. Even in French Québec, there were times when I could scarcely tell which side of the border I was on. Why, for instance, were Canadian school buses identical in every respect to their American counterparts? In Europe, you cross from one country to another, and everything changes: the language, the architecture, the cut of clothes, even cigarettes. Here in Canada, I accused, you don't even have the imagination to paint your school buses a different colour from the American bright yellow. Rotstein smiled. He was sympathetic, but said that the explanation had less to do with Canadian feebleness than with the terms of the 1966 Auto Pact, according to which Canadians retained the plants of the American Big Three auto manufacturers as long as they continued to produce Canada's market share, thus preserving employment for Canadian auto workers. That's why there are no Canadian car manufacturers and why Canadian school buses are indistinguishable from American ones.

'I take your point,' he said, 'but to me it's more important that you should be able to tell which country you're in when you turn on the TV.'

Rotstein's opposition to free trade may prove unnecessarily alarmist. Even supporters of free trade oppose any negotiation that would imperil Canada's welfare policies. The arguments in favour of freer trade are that increased access to markets and increased competition will in the long term benefit Canada; equally important, though advanced *sotto voce* by its supporters, is the tactical argument that since the United States appears to be moving in the direction of greater protectionism, it would do Canada no harm to be under the umbrella of the United States and share the benefits of such policies.

No treaty will be signed in a hurry. The United States will require any agreement to be binding on all the Canadian provinces; but under Canadian law, which guarantees provincial control over all-important natural resources, this could be difficult to obtain. Nor is it clear how a free trade agreement could override 'Buy America' provisions enforced at state level. Many other problems make any rapid conclusion to negotiations improbable. Some American plants were established in Canada specifically to get round tariff walls; if free trade comes to pass and American-based plants gain the same degree of access as their branches, it is probable that some of these plants may be closed. The United States and Canada also have different agricultural support programmes, and presumably these would have to be rationalized before any free trade treaty could be signed.

Rotstein admitted that most Canadians didn't give free trade much thought. Even businessmen, after decades of acquiescence in American takeovers of Canadian industry, are not easily stirred by the issue, nor much interested in the cultural integrity of the country. So what did interest Canadians in terms of defining their national integrity? Rotstein's answer, and I received the same reply from many other Canadians, though less elaborately, is land. Canada, he argues, is the homestead writ large. There's a local rootedness rather than a national adherence. I'd certainly noticed this myself in the Maritimes, where most people seemed almost oblivious of the Canadian federation to which they belonged. Rotstein thought the same was true to some degree of almost all Canadians, which is why it is acceptable, even mandatory, for provincial politicians to rail against Ottawa. The allegiance to the locality is often stronger than the allegiance to the nation. Canada, he argues, is not a people or a culture or a society, but a place.

'In 1969 we learnt that an American ship had sailed through the Arctic ice floes. Outrage! The Arctic may be to all intents and purposes empty of people, but Canadians were up in arms because an ally's ship had sailed through what we regard as Canadian waters.' Indeed, a similar incident was taking place as we were talking: another American ice-breaker was not only ploughing happily through the Northwest Passage but doing so without even troubling to ask the Canadian government, which claimed sovereignty over those waters, whether it was all right with them. 'These incidents infuriate Canadians, but when you give them far more significant information about American control of our economy, they're not very interested. That's because Canadian instincts are territorial. No trespassing! It's sentiments like these that buttress provincial politicians' bitching at Ottawa. It's almost a kneejerk reaction. Now, this strong distrust of central-ized power is healthy enough, but it's also negative because it means that there's no vision available for coping with national problems.

'Because we're preoccupied with our land, we excel when it comes to dealing with certain environmental issues such as pollution. That's why there's so much anger about acid rain, and such pressure on the United States to clean up their industrial plants near our border. But it's also why many people are instinctively wary about plans such as the one to turn James Bay into a gigantic freshwater lake. A scheme like that, whatever its economics, violates a deeply held taboo. Water, in Canadian eyes, is part of the homestead.'

Not that this vast scheme seemed likely to be getting off the ground in a hurry. So far, the only research done on its feasibility has been conducted by engineers; economists and environment-alists have yet to be heard from. The great hydro projects, the oil sands mining in Alberta, and now the talk of the James Bay lake, were about the only examples of Canadian entrepreneurship on a magisterial scale since the building of the railways. The relative smallness of the population is often given as an excuse for Canada's lack of initiative and vision, but countries such as Sweden have a population smaller than that of Ontario and yet maintain an economy far more vigorous. Canadians have never needed to be entrepreneurs; for centuries, they have been looked after by first the British and then the Americans. Since the majority of Canadian companies are foreign-owned, most Canadian businessmen implement rather than take risky decisions. Canadian entrepreneurs often choose the United States as their field of operations, presumably because their flair is more likely to be rewarded south of the border. It has become easier to supply the country's needs by importation from the United States than by manufacturing within Canada itself. Such ease of access to the world's mightiest economy is hardly conducive to the stimulation of incentive, let alone economic independence.

While economists and politicians grappled with these crucial issues, the municipality of Toronto was properly concerning itself with less weighty matters of more immediate concern to its citizens. Barrie, who was of a sceptical turn of mind, actually had high praise for the city's political system. Toronto's financial affairs are prudently managed, in part because the city is not permitted to go into debt. The municipality spends what it's got and that's it. Moreover, there is still room for open politics in Toronto. According to Barrie, 'If you've a brain in your head and the attention span of more than three minutes, you can get a lot done. In Toronto you can walk into the mayor's office and scream and something might actually come of it.'

Barrie's encomium put me in mind of a meeting I'd attended at City Hall the previous winter. I'd been shown round by Ray, an elderly gentleman steeped in local politics who thought it would enlighten me to observe the city's elected representatives in action. Some weeks before, a spokesman for a pensioners' organization had protested to the city about the failings of its snow clearance policy: old folks were slithering all over the streets, cracking limbs and dropping their groceries. The city responded immediately by establishing the Winter Services Subcommittee, known to its intimates as the Snow Committee, and it was to its opening session that I hurried one chilly February afternoon as the snow was sympathetically falling.

Ray, long retired from the fray, saw no reason to be charitable when introducing the cast of the committee to me. The meeting was chaired by Alderman Tom Clifford, for whom a two-minute delay mechanism appeared to operate when it came to understanding anything said to him. He was, said Ray, 'a simple, sweet guy – and a conehead. His assistant used to walk behind him muttering "Left, right, left, right", just in case Tom forgot how to walk. Tom represents a district that's half residential and half industrial, hard-working people like himself. He must be doing something right, as he's been reelected for twenty years now on a platform of Love the Queen, No Drinking, No Sunday Commerce, and pleas for an underpass beneath the rail lines so that kids won't have to cross the tracks on their way to school. Naturally, Tom struck out on that issue too, as the city eventually built an overpass instead.'

There were three other aldermen present, and representatives from the legal department and the Board of Health, and the Public Works Commissioner himself. The committee took its seats beneath a sign that read 'NO SMOKING – $100 MAXIMUM FINE' and puffed away. The general public was personified on this occasion by the old folks' representative, Ray, and myself. The meeting began, appropriately, with obfuscation, provided in this instance by the medical officer from the Board of Health, who mused aloud on methodology. Did falls on ice cause identifiable injuries? Which injuries could, without doubt, be attributed to slipping on snow and ice? How many people slipped on ice but sustained no injuries other than temporary discomfort? Alderman Anne Johnston contributed some delicious nonsense by requesting a comparison between ice and measles injuries. Another alderman, David Reville, disposed of her suggestion: 'Anne, this is the Snow Committee. We'll raise the case of measles with the Measles Committee.' When another alderman referred to 'my old lady' tripping on a frozen step, Reville, who was quite a card, interjected: 'Are you referring to your mother or your wife?'

Between guffaws, an alderman offered a practical proposal, based on the practice of the city of Buffalo. The Public Works Commissioner, a tough Scot, would have none of it: 'What Buffalo does is of no concern to the city of Toronto.' When someone pointed out that a woman who had failed to follow city regulations by clearing the pavements of her corner property had been socked with a snow clearance bill for about $700 by the Public Works department, the Commissioner smirked. 'Well, she'll be sure to clear her sidewalk next time.' The Commissioner dazzled us further with a thirteen-page report, complete with ten tables, outlining policies, exemptions, costs, all supporting a recommendation that the city stick to its current policy.

It was a splendid meeting, everybody enjoyed themselves thoroughly, the old folks' representative gave a long speech, and the aldermen made numerous quips that the chairman failed to understand. Only I can't recall what action was taken by the committee. I believe it resolved to hold a further meeting at some stage.

By summer, Toronto had seen the last of the snow for a couple of months. The city in August was warm but not hot, and I could now stroll through Toronto at leisure, pausing at art galleries and browsing through the dozen or so secondhand bookshops on Queen Street. One afternoon my wanderings took me back towards Mirvish Village. A few streets away lives Ronald Bloore, a distinguished Canadian painter. What interested me about Bloore is that he seems to have no link with the mainstream tradition of Canadian painting. I had spent much time gazing at the canvases of the country's best-known and most revered painters, the Group of Seven. I did not like what I saw. These painters had, during the first decades of this century, stationed themselves in various uncomfortable corners of the Canadian wilderness – the forests of northern Ontario, and the harsh unproductive rocky outcrops north of Lake Superior – and there they had tried to depict the isolation, the grandeur, the rich sunsets, the luxuriant autumn foliage, and the blanketing snows of winter. They tried too hard: the paint is jammily applied, there is an overall heaviness of touch that obscures more than it illuminates. Density is not the same as intensity. This is a heretical view. The Group of Seven are the artistic equivalent of motherhood and apple pie.

Ronald Bloore, however, was an abstract painter who shared my view. 'I tell my students: if God had intended you to paint with mud, he would have put it in tubes for you. It's curious, isn't it, the way Canadians used to paint by numbers. There's the Group of Seven, the Regina Five – someone once called himself the Group of One.'

His house was as cool and austere as his paintings, which are mostly white on white. The walls were limpid blue, and the fabrics that covered the furnishings were black and white checks of varying sizes, while the fabrics used in the adjoining dining room were a similar check but reversed out. The pale pine floorboards were as clean and shiny as those in a Quaker meetinghouse; on the walls hung some of his own paintings and one by Barnett Newman. Bloore himelf, who was recuperating after major surgery, was almost as pale as his paintings. Lean and still haggard, he reclined on a sofa while we talked.

Bloore had seen great changes in the Canadian art world since the Second World War. In those days there was little happening even in Toronto, where there were few commercial galleries. Aspiring Canadian artists headed for New York, just as Europeans and Americans made for Paris at the turn of the century. In the 1950s Bloore had gone to Saskatchewan to head the art gallery in Regina. He hadn't endeared himself to the small city by describing it as 'an unfortunate interruption of prairie space', and it took the citizens years to forgive him. Not that he despised the place entirely: Regina had always been a socialist hotbed, and there were still a number of old-time radicals around to keep the city on its toes. In those days, and well into the 1960s, it had been possible to be on first-name terms with every Canadian artist; but that was no longer possible and there was a great range of artistic activity right across the country.

'In the United States artists have to go to New York to make their reputation. But one good thing about Canada is that geographical location isn't seen as a reflection on the quality of your work. Christopher Pratt lives in Newfoundland, you've got Alex Colville in Nova Scotia, others in the West. Aspiring artists still go to the city to study, but they can't go off to New York any more as my generation did because they can't afford studio space there. It's much cheaper to find space in Montréal or Toronto, and there's a large artistic community in both cities.'

Although the clotted landscapes of the Group of Seven was the best-known Canadian style, it had long been superseded, despite evidence of its survival in debased form in Charlevoix and elsewhere. The dominating style at present favours a cool naturalism, and both the painters he had mentioned practised it. Theirs was an art both accessible and highly accomplished. Bloore himself represented an elegant and inward strain in a country not given to refinement. The gestures of Canadian art tend to be grandiloquent, on a scale appropriate to the country that nurtures them. With the singular exception of some Inuit carvers, Canada is not famous for its miniaturists.

Bloore, despite his pleasingly caustic tongue, was not saddened or downhearted by the state of Canadian art, and I had hoped to hear comparable good news about Canadian letters when I went to see the distinguished biographer Phyllis Grosskurth. The Canadian novels I'd read had not impressed me hugely; they had seemed heavy-handed, labouring their messages. But I had been reading the acclaimed novels of twenty, even thirty years ago, scarcely representative of what Canadian writers were up to now. Even the books by Margaret Atwood and Mordecai Richler that I'd read – and much admired – had not been recent works. Moreover, it seemed likely that the novels Canadian acquaintances recommended had been pressed upon me less because of their qualities as fiction than because they conveyed some important elements in Canadian life.

I sipped a gin and tonic out of what appeared to be a misplaced goldfish bowl in Grosskurth's pretty Cabbagetown garden, but its owner had little cheer for me. Canadian literature, in her view, consisted mostly of self-absorbed narcissism fuelled by the generous, well-intentioned but not always discriminating Canada Council. She lamented Canadian writers' ignorance of British writing, though she admitted that American novelists were much better known in Canada. To me, this seemed no cause for sorrow. American fiction is in a far more vigorous state than British fiction, which with honourable exceptions is anaemic and daintily self-regarding. I could think of very few British writers whose work I would wish to thrust into the hands of Canadians as models of the art. But to Grosskurth, the Canadian sense of identity was strongly linked to its British past. Once Canada ceased to be British, its whole sense of identity had loosened and it had become a 'country of separate isolations'. It puzzled me that she should speak of a Canadian sense of identity flourishing only when it could draw nourishment from the tired dugs of another nation.

She was, or had been, an intense nationalist. Her activism had been sparked when in the 1960s newly founded universities offered tax-free salaries for two years to American academics willing to come to Canada and teach. The result was both a stifling of Canadian academic talent and a wave of mostly second-rate American scholars and teachers occupying places that should have been taken by Canadians. She was irritated by what she took as a sign that Canadians lack confidence in their own abilities. It's not a feature of the country that has diminished with time.

'This is an envious country,' said Grosskurth dolefully, 'and everybody watches everybody else. In England people are more generous with their praise. But here in Canada people are suspicious of success, resentful of it. And that I also take as an indication that Canadians lack confidence in themselves. We feel anxious because we're not taken seriously in our own right, and most of all we're hurt by the indifference shown towards us by the

United States. But then what is there in Canada to catch their imagination?'

This was too depressing for words. I hadn't noticed that the English were conspicuously generous with their praise. The book review pages were crammed with hatchet jobs, often more entertaining than the books under review, and I myself had felt compelled, when provoked, to engage in some purgative literary thuggery. Then too the Americans were arguably more interested in foreign cultures, even Canadian, than the small-minded British and the fatuously ignorant French. And the following year some British readers would find their imaginations sufficiently caught by matters Canadian to nominate two Canadian novels for the Booker Prize. Phyllis Grosskurth's words, and the attitude they betrayed, while undoubtedly sincere, had the whiff of self-fulfilling prophecy. Chin up! I wanted to say, but didn't.

12

Schnitzel on a Bun

I never dreamed I would lay eyes on a mould of Wayne Gretzsky's feet, but I did. Gretzsky, as the world knows, is Canada's top hockey player, a national hero. His feet, or the moulds thereof, were on display at the Sports Hall of Fame at the Canadian National Exhibition, a jamboree held annually at Toronto since 1879, and combining a showcase for Canadian enterprises, an agricultural show, a peddlers' paradise, and a fun fair. The Sports Hall of Fame did not grip my attention, for apart from Mr Gretzsky's noble feet, sport doesn't display its best features behind glass. The puck that scores looks much like the puck that doesn't. All trophies and cups gleam alike. And the photographs of what are illiterately known as 'honorees' and 'inductees' freeze the animation that distinguishes sport from statuary.

So I moved on, and decided to get the animals out of the way. I made my way to the agricultural halls, led by my nose to the source of richly disgusting smells, and found myself witnessing a climactic event at the Mooternity Ward. No sooner had I arrived, than a large cow squeezed out a black and white calf. Birth attendants dragged the bemused calf – whose first notion of the miraculously volatile outside world was to be cheered at by small boys called Scott – to its mother, who licked it clean. No doubt a few days later the publicity and fun would be over and it would be back to the farm to await its transformation into veal. The piglets were cute too, a dozen pink nine-inch maggoty squiggles attached to a squad of nipples stiffly, bruisedly jutting from the belly of an overwhelmed sow. Elsewhere there were horse trials, observed by spectacled curly-haired women dressed in white or scarlet polyester trousers and their muted husbands, uniformly clad in check shirts and high-waisted trousers and capped with modified pork-pie hats. Reduced to silence by the ghastliness of their spouses, they sat in the bleachers while horses cantered round and round the track.

Viewing all this meat made me hungry, and I ploughed through the crowd to the hall called 'Good Things from the Land', which included the new edition of the *Encyclopedia Britannica*, water filter systems, the Christadelphians offering Proof That Christ's Return Is Imminent, and Tarot card readings. Some people will eat anything. I did find a stand promoting Ontario wild rice, Canada's only native cereal grain. Wild rice is, as its name suggests, a water-logged grass. The exhibitors had the good sense to brew up some wild rice soup, which I enjoyed thoroughly. From here I crossed the exhibition grounds to the Food Hall. Here all the edibles were provided by a complete range of fast food chains and 'donut shoppes'. There was a bargain going at Pizza Delight, the well-known franchise of Robin Hood Multifoods Inc. Here, for the price of a slice you could get absolutely free a 5 oz. Coke. Pepsi, an outfit that, I'm convinced, buy up half Coke's production and relabel it, were sponsoring an entertainment just outside the hall. On a makeshift stage, a dancing girl was whirling her chiffon cloak in time to recorded music. While ingesting my Pizza Delight, I read a pamphlet addressed to the world by Robin Hood Multifoods. They were, it said, 'looking for dynamic goal-oriented achievers with the desire and the financial resources to realize their entrepreneurial ambitions'. All that prospective franchisees require is 'a minimum personal cash base of $45,000 plus a bank line of credit'. If I had all that, I would retire.

I tossed the prospectus away and focused anew on the dancing girl, who was now doing magic tricks, changing bottles into bunches of flowers and vice versa. Her skills went unappreciated, for the large crowd was wholly preoccupied with wiping up after sick children or eating batter, plastic sausage casing, aerated buns, bile-green relish, and all the other staples of great American cooking. I then explored the Shoppers Market, passing on the way the First Ever Butter Sculpting Competition. In the Market, a woman with a mike round her neck was demonstrating a steaming device that produces wrinkle-free clothes without ironing, but no one was listening except me, and I dispensed with irons decades ago. Take it away, lady! Your time has been and gone. Equally useless but more diverting was a brand-new coin-rolling machine. The idea is that you take a stack of coins, and then roll them so that – reader, I have forgotten. But I do remember one brilliant invention, the beer hat. This has the simplicity of genius, for the beer hat is simply a hat that has on either side two clips, each of which will secure one beer can. When wearing it, you can delight your friends with quips about how drink always goes to your head.

Just down the aisle was the stall rented by Jews for Jesus, as though Jesus were busily running for office. Nearby I found a bingo hall. As I travelled across Canada I would learn that, after hockey, bingo is the national sport, one of the few ways to throw away money without moving a muscle.

Although, for obvious reasons, the CNE stresses Canadian products and enterprises, the polyglot nature of Canadian society was reflected outside the International Hall. Here stalls offered food from the world over. It was fascinating to learn so much about the exotic foods that come from exotic places. I knew, of course, that the national dish of England is breaded shrimp and that Swiss bankers and ski instructors alike lunch regularly off Swiss waffles with soft ice cream. But there were some surprises here too. I never knew that Gallic *haute cuisine* features cheese fondue baked fresh on a French stick with tomato and pepperoni, and that the national dishes of Poland and Iceland are, respectively, schnitzel on a bun, and hot corned beef on a kaiser bun. Poor old Hawaii, bled by decades of American colonization, couldn't come up with anything more inspiring than ice cream and iced tea.

The festivities at the fairgrounds continue until well into the evening, when rock concerts are mounted in the Grandstand stadium. Bruce Springsteen was due to give a concert a few days later and a new cottage industry had sprung up in Toronto: forging tickets. As I walked past the Grandstand I couldn't help noticing the crowd of about two thousand young persons around the entrances. Perhaps Springsteen was performing that evening? I approached and made inquiries of a clutch of fourteen-year-old girls with glinting teeth braces and pink nails twinkling with silver glitter dust. They were, they informed me, waiting for Power Station to arrive. The name meant nothing to me, philistine that I am, and I prepared to rejoin the grown-up world. Then I recalled that the two buses I'd seen at the border on my way to Toronto had carried a small card in the window reading: 'POWER STATION TOUR'.

'Ah,' I murmured to the teeny-boppers, 'I think I saw Power Station near Buffalo the other day.'

'EEK!'

'Yip!'

'Did you see Andy?'

'Mike?'

'I don't know. One had a mop of dirty sandy blond hair –'

'Yeek! It was John!'

'No Andy!'

' – and a bushy moustache.'

'John's grown a moustache! Yech!'

'Did he have his hair in a ponytail?'

'No, the ones I saw looked as though they'd just crawled out of bed. After a nightmare.'

'That's Andy.'

'He's lying, he's lying.'

I was so enjoying my vicarious celebrity – it appeared that the next best thing to being Power Station's lead guitar was to have glimpsed them for three seconds – that I decided to prolong the interview. We exchanged views on funny accents (mine) and I explained to them where Birmingham, the seat of Power Station, is in relation to London. But these matters overtaxed their brains, which, like needles drawn to magnetic north, kept reverting to the objects of their passion. Two of the girls, still sheathed in pubertal plumpness and misting over with unfocused sexual sizzle, fished in their bags for badges that portrayed their heroes. The lads didn't look remotely like the scruffs I'd seen on the bus, who were probably technicians or security guards.

'Andy used to be with Duran Duran. Did you ever see them?'

'As a matter of fact I did. I arrived at Heathrow one morning and found a crowd as large as this waiting for them, and two minutes later out they came.'

'He's lying again.'

'You'll be asking me if I ever saw the Beatles next.'

'Who?'

'Must be going. Nice talking to you. Hope it's a good concert.'

'Gee thanks. And if you see John – '

' – or Andy – '

' – tell him two cute Canadians are crazy for them.'

While the Power Station concert was being drowned out by the screams of young girls practising orgasms, I was sitting on the balcony of an apartment block in Yorkville chatting to William Kilbourn. A distinguished historian who had also served as a Toronto alderman, he had been a leading member of the reformist council that helped to preserved downtown Toronto as a residential as well as a commercial district, and that prevented the destruction, in the name of development, of some of the city's oldest buildings. I told him how depressing I had found my conversation with Phyllis Grosskurth some days before. Perhaps her mood had been soured by some private event of which I'd been unaware – a headache or an unwelcome letter – but I couldn't help contrasting her glumness with the attitude of even the most acerbic American critics of their own country, who maintain a passionate fierceness, an energetic determination, however devastating their critique. Lassitude is not an American characteristic. Is it a Canadian one?

Kilbourn, a large shambly man whose speech is more elegant than his clothes, stared into his glass for a while. 'You must remember that Canada is a collection of refugees and defeated peoples. This is a second best destination for those who didn't make it to the United States. But I don't think that makes us feel sorry for ourselves.' On the other hand, he considered that Canada's political structures had moderated the entrepreneurial drive, which was not the case south of the border. The American frontier had been wild and lawless. The Canadian frontier, while just as wild and just as dangerous, had never been lawless. By the time the pioneers got out to the prairie or the Yukon or wherever, they would find that the authorities had usually arrived there first. They might be missionaries, or the railway agent, or the Hudson's Bay factor, or the mounted police, and their institutions were already in place. The colonization of Canada's outposts was directed from the metropolis, and has been ordered and orderly. There has never been a revolution here, and Canadians show an almost instinctive respect for authority. With so stable a structure in place, there's been less need for the aggression, the willingness to take risks, that you find in the States. But, Kilbourn insisted, Canadians possess other qualities just as estimable. He admired the way Canadians preserve their ethnic origins, the way that communities such as the Scots of Cape Breton and the Ukrainians of the prairie provinces had kept their language and culture alive through many generations. Canadians also have a different outlook from that of Americans, even though close contacts between the two nations were causing them to homogenize in other respects. Canadian governments may follow the American line on certain issues too closely, but in general Canadians stubbornly insist, according to Kilbourn, in doing things their own way. Unlike Abe Rotstein, he didn't feel that local rootedness was the clue to the Canadian outlook. 'The United States sees virtue rooted in small towns and the country – but in Canada country is fearsome wilderness. Perhaps most important of all is the absence of a Canadian ideology. We're less jingoistic than the Americans. Hugh Hood once observed that it's inconceivable that there could ever be a parliamentary committee to investigate un-Canadian activities. It comes down to this: there's no such thing as the Canadian dream.'

I mulled over what Kilbourn had said as I walked back towards Cabbagetown, but I was soon distracted. It was on Church Street that I suddenly became aware that the six girls clustered around a bench were not teenagers out for a smoke and a giggle, but teenagers out to sell their bodies. One stepped forward and plucked at my sleeve: 'Wanna date?' I shook my head. A block away, another long-legged girl approached: 'Are you lonely?' Again, I shook my head, and friendly exchanges along these lines were repeated half a dozen times before I made it back to Barrie's house.

'What's all this rubbish about Toronto the Good?' I challenged her. 'I've never seen so many hookers in my life.'

'There's no law against soliciting.'

'Evidently.'

'Want a tour of the hookers? I'll show you a thing or two round here.'

'Sure. Anything to fight vice.'

So I climbed into her car, tipping off the seat a year's accumulation of socks, candy wrappers, school reports, political pamphlets, and hockey pucks.

'Yonge Street was where the hookers used to hang out in the 1960s. In fact they used to hang out of the windows and yell down at the johns on the street. Then the police cleaned the place up and the action moved into the neighbourhoods. Mostly this neighbourhood. When there are enough complaints from local residents, the city changes the directions of the one-way streets. This means the johns have to use different routes for cruising around, and that distributes the girls into different streets until those residents wake up and start complaining too. Then the city changes street directions again. It's a neat system.' Barrie drove slowly down Church and Jarvis, Carlton and Sherbourne, her nose close to the windscreen as if sniffing her way to every street corner, each embellished with at least one prostitute, leaning forward whenever a cruising car approached.

'I used to have fun parking down some of these side streets south of Wellesley. When I'd see a car slowing down to pick up a girl, I'd pretend to be writing down their licence number and I'd yell, "I'm gonna tell your wife!"'

I looked at her as though she were insane. 'People have had their throats cut for less.'

She grinned. 'The other thing that's fun to do is pretend you're a cop.'

'How can you do that?'

I shouldn't have asked. 'I'll show you.' A minute later, down a side street, we spotted ahead of us a white Mercedes. The driver, a swarthy moustachioed man, was leaning out of the window talking to a girl on the kerb.

'Greaseball . . .' murmured Barrie, scenting blood. She let the car idle while he negotiated.

'We'll follow them.' And she did. It wasn't long before the Mercedes driver realized he was being followed, and he pulled over to let us pass. Barrie eased by, and then fifty yards down the road she too stopped. She stared at him. He stared back. We moved off again, and he followed. For some minutes he tailed us, pursuing us down side streets.

'I knew I should have brought my rosary with me.'

'Relax. We'll shake him.'

'If I'd known I was going to die, I wouldn't have said no to all those girls earlier on . . . .'

'Hold tight. I'm pulling over.'

And by various strategems, Barrie did indeed shake off our pursuer. Next stop on our tour was what she called Needle Park, a patch of grass on the corner of Parliament and Gerrard frequented by drunks and pushers. Not much happening there. Then we stopped near a laundromat, still open despite the late hour. It looked inoffensive enough, but the establishment was owned, I gathered, by the sister of leading Toronto Mafiosi.

'You get some strange cars parked here sometimes,' mused Barrie. 'Cars with New York plates full of Chinese guys. Don't ask me what goes on in the upstairs rooms. They don't let me in. The woman who runs this place, she's nice enough. She's still around most nights, which is more than you can say for some of her brothers. One vanished and a couple of others were found stuffed into the trunk of a car – Hi, Mollie!'

Barrie, who knew everyone in Toronto, it seemed, spotted an old friend collecting her laundry, and the two women exchanged indiscretions for a few minutes.

'Okay,' yawned Barrie, 'time to check out the pimpmobiles . . . .' As we headed towards Wellesley, we spotted a handful of people gathered around a man lying face down in the gravel along the kerb. We investigated. No one seemed sure what the problem was, and Barrie offered to call for an ambulance. The nearest telephone just happened to be located inside a café that just happened to be the dump where the local pimps hang out. While Barrie was on the phone, I saw an ambulance arriving at the scene, so we hurried back to the unfortunate youth, who by now had perked up, and instead of just lying on the gravel was attempting to eat it. The grubby lads who had been keeping him company vanished into the night, so Barrie and I explained the situation, such as it was, to the ambulancemen and the occupants of the fire engine that, with an excess of zeal, had also roared up. We left them to it.

'Don't think I've forgotten about the pimpmobiles,' said Barrie, and she turned down the side street. Here a van was parked with the side doors open. 'This is where the hookers check in with their pimps before they go off with the johns. See, there's one in there now. We're laughing, but it isn't that funny. Some of these kids, they come in from small towns like Guelph and they're no more than fourteen years old. Most of them get beaten up from time to time, and some are killed – and most of this stuff goes unreported. The whole thing stinks. Let's go back. Hey no, let's not forget the gay scene. There's a street back of the Y . . . .'

But the street was empty. One boy in white slacks sat on a wall swinging his legs, eyeing the cars that passed.

'A year ago you couldn't move for hustlers. Now there's just one guy. That's the power of AIDS.'

Driving back to her house, Barrie told me how her kids had been wrongly arrested some months before. The police, in her view, had behaved not just wrongly but with incredible stupidity, and there had been talk of filing complaints and various other repercussions. Barrie was not the kind of person who responded docilely on seeing her tearful boys quaking in the back of a police car after having been picked up for an offence they couldn't possibly have committed.

There is, however, a mortifying sequel to this tale, one of many that shows Barrie battling against thick-skinned authorities. Canadians may, as Kilbourn said, instinctively accept authority, but Barrie was far from typical in that respect. Her instinct was to distrust anyone in uniform, anyone with a badge, anyone on a committee. Some months later she had been sitting up long after midnight, reading and smoking, when she heard strange sounds emanating from the house next door, which she knew to be unoccupied that week. Peering out of her back door, she detected signs of unlawful entry. Then a voice muttered, 'Dammit, someone's heard us.' Barrie dashed to the front door just in time to see two men running down the street. Clad only in nightdress and slippers, Barrie gave chase through the snowy streets. By happy chance, her former sparring partners, the police, were patrolling the neighbourhood and arrived on the scene just as Barrie caught up with the burglars and flung herself at them. Arrests were made. And Barrie, to her everlasting shame, was rewarded for her bravery with a special police citation.

13

Licked by Wolves

It was a long way to go for lunch, especially in the middle of February across roads newly polished with snow, but I needed advice on visiting northern Canada and R. D. Lawrence was the man to give it. English by birth, he had come to Canada in 1954 and established himself as one of Canada's best writers about the North and its wildlife. He had a taste for solitude that enabled him to burrow into remote valleys of northern British Columbia for month after month, sometimes in deepest snow-bound winter. There, one year, he had built himself a cabin from which he emerged every day to observe the activities of mountain lions. Such was his rapport with these elusive and dangerous animals that he was eventually able to sit beside one of them as it devoured its prey. Lawrence had written eloquently about this spell in the wilderness in *The Ghost Walker*, and in *The North Runner* he had recorded his relationship with the wolf dog Yukon that had often accompanied him across the Canadian wilderness and saved his life. Lawrence had described his relationships with animals without mawkishness, no mean feat.

It took me about three hours to drive northeast from Toronto to his house on the edge of Algonquin Park. Ron Lawrence proved to be much as I expected: a tall man with a lined serious face. He indulged in little small talk, and over a lunch of cold meats and cheeses reminisced about the north he knew, the north that no casual visitor such as myself, however diligent, could hope to know. He had had the courage to expose himself to it, and in Canada that implies the certainty of discomfort and the possibility of death. I had neither the time, nor, I admit, the inclination, to follow his example. Lawrence, who spent years of his life winning the trust of wild animals, was less enamoured of the human race, with the obvious exception of his wife Sharon. He was not unsympathetic to the plight of the desperately dependent Indians they had lived among in the north, but it was clear that he felt some disdain for those who, for whatever reason,

145

lacked self-reliance. There was a sententious streak to his talk, as though long periods of isolation had led him to formulations about the human condition that he had elevated into certainties.

His neighbours in this thinly populated corner of Ontario were mostly Anglo-Saxon, who had cross-bred through the generations with not always admirable results, and various refugees from the cities, some of them creative and lively people, including scientists and musicians. And, inevitably, these backwoods held more than a few people who were unable to find work and thus lived off welfare. I couldn't imagine any circumstances that would induce Ron Lawrence to collect a cheque for unemployment benefit. He would survive on his own resources wherever he was dumped, not solely because of his resilience but because of a profound sympathy with the natural world, an environment that he perceived as essentially supportive and only incidentally hostile, whereas my own inescapably urban perception of the natural world is the other way round.

After coffee, he said: 'I suppose you'd like to see the wolves.'

'What wolves?'

'I thought that's one reason why you came here. Didn't they tell you about my wolves?'

'May have done . . . .'

'Come on. We'll find you some boots.'

I knew that Lawrence had tamed Yukon, an exceptionally fierce dog, but raising and keeping wolves was another matter. I'd heard all the radio documentaries about how wolves were scarcely more formidable than hamsters, but I'd never believed them. A hundred yards from the house, behind a wire fence stretched across the property, a hut stood at the edge of the woods. The three of us were just beginning to clomp through the fresh snow, when two silver-furred beasts came tearing out of the hut and began a fugue of howls and yelps. I slowed down.

'They're perfectly friendly . . . .'

Oh yeah? I am bitten regularly by dogs, and the likelihood that these howling wolves would help themselves to *Brook tartare* seemed high. But they were, at that moment, secure behind the fence, so I approached with faked jauntiness.

Ron tried to hush the wolves, and explained to me that they were only making so much noise because they were excited to meet someone new, a statement that merely doubled my anxieties. Ron urged me to step closer, assuring me they would do me no harm. I did so. Then he told me to put my hand through a gap in the fence so that the wolves could inspect it. The man was obviously out of his skull, deranged by all those solitary months in the wilderness. I stepped back again.

'They want to lick your hand . . . .'

'I know they're hungry, but can't you find them somebody else to eat?'

Lawrence showed signs of impatience with me, and insisted that it was essential that the wolves should get to know me, that they were more frightened of me than I was of them – impossible – and that the swiftest way to initiate détente was to allow them to slobber over my hand. I stretched out my left hand, more dispensable than the pen-clutching right, and thrust it towards the drooling maws of the excited wolves as their beautiful heads strained forward towards their human lollipop. Ron was right, of course. After a thorough slurping, the boys calmed down, went for a romp through the woods, and then engaged in a little Sumo wrestling with their master.

And so it was that I explored the Canadian wilderness and became chummy with a pair of full-grown wolves. It took courage to do what I did, but you can't get to know the place unless you open yourself to it. I'd survived a visitation of leeches in the Malaysian jungle, and the lash of jellyfish half a mile out in the Adriatic, and now I'd won the trust of two determined predators. It takes a special kind of man to be at one with the natural world, and it's a gift on which I pride myself. Later that day, as I sat in a Chinese restaurant on Spadina nibbling on prawns baked in salt, I looked around me at the flabby city types chortling over their spicy beef and Molson's beer and I wondered how many of them had spent the afternoon being salivated over by animals whose standard equipment includes two-inch fangs.

When I returned to Toronto the following summer, I had intended to visit the Algonquin Park, and hoped to renew my acquaintance with the Lawrences and with Spot and Fido. But there was insufficient time for this excursion and I had to content myself with shorter journeys into the less challenging countryside around Toronto.

One Saturday morning I made my way west to the farmers' market at Kitchener. When, almost two hundred years ago, the town was founded by German settlers, it was known as Berlin. This is a corner of Canada thickly populated by German Mennonites and Pennsylvania Dutch Amish, sects that still preserve their puritanical ways. They scorn modern appliances, don't vote, shun liquor and tobacco, wear unbecoming clothes, cover any parts of the body that could conceivably inflame desire, and, more positively, display a communal spirit that is both admirable in itself and much appreciated by the other inhabitants of rural Ontario.

I had long had a fascination with these austere sects, ever since I visited the Amish townships of Pennsylvania, where German is the first language, smiling is frowned upon, and the horse and buggy the only approved method of transportation. Indeed, I had once successfully impersonated a minister of the Hutterite community, another sect of equally stern outlook. While sharpening my pencil as a junior editor on the *Atlantic Monthly*, I had been promised greater responsibilities, which not only failed to materialize but were evidently receding. Inevitably, I grew bored. To amuse myself, I took to writing fake Letters to the Editor. My first effort alleged that, as the consequence of seeing a particularly graphic cover of the *Atlantic* that depicted a guillotine designed to lop off penises, my little son had built a model of this device in woodworking class and only my timely intervention prevented him from demanning himself. This letter was immediately accepted for publication. Only after I corrected the proofs did I come clean. My senior colleagues chortled, but the bogus letter was pulled from the proofs. A few months later I struck again after editing an article about the Hutterites.

In my letter, which was signed by Gustav Bimmel and dispatched from Yaphank, New York, I wrote the following authentically awkward prose:

Not all Hutterites who arrived in New York in the last century trekked to the Midwest. A small colony remained as farmers on Staten Island. In 1924 the farm discontinued, but Jakob Hutter Colony still thrives as a religious body here in Yaphank, though we no longer live communally. Communal living still works in the prairies, but here in the urban East proximity to sinful ways harmed the ideals of our colony.

Nevertheless, our colony still gathers once a week for *Platteabend*, where we eat in praise of Our Lord. And of course we observe together the Sabbath Day and keep it holy. Because of a theological controversy in the early years of this century, and because our lifestyles are now different, there is no formal contact with our brethren in South Dakota. The issue of the authority of the *Stimme* (voice), and to whom it may rightfully speak, still divides us.

We do not consider our concept of *Gemeinschaft* has been under-mined in essence, though it has of necessity been modified. For instance, our colony will permit dancing, provided the partners do not touch except to clap hands with each other.

Und so weiter.

Needless to say, the editors of one of North America's leading intellectual monthlies instantly accepted this drivel for publica-tion and once again I had the pleasure of correcting the proofs of my own work. I confessed, and Bimmel's tedious letter duly ended up in the waste paper basket. My superiors were less amused this time around, so I resolved that the next time I made a spontaneous contribution to the magazine I would forgo the courtesy of a confession. My career as a magazine editor did not continue for many months more.

I was still intrigued by these dour Protestant sects. I like to brush against the habits of passing nuns for much the same reason, testing their purity against my lack of it. Nuns, sad to say, now adopt civvies, but Mennonites still wear their traditional garb. The Mennonite women behind the trestle tables at the Kitchener farmers' market were stout and strong, their hair hooded beneath starched white caps, their full figures loosely wrapped in dresses made from dark flower print material. Their apple-cheeked daughters wore similar dresses of lighter material, but no caps; instead their hair was tightly braided into double pigtails, and their spindly legs were encased in unbecoming brown knee socks so that they resembled furniture. As in the Pennsylvania markets, there was a plentiful supply of Dutch baked goods, such as shoo fly pie, a sticky slab composed of molasses, corn syrup, and brown sugar. It was surprisingly lacking in taste, but it has other uses, including roof insulation.

Most visitors to the market were simply local people stocking up the larder for the week ahead. But there were also a few members of the ugly squad in town, people who humourlessly forsake the city for an honest life of toil on some patch of earth where they can cultivate their primitive smug ignorance and bad breath, and where their dribble-powered babies can run around naked and scare the animals. A number of ugly squad mums were in Kitchener that morning, instantly identifiable by their absence of make-up, their lifeless hair, their turned-up jeans, their pendulous breasts, and their babies tucked into back-pouches; their hus-bands tended to have sparse beards and hounded eyes and walked as though attached to an invisible leash. This branch of the clientele was catered to admirably by some fruit growers from Northern Ontario, who were selling blueberries advertised, irresistibly, as 'pesticide free, student picked'. Yes sir, nothing like student picking to give that country-fresh flavour.

The following day I revisited Niagara Falls, last honoured with my presence in 1965, because it seemed perverse not to. Its glories have been splendidly documented by earlier visitors – including Dickens, Kipling, Rupert Brooke, and Oscar Wilde – and although words are inexhaustible, mine certainly can't soar any higher than theirs. Of course the Niagara that earlier observers described is not the Niagara one sees today. The ferocity of those sheets of water, the immense vista across the churning rapids behind the lip of the falls, the veils of spray – all this has become an enclosure against which the unsightly encroachments of urban Niagara nuzzle up. The throngs of tourists – including the honeymooners in convoy, their cars tagged with ribbons and flowers, who inexplicably celebrate their nuptials in one of the most public spots in North America – have to be sheltered, fed, and entertained. Niagara is not just a waterfall but a resort. Since the splendour of the falls alone can scarcely supply sufficient excitement to carry holidaymakers through a week of pleasure-seeking, their quest for jollity is given a helping hand by a barrage of tacky paraphernalia.

On the one hand there are the facilities that offer you a different angle on the falls – either from the top of an observation tower, from helicopters, from the Spanish Aero Car, or from the innumerable little tugs all called *Maid of the Mist* that ferry raincoated tourists into the spray at the foot of the white walls of water. Different vantage spots are connected by buses frankly named People Movers, and red double-deckers from London Transport's surplus stock perform a similar function more expensively. To add an authentic touch, the double-deckers retain their route numbers and destinations, but the research is slapdash, for the 68 doesn't run to Southall, any more than the 105 will take you to Clapham. A complex of hotels and roads and bridges ring the falls lest a viewpoint should escape. And for those who have had their fill of the falls, there are the sideshows: the landscaped parks, the world's largest roller coaster, Marineland with its killer whales, Louis Toussaud's Waxworks ('New for '85: Boy George'), Ripley's Believe It Or Not Museum (featuring the Mystery Faucet), Miniature World, the Elvis Presley Museum, Reptile World, the fast-food troughs on Clifton Hill, and the prostitutes along Queen Street imported from Buffalo. You, and the fourteen million other visitors each year, can dine at Mama Mia's ('a standout Italian restaurant') or at Hungarian Village ('a landmark restaurant') or at Carlos O'Brian's ('the most unique eating emporium in the Niagara area'). And if you're still hungry, jog over to Swiss Fudge, where the goo is stirred up according to 'the Collins family's secret recipes'. By dusk, I found, the crowds had cleared to fill their stomachs, and by walking to the observation point just behind the awesome spot at which visual expectations are confounded as the sweeping complex of rapids simply tumbles over the edge of the Horseshoe Falls, from here, with the sounds of the roaring water obliterating all else and with the spray splattering against my face, from here I could enjoy not so much a view as a contemplation of the inhuman power of Nature.

A sense of scale is restored at the nearby village of Niagara on the Lake, a village both pretty and prettified. Mature trees line the broad streets, including some copper beeches that were beginning to darken with the early approach of the Canadian autumn. The modest nineteenth century houses are decked with twee signs, evidence of a self-consciousness that almost negates the charms to which they draw attention. The village sustains itself by self-advertisement, and then, having attracted bus loads of tourists, has to divert them not with the delights of the village itself, which, with the singular exception of a charming apothecary's shop of 1820 delightfully restored as a museum of pharmacy, are minimal, but with ways of spending their money, as though an excursion can only be justified by bringing back tangible proof of one's visit. Thus there are shops that in August sell Christmas baubles, others that peddle mass-produced ornaments as 'collectibles', outlets for Scottish woollens, 'Special Gifts for Special People', and souvenir shops that provide knicknackery from the Falls as well as from the village. This is no way for a former capital of Upper Canada (from 1792 to 1797) to disport itself.

In summer, the village remains crowded into the early evening, for this is the home of the Shaw Festival. The more famous festival at Stratford, Ontario, pays partial homage to Shakespeare, and the Niagara on the Lake festival does the same for Shaw. I took a double dose, and attended a matinée of Noel Coward's *Cavalcade* as well as an evening performance of Shaw's *Heartbreak House*. Thus the day was a dual tribute to a nostalgic view of Britain to which none of its natives subscribe. *Cavalcade* seemed vapid and grandly sentimental, though it had the merit of unfailing theatricality. *Heartbreak House* does of course present a more troubled view of Britain lurching into the twentieth century, and this particular production captured beautifully the fantastical element in the play, especially when the curtain rose on the first act to show Ellie dozing, and moments later the very walls of the room in which she sits rise to a great height, a Lewis Carroll-like entry into a dream world. The theatre was packed for both performances, not just with Canadians but with Americans, mostly from New York State, who had driven up for the day. What a bizarre view of Britain this very Anglophile festival must convey, and I wondered whether Canadians, who affect, some of them, a connection with Britain that Americans shrugged off two hundred years ago, felt that these imaginative visits to a vanished Britain brought them into a real communion with the land which their ancestors had left a century or more ago. For the likes of Louise Hill, Britain was, imaginatively, much as it had been in the days of George V. Even *Coronation Street*, touted in *Britannia*, would have been incomprehensible to her. Nor did I believe she was isolated in this, for any nation that continues to celebrate Queen Victoria's birthday eighty-five years after the sour-faced duck breathed her last must hold in its psychic cupboard of toys any number of archaic baubles that can't help but render ineffective any emergent sense of a distinctly Canadian national identity.

Part Five

The Prairies

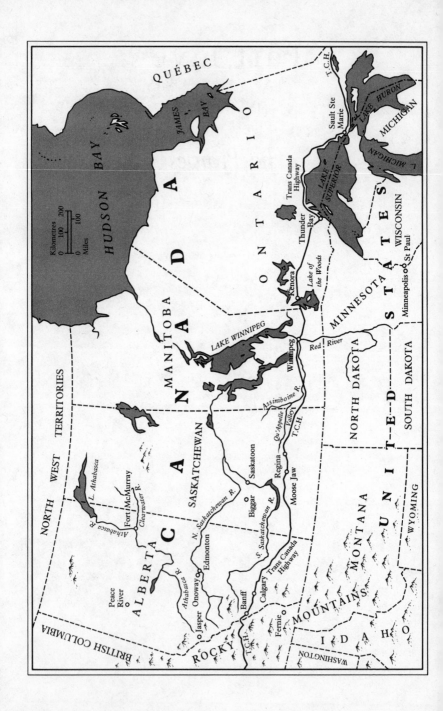

14

Mr Cropo's Evening Out

I now pulled from my kitbag of preconceptions the one telling me that the 'real Canada' didn't begin until the shores of Lake Superior were glimpsed some hundreds of miles northwest of Toronto. Central Canada and the Maritimes, while no Liechtenstein, had a palpable coherence. Distances were great but negotiable. The forests of New Brunswick and rural Québec may have stretched to the horizon but they were not unbroken, and every thirty or fifty miles a small town would appear. The landscape was not unrelated to the vistas of Europe or New England; it was unfamiliar but not alien. Only at James Bay had I truly felt the vastness of Canada and sensed the panic that could overtake one in a malnourished landscape that stretched for hundreds of miles unchangingly in every direction. The same was true of northern Ontario and of the immense thousand-mile tract of the province from Georgian Bay north of Toronto to Thunder Bay and the Manitoba border to the west.

This was a landscape of rock and water, trees and hardy shrubs providing the scraggly toupee on the great bald surface of the Canadian Shield. Although the desolate terrain north of Lake Superior was, in relation to the Northwest Territories, a southern outpost, its climate was far from tropical and the winter weather could be as malign as in the Arctic regions. Storms and wintry winds tearing across the endless plateau had whipped up some of the very worst conditions encountered by those who built this stretch of the Canadian Pacific Railway. Two roads crossed this part of the province from east to west, and north of them there was nothing, no habitation apart from isolated bands of Indians and, by the Arctic shores, tiny Inuit settlements. The only sizable communities in this part of Ontario were the shipping ports of Sault Ste Marie and Thunder Bay, the most westerly terminal of the St Lawrence Seaway. Between Thunder Bay and the Manitoba border were a handful of mining towns, for the Canadian Shield is rich in minerals, though the cost of extraction and erratic commodity prices have impeded their exploitation.

From Thunder Bay straight roads rip through the forests and then fade out. Beyond, the wooded landscape seemed to have only barely risen above the surface of a vast lake, as though the natural condition of the terrain was aquatic and pockets of rocky land were concessions granted by the water. It's an obstacle course of woods and lakes and noisome marshes, a trackless morass, a monument to inhospitality, a defiant snarl of nature. At Kenora water begins to overwhelm the land, and the aptly if unimaginatively named Lake of the Woods stretches like a great wet flag as far as the border. A hundred miles further west, just before the shores of Lake Winnipeg, the landscape is transformed, and wilderness gives way to bands of rectangular fields, a quilt of pale green grains and dark green woods and the straw colour of ripening wheatfields. In the corners of some fields lines of willow and poplar stand like sentinels to guard farmhouses or barns from wind and storm. All along this easterly strip of Manitoba are farms that constitute the last patches of cultivation for a thousand miles. Their proprietors can look east to the barren lands of northern Ontario, and, swivelling on their heels, can gaze out over flat unsullied prairie that sways in the breeze for a further thousand miles.

Manitoba was, as the first fertile spot beyond Lake Superior, the gateway to western Canada. Indian bands have been roaming its forests and fishing its lakes for at least 12,000 years. No European set foot here until a certain Captain Button did so in 1612; in the 1730s the French established outposts here, followed by the Hudson's Bay Company later in the century. In the Anglican Cathedral in Winnipeg the heraldic east window contains the Company's crest alongside that of Manitoba, a visible tribute to their mutual interdependence. In 1812 Lord Selkirk chose this junction of two rivers as the centre of his newly founded Red River Settlement, which he stocked with dispossessed crofters from Scotland.

Manitoba joined the Confederation when in 1869 the Hudson's Bay Company agreed to cede control of the Red River Settlement, which included most of Manitoba, to the Canadian government. Louis Riel led the resistance to these plans, arguing that the position of the Métis (Indians who interbred with the early French settlers but usually maintained a way of life more Indian than

European) within the proposed Confederation was unclear and that Méti lands were in danger of being taken over. He led the formation of a provisional government later that year but confrontation with Canadian officials resulted in the injudicious execution of one of them. Prime Minister John Macdonald cooled the situation, not without some noisy sabre rattling, and subsequent negotiations led to the colony's absorption into Confederation in July 1870.

Riel emigrated to the United States. Had he stayed there he would have died an elder statesman, but fifteen years later the Métis of Saskatchewan found themselves facing the identical problem that had troubled their brothers in Manitoba, and Riel was urged to come to their rescue. He did so, but on this occasion there was serious violence; once the rebellion was crushed, Riel was brought to trial on a charge of high treason. Although his lawyers maintained that Riel, who was prone to religious megalomania, was insane, Riel himself would have none of it. He was sentenced to death and Macdonald refused to commute the sentence. So Riel, who was by this stage clinically mad despite the strength of his political arguments, went to the scaffold a martyr on 16 November 1885. He is buried in the graveyard of the cathedral at St Boniface, the sizable French district of Winnipeg. By his gravestone someone had tossed a fresh marigold, its orange yellow splashing against the grey of the stone. The Riel family house, a modest farmhouse of 1881, still stands on the edge of the city. Although never Louis' permanent home, it remained in the Riel family until 1969, when it was turned into an attractive little museum, refurnished to resemble its probable appearance in 1886.

By the late nineteenth century Winnipeg was a boom town, and fortunes were made and lost in real estate speculation as the vast wheat reserves of the prairies began to be turned into ready cash and new settlers were lured westward in hopes of a free ride to prosperity. The commercial district of Market Square contains warehouses and banks built to a grandeur of scale unmatched in any other Canadian city. Some of the commercial buildings still maintain their original function, others are partly converted into spacious bars, clubs and shops, others stand empty. The Victorian blocks of Vieux Montréal, though solid and imposing, are modest compared to the splendours of Winnipeg. The business boom came later to Winnipeg than to Central Canada, and new construction techniques made it possible to build high. Some of the office blocks seem modelled on the magnificent turn-of-the-century towers of

Lower Broadway in New York; one in particular resembles Louis Sullivan's beautiful Bayard Building. Commercial blocks still pristine in their skin of white terracotta stand alongside more sombre neo-Romanesque warehouses of rusticated stone and hefty round-arched windows.

The boom had begun in 1878, when the railway linked Winnipeg with St Paul, Minnesota. Twelve years later a dozen separate railway lines flowed out of Winnipeg, which had become a centre not just for the booming grain business but for all trading operations in the west. With the Grain and Produce Exchange vigorously shaking its floury skirts through the last decade of the century, it was only a matter of time before more formal institutions in the shape of large Eastern banks opened branches in Winnipeg. These banks sought to present an image of immovable reliability, and this is certainly achieved by the pompous neo-classical porticos along Main Street. With the outbreak of the First World War, Winnipeg's prosperity dwindled and such commercial development as there was moved south of Portage, where it left a far less distinguished legacy. Grain nonetheless remains crucial to Manitoba's economy. There are almost 30,000 farms in the province, and one third of their production consists of wheat; barley and rapeseed are other important crops, and livestock production flourishes to the west.

There is nothing monochrome about Winnipeg. It's a city of many aspects, and of hideous contrasts. The prosperous middle classes live in spacious suburban enclaves, while new arrivals cluster into the more modest suburbs, such as those I had passed through on my way into town from the airport. On one side of the street was a Greek grocery, and the plate glass window of the European bakery offered a glimpse of fleshy breads and pastries. There was a Chinese cinema on one corner, Italian delicatessens, and the dingy offices of the Free Vietnamese Association of Manitoba.

Yet there was more than ethnic cosiness to Winnipeg. The city had an unexpected grandeur, a pomp that blended unhappily with the routine violence and misery I was soon to observe on its streets. The Legislative Building is a vast edifice of mottled beige Manitoba limestone. This hefty four-square structure is, my guidebook eagerly insisted, 'one of world's great examples of the neo-classical style', a statement that would make Palladio or Lord Burlington turn beneath their steles. But in its own hybrid way it's an imposing pile, inside as well as outside. Sphinxes loll beside the pediment above the main entrance, while inside, the Great Staircase flows upwards between the bronze shanks of two mighty bison, their presence a weighty and poignant reminder of the vast herds that were eradicated when the prairies were settled. Columns and flagstones of Italian and Vermont marble lend a luxurious touch to the public halls. Inside the ceremonial Manitoba Room were allusions to Canada's links with a now defunct imperial Britain: large portraits of King George V and Queen Mary in full regalia.

This imperial legacy is, however, presided over by Canada's version of socialists, the New Democratic Party. Nor is this a recent development, for there has always been a strong socialist presence in the prairies, which were settled in large numbers by Scandinavians who had packed their social democratic traditions along with their ploughs and hoes. The NDP under Howard Pawley seems to be riding high: unemployment rates are among the lowest in Canada, and a new hydro project on the Nelson River in northern Manitoba was requiring an investment of $2.1 billion but would, it was hoped, create 19,000 new jobs, especially for the native peoples of the area, and large profits from the sale of hydroelectricity to the American Midwest. Manitoba's share of economic woe is provided by unprofitable crown corporations, such as Manitoba Forest Industries and Mackenzie Seeds, organizations that have been losing money for years, whatever the colour of the government.

Downtown Winnipeg is little more than a dispersal of department stores and car parks. Tall glossy office complexes, with underground shopping arcades beneath them, line both sides of Portage, and the famous intersection of Main and Portage, once a symbol of Canadian prosperity as potent as Toronto's Bay Street or Montréal's St James Street, has become even more gale-swept than before by the presence of glass skyscrapers that form wind tunnels. Nearby are the museums of Main Street, while on the opposite corner of the downtown district are the landscaped parks around the Legislative Building and the new Art Gallery built of sculptural concrete. Most of the people pressing through its doors at lunchtime were on their way to the rooftop restaurant, not the galleries.

Two rivers, the Red and the Assiniboine, twist through the city. One of the oldest corners of Winnipeg is not downtown but along the banks of the Red River. Here the first Anglican church in western Canada was built in 1822. The present structure dates from 1926, but it does form part of a more ancient complex, set in a beautiful churchyard; its elms shade the oldest cemetery in western Canada. Inside the wagon-roofed cathedral are memorial tablets to early settlers, such as Ann Charles, who, dead a month after her father, 'received the reward to filial anxiety and watchfulness' at the age of twenty-four. On the other side of the Red River is the substantial French quarter of St Boniface. Apart from the French street signs, the district doesn't look very different from the rest of Winnipeg. Only around the cathedral is there a Frenchness as palpable as that of Québec. A soaring west front is all that remains of the splendid neo-Romanesque structure that burnt down in 1968. The nearby convent of 1846, a cheerful shuttered building, is now a museum, but could pass for a resort hotel in New England.

Between downtown and suburbia lies Osborne Village, Yup-piedom's contribution to Winnipeg. Restored houses are now filled with restaurants, ice-cream parlours, and boutiques selling scented candles, wrapping paper, Giorgio Armani pimple cream, hand-blown chocolates, and other accoutrements essential to maintaining an upwardly mobile lifestyle. Beyond Osborne Village curls Wellington Crescent, the front line of the grandest Winnipeg suburbs: River Heights and the appropriately named Tuxedo. Elegant elms shade the streets, cooling them in summer, providing mere adornment in winter. Beyond the suburbs are two parks, one tame and the other wild. Assiniboine Park has a riotously planted and colourful English Garden and in summer the exquisite feet of the Royal Winnipeg Ballet's dancers flit through the grass giving free performances. The Assiniboine Forest lacks high culture, but offers instead cross-country ski trails and thick woods that are particularly treasurable in a land where trees don't grow unless you plant them.

The moneyless are advised to head east from the Red River to the Royal Canadian Mint, a building far more attractive than its function would suggest. It is housed in a lovely glass tower with a steep-pitched roof, and in symbolic recognition of the desirability of wealth the Mint is moated. A fountain splashes merrily and brightly coloured flowers divert your attention from the primary concern of this birthplace of coin. Inside, in a long low shed tucked behind the elegant glass tower, is the mint itself, clanking out three billion coins each year not only for Canada but for the nations of Australia, Spain, Honduras, and Papua New Guinea, which proudly displays not a sovereign's head but a shrunken one.

From the Mint I returned downtown, intending to lunch at the city's one and only Native Canadian restaurant. When I located it, I found it had been transformed into a distinctly non-native steak house. So much for buffalo stew and bannock. Instead I ended up in Little Old Lady Land, at the Georgian Room in Eaton's department store. The waitresses as well as the clientele were old enough to have attended the funeral of George III himself, and service was thrombotic. The food was worse, though there was something heroic about the dedication to carbohydrates evidenced by garnishing my overcooked omelette with both chips and toast. On emerging from Eaton's I took advantage of DASH, the free bus service that follows the perimeter of the downtown area. I was also impressed by special buses for the handicapped that I kept seeing. In my country, had they existed, they would have been sold off and converted into delivery vans for Fortnum & Mason's.

Multicultural Winnipeg may be the gateway to the west, but it is no frontier town. It lost its rawness almost a century ago, and now breathes with ease and assurance and confidence, though some Torontonians told me they would sooner sell their children than move there. True, the winters are foul, but it's their length more than their severity that taxes the temper and the constitution. Given that Winnipeg has only a sixth of Toronto's population, it can boast of its cultural assets – its orchestra, its ballet company, its many museums – with more justification than most Canadian cities, all of which like to claim a unique sophistication and cultural splendour.

I called on the brightest ornament of Winnipeg's cultural scene in the person of Arnold Spohr, the artistic director of the Royal Winnipeg Ballet. The company's school and offices, on a dingy block along Portage, contained ill-ventilated offices leading off narrow corridors made almost impassable by crates of costumes and jettisoned filing cabinets. Corners were obstructed by leotarded dancers clutching plastic cups of coffee and gossiping between bouts at the barre. Spohr's office, which actually had a window, was reached across a creaky gallery that overlooked the main practice hall. Spohr welcomed me warmly. After we had shaken hands he stood before me, well over six feet tall, his whole body shimmering with a taut restlessness. Although a former dancer himself, he did not seem entirely at ease within his tall frame and his shoulders were slightly hunched. He talked fast and breathlessly, the flow of words impeded by a slight lisp and a failure to part his lips.

Spohr had been associated with the company for almost thirty years, and had been its director since 1958. During the 1960s many of his dancers were recruited from outside Canada, especially from the United States, but when in 1970 the Canada Council began to give the company financial support, it also demanded a larger proportion of Canadian dancers. Recruitment began and so did training programmes, using the Kirov method. These days most RWB dancers begin their training at the Winnipeg school, which is clearly capable of turning out world-class dancers. Spohr deliberately presents a diversified repertoire of about 200 works, fifty to sixty of which may be performed in any year. The company also spends a good deal of time outside Canada, and has toured thirty-two countries, including a courageous but triumphant tour of Russia in 1968. Although Spohr himself did not make this point, other Manitobans regretted that the RWB was better appreciated outside the province than within it.

Since the RWB was not performing while I was in Winnipeg, I asked Spohr whether I might sit in on the rehearsal class taking place in the hall outside his office. He had no objection, and so I sat up in the gallery looking down on the hard-working dancers below. They were being kept in line by Galina Yordanova, a guest teacher from Bulgaria. 'Boyss, boyss, look at me,' she called, as she demonstrated some steps with a nimbleness and precision that sprang oddly from her short stocky body. As the repetiteur banged away at the piano and the dancers leapt and twirled and lifted and swooned, her voice rose clearly above the hubbub: '*Assemblé, assemblé, changement, changement, jeté, boyss, jeté!*' The school principal, David Moroni, was leaning against a wall, and as the dancers began to hurl their bodies into a new routine, he stepped forward and took the hand of a dancer in a black leotard. With tact and restraint he led her through the steps. Moroni himself was not dancing at full throttle, but merely facilitating the steps of his partner. And she, the dancer in black, moved beautifully through the steps, with impeccable line and grace. I was not the only one to notice the sheer loveliness of her movements, and within a few minutes all the other dancers had come to a halt and watched intently. When the *pas de deux* came to an end, they applauded.

I asked a man seated nearby who the entrancing dancer in black was. He looked at me in astonishment and told me it was Evelyn Hart. Since she is one of the very finest ballerinas in North

America, I could well understand his amazement at my ignorance. It was the very absence of any audience except her colleagues that made her dancing not only beautiful to watch but moving. The emotion was mine; for the class it was routine, though they were privileged in their access, and the rehearsal soon resumed. But a few minutes later it was interrupted again as a girl carried in a large cake, its candles fluttering as she moved gingerly across the hall. It was the birthday of Tracy Koga, another RWB ballerina. Again the company applauded and Tracy was kissed by one and all. By now I felt that I was intruding on a private party and slipped away. But memories of that morning, with that unexpected and ravishing *pas de deux* performed, I fancied, solely for my unsuspected pleasure would warm me through many of the more desolate moments to come as I continued my journey across Canada.

My walks through the Warehouse District took me repeatedly past the prostitutes showing a leg on most corners. Since they remained at their stations for the hour or so I was tramping these streets, business was evidently poor. I dare say most Manitobans have other occupations at three in the afternoon. The District, spread behind both sides of Main Street, dovetails into the section of the street dominated by cheap hotels and seedy bars. 'Drunken Indian' is almost a term of abuse, but on this afternoon, and indeed at almost any time of the day or night, it accurately summarized the condition of most of the people walking the streets. There are 40,000 Status Indians (natives from bands that signed treaties with the Canadian government) and 20,000 Métis in Manitoba, and a sizable proportion of them crowd the bars.

Their poses were not attractive: many were slumped, or at best huddled, in doorways, their shiny black hair matted and grubby, their eyes withdrawn and expressionless, their sturdy bodies drooping and listless. Along Main Street the human wreckage was even more widely strewn. A drunken woman weaved along towards me, no longer attempting to walk in a straight line, and all the determination of her jaw was concentrated on remaining upright, a battle that some of her companions along the street had lost. On the next block another drunk, not an Indian, was stumbling along the pavement, singing loudly and cheerfully; over his shoulder he had slung an axe, and though he showed no signs of intending to lop off the limbs of passersby, he was given a wide berth. Near the museums along Main Street I came upon a police car disgorging three cops, who gave brief chase to a heavily built Indian. As the policemen hurled themselves towards him, he took flight but was soon tackled and brought to the ground. He was unceremoniously dragged back to the kerb and bundled into the waiting car. At the bus stop just a few yards away, the crowd scarcely looked up from their newspapers and crossword puzzles. I was, I realized, witnessing an event so common as not to be worthy of attention.

I entered the bar of the McClaren Hotel by pushing past the swaying, red-eyed bodies by the door. The large saloon was packed with men and women, mostly Indians, mostly drunk. There was noise in the bar but no animation. From time to time a man would rise to his feet and stagger to the bar for fresh rounds of beer, while at the tables his companions would mutter listlessly or stare into the middle distance. Only at the pool tables was there any liveliness, a slap on the back, a loud laugh, a cadenza of swearing. I became conscious of the relative swiftness of my movements. I'm no slouch, and my quick strides into the bar seemed to throw out a field of energy that disturbed my fellow drinkers, some of whom stared at me uneasily, although many were too comatose to lift, or even open, their eyes.

I downed my beer in less than a minute. The scene was too distressing. Winnipeg is a prosperous and cultivated city that also embraces the largest Indian slum in North America. It's been there for years, and, despite the presence of Salvation Army hostels and refuges for alcoholics, the situation never improves. Indians come down from the reservations in search of jobs and an income. Those lucky enough to find a job don't hold it for long, and within a month or so the majority of new arrivals have succumbed to the mind-numbing lures of the cheap beer halls and, if they have enough money left, ride their nightmares in the grubby old hotels adjoining the bars. Of course many Indians do not conform to this bruising stereotype, but it seemed dismayingly accurate as I weaved between lurching bodies, my feet slipping in pools of spilt ale, my eyes smarting from the folds of pale blue cigarette smoke tumbling in the sweat-moistened air. I finally made it back to the door and out into the bright sunshine.

The relief was short-lived. Coming towards me along Main Street was more human wreckage, stumbling towards the hotel entrance. I veered down a side street and into the alley behind the hotel. Here were two young Indian women, no more than twenty, their heads thrown back as they drained their beer bottles, which they then tossed expertly into a skip already overflowing with the hotel's garbage. It seemed hard to believe that I was still in clean, honest, decent, socially responsible Canada. Indeed, the widely acknowledged paradox is that the very generosity of Canada's social programmes has helped destroy the centuries-old system of hunting and food-gathering that sustained Indian bands in their remote northern outposts, and replaced it with a steady supply of welfare cheques that could purchase immediate gratification, usually in the form of alcohol. Many liberal Canadians were convinced that the problem was both desperate and intractable. Here, in my first encounter with large numbers of Indians, I was face to face with the despair and the intractability. Only later in my travels would the full complexity of the problems of the native Canadians, with its rays of hope and wells of darkness, become more apparent.

As I walked towards the dock, I could hear the faint but bright sounds of a steel band. Yes, this was Winnipeg and I was about to go on a Caribbean cruise. This unlikely way to spend the evening has been devised by the proprietor of the *Lord Selkirk II*, a pleasure boat that used to cruise Lake Winnipeg but is now demoted to the less taxing voyage up and down the Red River. This exotic adventure has been dreamed up by a Hungarian who came to Winnipeg after living sixteen years in East Croydon, an ordeal he has survived remarkably well. The *Lord Selkirk* was packed, since the cruise had been selected for an office outing by a large oil company. Shyly accompanied by spouses, guests shuffled up the gangway; long dresses were gathered up in one hand while the other clutched the railing; men in blazers rubbed their moustaches and cheerily greeted colleagues they probably despised in the office. Mr Cropo the undertaker, a large man with broad Slavic features and pale sandy hair that complemented his pale blue suit, had in tow six Ukrainian nuns, who acted with that crisp jauntiness shown when those who live by the Rule are given the evening off. Mr Cropo was the most solicitous of hosts, a model of benign courtesy and effortless patronage. Even a nun will one day be a corpse.

The ship's whistle blew, and a few of us gathered by the rails to watch as we cast off. Gina the restaurant hostess, wearing nothing but a tight sarong and shivering in the rapidly cooling evening air, handed out streamers. As the ropes uncurled and the *Lord Selkirk* pulled away from the dock, the half dozen of us on deck, urged on by Gina, flung our paper streamers towards the shore. A vast crowd, consisting of the ticket clerk and the car park attendant, stood on the quay to wave farewell. I stayed on deck for a while as we moved downriver. For a mile or so the french windows of pleasant houses seemed to promise endless garden parties as they unrolled their lawns down to the willow-shaded banks.

On the deck below, the Shell party were knocking back the fruit punch and the nuns were nursing their Fantas. After an hour of increasing conviviality most of the two hundred people on board went to the dining room to pick at the Caribbean buffet, while I joined a small group in another dining room for a more formal and surprisingly good meal of lobster quenelles and prawns in whisky and cream. After dinner my high-spirited fellow passengers began to whoop and yell to encourage the limbo dancers who had suddenly materialized, and I returned to the deck.

The creamy but fading light of the sunset, partially obscured by the tree-lined riverbank, spread across the western sky, which was darkening into ever more profound shades of blue, as though working its way down a paint chart. Dramatic backlighting was provided by a full moon that coyly peered out from behind banks of low cloud. Romantic Winnipeg! It was too, though I was the only person on deck to savour it. As the boat glided back towards the city limits and the dock, the cupolas of the Greek Orthodox church rose behind the trees, and the sky was subtitled by the red and blue neon of another local landmark, the Carling O'Keefe brewery. This Caribbean cruise through the cold waters of Manitoba was anomalous but not absurd, as I had expected it to be. For Canada has long been receptive to escapees from the rest of the world, and all the hokum of the cruise had some connection with reality. Canada is no theme park. Andras the Hungarian from Croydon must have chuckled as he mapped out his curious little enterprise, but since all of western Canada is a ragout of cultures a Caribbean cruise for Ukrainian nuns is no more unlikely an entertainment than any other that could be devised. This cultural eclecticism did of course confirm the tenuousness of Canada's own claims to a national cultural identity. What could Manitoba offer that was uniquely Manitoban? There were country fiddlers in neighbouring Saskatchewan, and I dare say country fiddlers in Manitoba too, but that was a threadbare flag to fly. In western Canada, which is still shaping itself, you give what you can from your own culture and in return you are invited to take as much as you please from others. It's an unsettling state of affairs for those, such as myself, who prefer set meals to buffets, but it didn't seem to trouble the Canadians at all. While I was moping in a contented inward way up on deck, the two hundred other passengers down below were, without any doubt, enjoying themselves to the full.

15

Vivat Regina

'The best way to see Regina,' advised Ronald Bloore when I spoke to him in Toronto, 'is through a double martini from 35,000 feet.' Regina, of course, is a mere dot on the prairie, and as the plane slipped into Saskatchewan from Manitoba, I peered out of the window at what looked like old linoleum patterns; the colours of the soil and crops varied only within a narrow range of colour. Greens and buffs were here a shade lighter, there a tone darker. Closer to Regina, the patterns lost their uniformity, and were fuzzed at the edges by amoebal configurations of trees and ponds. These natural features had compelled farmers to deviate from straight lines and right angles, and to erect fences and ditches along the curves that marbled the geometry of the landscape. Trundling up and down the long fields, giant harvesting machines created extraordinary patterns: there were diamond shapes diminishing towards the centre and what looked like mazes with the gaps filled in. Scarcely any two fields had been harvested in the same way and it appeared as though a computer had been fed a basic geometrical design and then generated and displayed every conceivable permutation over hundreds of square miles.

Regina itself was astonishingly empty, even though a major football game that weekend had brought hundreds of supporters, laden with tooters and crates of beer, into town. Perhaps the permanent population had fled for safety. From my room at the Westwater Inn (fondly known by local folk, until recently, as the Wastewater Inn, in tribute to Regina's notoriously poor water), I had a fine view onto the Regina Inn opposite; from its balconies supporters of the away team from Winnipeg exchanged yells with the scattering of Saskatchewan Roughriders fans down in the street. At the Norman MacKenzie Art Gallery, which for some reason has quite a good collection of German expressionists, there was only one other visitor, and the same was true over at the Legislative Building. If you've seen Winnipeg's Legislative Building, you can skip Regina's and vice versa, since both are neo-classical structures of some grandeur and little interest. I had to admire the presumption of the huge building. Even today there are only 175,000 bipeds in Regina; when the Legislative Building was built over seventy years ago the entire population of Saskatchewan could have sheltered beneath its dome. From the top of the steps I looked over riotously planted gardens to the lake of the Wascana Park; beyond, in the not so far distance, rose the modest towers of downtown Regina. The city fathers had made a good job of the landscaping, and the Wascana Park, a public works project which provided an artificial lake and flower beds among the lawns and a waterfowl park, was enchanting. It was also deserted.

My sole companions as I trod the paths were grasshoppers. Even a hesitant step prompted half a dozen vertical takeoffs. To the 70,000 farmers of Saskatchewan they were an unwelcome sign. Parts of the province had been severely affected by drought, and while Saskatchewan does have substantial reserves of potash, uranium, oil and gas, wheat is still the mainstay of the economy. The previous year bad harvests had cost the farmers about a billion dollars; this year, it was feared, the economy would be hit for twice that sum. Over southern Saskatchewan and southern Alberta some sixteen million acres were affected. Yields which in most years averaged twenty to thirty bushels per acre were down to about two, though Nature's sense of injustice had ensured that northern Saskatchewan was enjoying bumper crops of about sixty bushels. Where the wheat had managed to grow, the farms were plagued by millions of grasshoppers, and I was now encountering hundreds of plump frisky insects who'd wandered into town for the day.

I'd been to the art museum, and to the Wascana Park and through the marble halls of the Legislative Building, and I'd only been in the city for an hour and a half. So I drove to the outskirts to visit the Royal Canadian Mounted Police Museum. It was not wildly interesting. I dutifully peered at glass case after glass case filled with documents, uniforms, weapons, models of forts. A few exhibits did engage the imagination: I saw photographs of Sitting Bull from the 1870s and the handcuffs that locked Louis Riel's wrists and the frayed rope that broke his neck, and archaic electronic equipment secretly employed by a German spy the Mounties had exposed. Near the museum stands the RCMP chapel, which dates from 1883 and is thus the oldest building in town. I had now been in Regina for two and a half hours. I returned to the hotel and leafed through my address book. A kind friend had given me the name and number of a local tycoon. If I was going to be bored, perhaps I could arrange to be luxuriously bored. I phoned the number and asked to speak to the gentleman. He had, I was soon told, died the year before, and as my informant happened to be his widow, she was none too pleased by my inquiry. My only other contact in town was a friend of Barrie's – no farmgirl, but a doctor called Cynthia, who obligingly invited me to come and gnaw some pizza. Hugely relieved that I didn't have to spend any more hours in downtown Regina (which, I was not surprised to learn, has the highest suicide rate in Canada), I sped to the suburbs.

Cynthia's background must have made her an oddity in Regina. A New Yorker by birth, she had come to Toronto in the late 1960s. Like Barrie, she had been a pioneer in Cabbagetown, where she rented a former cockroach control centre and moved in. After many years working as a doctor, she became disgruntled and wrote a book attacking the medical system in Canada. She then went off to take a degree in public health care. Newly qualified, she had been offered a job in Regina. Her Torontonian friends thought she was mad even to consider it, and I suspect their reaction helped her decide that she would accept the position.

'It was a challenge,' she shrugged. 'But I did make two conditions. First, they had to find me a new husband, and secondly, he had to be Jewish.'

'Any luck?'

'None. Yet.'

Like most of the people I was visiting in Canada, she was recovering from surgery. This entailed lying on a couch while her two daughters waited on us hand and foot. The daughters weren't yokels either; Rebecca was hitchhiking through the west of Canada with her boyfriend from Toronto, and Lisa, who had married an ultra-Orthodox Jew and adopted this most strenuous of faiths – ritual baths, the works – was just visiting for a week. Lisa stood by the door, hands on hips.

'The cat has shat.'

'So? Clean it up.'

'It hasn't shat,' corrected Rebecca. 'It has puked.'

'That isn't puke, that's shit,' insisted the ritual bather.

'Whatever it is, just clean it up. And when you've finished, bring me another bottle of wine from the icebox.'

Cynthia's experiment in provincial living had not, she admitted, been a success, and it was only a matter of time before she packed her bags again. After only two months she had resigned from her job and taken another, working closely with Indian bands in northern Saskatchewan. Their plight, she confirmed, was as desperate as everywhere else in the prairie provinces. Most of them tended to stay on the reserves, which were located in the north, where there was no work. The unemployment rate was 90%. Such work as there was never seemed to last for long. Uranium City had had a population of about 3000 and though the majority of the workers were non-natives, the mines and various service industries had provided some jobs for Indians too. Then a few years ago, the government closed down Uranium City and the population shrank to 200. The newly erected houses were either boarded up or shipped elsewhere, and the Indians went back on welfare. Cynthia suspected the only hope for the Indians was to encourage a resurgence of pride in their identity instead of their present defeatism, however understandable that fatalism might be. It was not an easy policy to put in practice. 'We've been training community health representatives on the reserves. We're given twelve weeks to train them in modern nursing techniques, and we're talking about girls who are barely literate. No sooner did we complete their training on one reserve than a new chief was elected. He dismissed the CHRs we'd trained and installed his cousins. So we're back where we started.'

At eight we sat down to dinner. Lisa's plate was empty, as the Sabbath still had an hour to run. Our watches were synchronized so that she could be alerted at the exact moment when the Sabbath expired. Just after the minute hand liberated her from the iron laws of orthodox Judaism, the telephone rang. It was her equally orthodox husband phoning for a chat. After our meal, the daughters invited me to join them on an outing to the cinema. It was an attractive idea, but that summer the only films enjoying wide distribution across North America were aimed at the teeny bopper, whimsy or moronic market. That evening Regina offered a choice between a film about a high-school boy who was good at science and a high-school boy who was a werewolf in his spare time and a film about old people who get whizzed away in a flying saucer. I declined the invitation and opted for tending the invalid. I wanted to know why Cynthia was disenchanted with Regina.

'It's no place for single people, I guess. When I first arrived, I loved Regina. It's so easy to live in. I can do all my shopping in five minutes from here, parking's easy, nothing I need is very far from here. It's the people that are the problem. Everyone says how western Canadians are real friendly, and in a way it's true. In shops and at gas stations, people will greet you by name and wish you a nice day and smile a lot. But in over a year I have hardly ever been invited into somebody's home. I experience friendliness every day, but I have no friends here. I guess it's because people here are very suspicious of anyone who isn't married. This is a family oriented city, and single people don't fit the pattern.'

Many Canadian place names are like pretentious menus: they tempt more than they satisfy. Thunder Bay lacks thunderousness, and Moose Jaw, Saskatchewan, is no repository of wind-dried bones scattered across the prairie, but just another industrial town usurping the wheatfields. I spent one night at the Heritage Inn. A wedding reception was in full swing as I arrived. The broad corridor was filled with the insecure figures of men in cummerbunds searching for the vomitorium; though the party itself was no bacchanalia and all the guests were getting drunk in a most seemly manner. My room effectively insulated me from the distant sounds of decorous revelry. The air was a trifle stuffy, so I strode over to the curtains and pulled at the drawstrings. They parted, and I found myself gazing at a brick wall. I was in a spacious but windowless room. The architect had stumbled. I closed the curtains, preferring a view onto cloth to one onto brick, and went to bed.

Despite the disappointments of the Regina museums, I drove the next morning to an outlying tooth of Moose Jaw to visit the Western Development Museum. There are a number of these museums scattered over the prairies, each devoted to a different aspect of the region. The Moose Jaw museum, which concentrated on transportation, exalted technology rather than those who made use of it. Machines of various kinds were lined up in the vast shed of a building: steam engines and covered sleds, carts and wagons, air ambulances and old aircraft, railway carriages and a reconstructed Canadian Pacific station. This collection of objects did, unexpectedly, convey a sense of the prairies, for with distances so great between any two points, modes of transportation are lifelines, not toys. The only personal touch was provided by the display of – wait for it – the last car that Prime Minister John Diefenbaker, a local boy, owned. It was, for the record, a 1977 Oldsmobile.

I drove back towards Regina. From the air the countryside had looked entirely flat, so it was a pleasant surprise to find it rolling lazily towards the horizon like slightly crumpled cloth. The road passed farm service centres and the Great Plains auction house, which specialized in farm equipment. No doubt its warehouses were stocked with the harvesters and tractors of the many farmers defeated by yet another drought. The railway had drawn its steely lines parallel to the road and for a mile or two I raced a freight train; the telephone poles and wires framed the engine and reduced it to the size of a working model. I turned onto the farm roads and stopped for a picnic. I was joined by three million grasshoppers. A handful of these insects had splatted themselves against my windscreen, but their innumerable grieving cousins were waiting for me as I dredged my bread and cheese from the back seat. They left my lunch alone but clearly they hadn't been ignoring the delicacies of the fields. Odd how the prairie was fully cultivated – wheat on all sides, and grain elevators with steep pitched roofs giving a thumbs-up over the horizon – yet empty. Few cars passed as I munched, the train had long since chugged its way eastwards, and no farm vehicles clumped along the lanes. Only the warm sunshine and the racket of the grasshoppers kept desolation at bay, and the same spot in winter must be terrifying in its openness to the elements, its lack of shelter.

As I approached the Qu'Appelle Valley, the plains suddenly dipped and the road passed through soft grassy dunes that fell steeply towards the river. Clumps of trees huddled in the creases of the slopes, and the valley had a cohesion and verdancy in startling contrast to the expansive treeless plains all around. The small town was enjoying its Sunday afternoon. The laundromat was busy and the bingo hall was packed with about three hundred players eager to win the worthless gifts on display. I was surprised to find Qu'Appelle a pocket of political liberalism. Along the broad main street was The Peace Place: Your One-Stop Peace and Justice Information Centre, a cramped office that could have been airlifted from Islington or Greenwich Village. The shop dispensed posters and pamphlets and lapel badges, and advertised forthcoming anti-nuclear meetings. A few doors away Spike's Restaurant specialized in pizza but also offered an 'ethnic menu', which featured such exotica as veal parmesan and spaghetti. All dishes, the menu trumpeted, 'were prepared in old world fashion with traditional kitchen equipment.' Around the corner was the local drive-in, which was doing a roaring trade at the ice-cream counter. Here I tasted for the first and last time the flavour known as Tiger, a combination of orange and licorice that looked like mud and tasted worse.

There was more mud – perhaps it was the Tiger depot – around the corner behind the RCMP post. This large beige lot was marked out with surveyors' poles and planks that traversed the muddy bottom. These few square yards of muck were provoking a thoroughly divisive rumpus. A local car dealer, Cal Davis, had acquired this lot with a view to erecting a condominium block on it. His workmen had begun to dig to lay the foundations when a back-hoe operator hit bone. Local archaeologists rushed to the site, identified it as an Indian cemetery, and uncovered twenty-seven skeletons that had apparently been interred about 130 years ago. Mr Davis was forbidden to continue his diggings; work on the site came to a halt. Mr Davis was sympathetic to the notion that a burial place should not be desecrated, but he nevertheless wondered who was going to compensate him for the obliteration of his investment. At the Qu'Appelle museum, an old lady told me she found the whole affair puzzling. 'When my grandparents arrived here in '83 the Indians buried their dead in the trees, but the bodies on Cal's lot were found, all but one of them, in caskets. It seems a Christian mission we don't know about must have had them buried there, but how can we be sure they're all Indians?' Not all the bodies were accompanied by the ornaments commonly found at Indian burial sites. Another old lady – everybody under eighty was either playing bingo, washing their clothes, or out fishing – told me that Davis was worried about the $100,000 he already claims to have lost but the Indians, who comprise half the town's population, 'don't give a hoot'. Indian leaders, on the other hand, have expressed willingness to buy the site, though how the funds would be raised was less than clear. Reburial at another site won't do, since band elders have warned that the removal of ancestral graves carries a curse. Eventually the whole matter would be settled, but not, the old ladies were sure, without considerable bad feeling on both sides.

The museum down by the river occupied the former trading post of Qu'Appelle, which was founded in 1864. Its attractions were modest, but in the context of the uniform ocean of wheat that covered most of southern Saskatchewan it counted as a resort area. A few small boys hopefully fished off the bridge, but that was the only recreational activity I noticed that day. Except for bingo. I pressed on, heading vaguely northwest towards Saskatoon. My determination to stick to minor roads meant that I had to move at right angles across the checkerboard landscape. The long straight empty roads encouraged me to drive fast, with the windows down to cool me on this hot afternoon – until I tired of having my face battered by grasshoppers sucked into the moving car. They were all over me: floundering within the creases of my rolled-up shirt sleeves, frolicking between my thighs, dead beside my feet. I stopped the car, swept the corpses and the wounded onto the roadside, rolled up the nearside window and continued on my way. The gentle undulations of southern Saskatchewan had given way to an entirely flat landscape, and I began to understand the appeal of the prairies. I could also understand how hard it was to convey that they had any appeal at all, and it no longer seemed bizarre to me that the 1943 movie *Saskatchewan* was shot in Alberta.

In Europe you look up at the sky; on the prairies you look straight at it. I was astonished to find myself observing three weather systems simultaneously. To the east there was an expanse of clear sky and wispy cloud, while directly above me were vast suspensions of cumulus at their most three-dimensional; and over to the west were banks of threatening storm clouds with dark grey fringes of rain and hail falling like needles on the horizon. Here was a liberality of choice: to be able to stop the car, observe the skies in all directions, and then choose whether to head for good weather or bad. The skies impressed with their immensity, to be sure, but also with their accessibility. It was like standing in London and being able to observe the weather in Paris and Liverpool. Saskatoon lay beyond the curtain of hail but by the time I reached the fringe of the steely gray, it had considerately moved aside to let me pass and I arrived in Saskatoon in pallid early evening sunshine. It was Labour Day weekend, a festivity borrowed from the United States in which the dignity of labour is celebrated by not working. Saskatoon had understandably shut down for the weekend. At the downtown hotel where I took a room, the clerk increased the warmth of her greeting when she saw my passport. She had emigrated from Scotland ten years earlier and her tone indicated she was having second thoughts about the wisdom of the move.

On Third Avenue I found a Chinese restaurant called the Marigold. Here I enjoyed my first Chinese Smorg. In a marriage of cultures, Scandinavian smorgasbord had been retained in form but altered in content, for the dishes were mostly Chinese, though they also made numerous concessions to Western tastes. Those who were suspicious of Chinese food were mollified by the provision of fried chicken and apple pie. I ate like a trucker, being in greater need of ballast than of *haute cuisine* at this point in my travels. As the waitress cleared the table, she asked me 'Is everything okay?' in a tone of voice that implied she didn't expect it could be. I responded serenely. This was no time for a restaurant review. Walking back to the hotel I encountered a dozy Chinese whore. Since I usually stay in downtown areas, I was invariably finding myself in what passed for red light districts. Following Canadian traditions, the girl was friendly, and I stopped to chat. Rapid market research established that the rates across Canada were almost identical, a surprising discovery given that the profession is non-unionized. Rates also struck me, though no expert on the matter, as high. By parting with sixty dollars I could purchase a 'straight lay', and for an additional twenty dollars I could have, according to my stoned informant, a 'half and half'. I asked for an explanatory footnote, which she provided. I had more questions to put to her, but the dear girl looked sleepy and, besides, I was keeping her from her work. Back at the hotel I turned on the television. Fluttering across the prairie air came two irresistible programmes: Joan Sutherland in *Anna Bolena* on one channel, and Willie Nelson in *On the Road Again* on the other. I alternated between the two and in an increasing delirium of cultural confusion lulled myself to sleep.

By morning, the town presented an appealing aspect, for the day was bright and No Labour Day brought whole families onto the streets and into the parks. According to a newspaper survey I'd been reading, Saskatoonians had reacted with contempt when asked what they thought of Regina. Saskatoon, in the eyes of its residents, outclasses the capital on two grounds: it has a river and the streets are wider. I came to support their view, in the same way one comes to back poisoning over drowning, or vice versa. Along West 20th Street, a tolerably wide street and Saskatoon's answer to Lexington Avenue, few shops were open but the streets were busy. Outside the Vietnamese restaurant stood a man in a Stetson and neckerchief, for many western Canadians affect the same cowboy styles as Texans and Wyoming ranchers. His lumbering passage reminded me of western Canadians' grumble that their countrymen from further east regard them as Neander-thals with clothes on. There was something to it after all. Down the road, at a delicatessen that also stocked sausage-making equipment, beef jerky was on sale for $35 a pound. Nearby an Indian was contemplating the window of a pawnbroker's shop.

Saskatoon's Western Development Museum proved of greater interest than its brother in Moose Jaw. Enclosed within a space the size of an aircraft hangar, a fictional Boomtown of 1910 had been reconstructed. The telegraph operator's house gathered under one roof all the elements that must have matted daily life with their greyness and orthodoxy. Victorian photographs of hostile ancestors glared from the walls; oil lamps cast their warm musty glow over the harmonium, which would have wheezed out incessant hymns; hideous glassware and crockery filled the shelves of dressers; a rocking chair stood motionless in a corner, no doubt the private reserve of a toothless elder of implacable needs. In another room the museum authorities had placed a waxen model of a girl within a bed, mistakenly believing that the provision of dummies suggested life rather than death. Death too has its place in Boomtown, and among the ancient threshing machines and tractors stood a Jewish hearse dated 1908. In the doctor's office a list of fees was posted: each mile travelled by the physician would have cost the patient $1.50, but the actual surgical fees were relatively modest. For $3 the doctor would fit an artificial eye, though an amputation would, at $100 per limb, cost you an arm and a leg. Entertainment at Boomtown was provided at the pool hall behind the barber shop, though I dare say the community would have thrown up a Chinese whore or two then as now.

The cosy but horribly confined interiors reminded me of my old farm in Maine, which I had bought from a matriarch who had evidently tyrannized her family in the cause of godliness. I had found the five-year diary kept in the 1940s by one of her daughters, a document that confirmed my worst suspicions. With each new year the young woman had briskly entered the daily record of her life: laundry on Tuesdays, visiting sick neighbours on Friday, and, of course, repeated churchgoing on Sundays. By March even the stout heart of this good and dutiful woman could no longer pretend to celebrate the hideous sameness of her days, and the entries would peter out until the bold resolution of the following New Year's Eve would spur her to a fresh attempt. After four years the wretched diary, with loneliness and the tedium of her wasted life aching from every stuttering line, was chucked into the barn, where I came upon it thirty years later. Since then nothing has been able to persuade me that life in remote rural outposts is enviable, whatever claims are made for its virtues by its chroniclers. For the pioneer farmer there may have been challenges and dangers that were stimulating to overcome, but for the support team – mostly wives and daughters – there would have been few such compensations.

Trailing behind me, and viewing these constructs with a rich and articulate bemusement, was a family from Pakistan, who must have felt they were visiting another planet. Natives of Islamabad, they had emigrated to Calgary, though their attire and the boom and shrill in their voices seemed more suited to the bazaar than the halls of Saskatoon. I took it as a tribute to Canada's open heart that a whole Pakistani family, while no doubt embracing their new Canadian home with fervour and relief, nevertheless exhibited an unmistakable pride in their origins. The women, plump and sleek like their menfolk, wore Indian trousers and their hair was lavishly braided with silver. They had no more connection with Boomtown, Saskatchewan, than I did, yet their studious examination of the museum's exhibits suggested they were at least attempting to take on board the heritage of their newly adopted home. They were Pakistani, and they were Canadian, and neither allegiance encroached on the other. Yet.

While Regina derives such animation as it possesses from the presence of government offices, Saskatoon feeds off its university. I found youthful joggers thumping along the ten miles of paths that line the South Saskatchewan River. The university perches above wooded slopes on the far bank of the river, which was being ruffled by water skiers. Walking along the paths of the landscaped riverbank proved hazardous, since daredevil cyclists took delight in minimizing the gap between fast-moving bike and slow-moving pedestrian. Eventually I came to the Mendel Art Gallery, a sizable and well-stocked museum with – an inspired idea – the civic conservatory attached to it. A block away was the Ukrainian Museum, full of photographs of eminent Slavs that no doubt Mr Cropo of Winnipeg had helped box and dispatch. Beginning in the early 1890s 175,000 Ukrainian immigrants had come to the prairies, settling on fertile lands from south of Winnipeg to north of Edmonton; 70,000 more arrived between the wars. It is said that they settled here because the landscape reminded them of Carpathia. I couldn't help wondering whether, had the immigrants discovered that the landscape in fact more closely resembled Ruthenia, they would have turned around and made the 8000-mile journey back to the Ukraine. The museum was stacked with their artifacts, specimens of weaving, brightly coloured painted eggs (*pysanka*), and carved plates and boxes (*riz'ba*).

I could have used a good Ukrainian restaurant that evening, but there was none open, so greed drew me to another Chinese Smorg. This spread was offered by my hotel, but the food was tired, the staff was tired, the customers were tired. After my wonton soup, fried rice, and apple pie, I wandered next door to the Baldwin Hotel, an unsavoury looking joint. The immense bar accommodated two pool tables, two video screens (playing different tapes), two jukeboxes (playing different music). The grubby carpet resembled green crazy paving; staring at it for five minutes could induce delirium tremens. Behind the counter jars of pickled eggs conjured up an abortionist's library. There were perhaps twenty drinkers in the bar, most of them doggedly silent, stupefied by video. Only a small group of cutthroats at the pool table expressed any liveliness. A fat and elderly couple who had been drinking silently at a table opposite staggered unsteadily towards the door, a trek of about a hundred yards. Some minutes later, I followed them out. The couple were standing out on the pavement. He was yelling at her, and she was weeping, the tears falling haltingly down her bacony cheeks. It was unseemly for these sixty-year-olds to be brawling on the street, but I felt sure this was not a tiff I was witnessing; it was an utter collapse of dignity prompted by an extreme of misery. A sea of mutual misunderstanding seemed to swell between them as he screamed the grievances of decades at his wife, who, not listening, wept as though her tears might carry away the wretchedness of her life.

16

Royal Festival Mall

The train that, among its other duties, was to bear me from Saskatoon to Edmonton was on time. For this I was grateful since I had risen at 5.30 a.m. in order to catch it. The train was equipped with a restaurant car and snack bar and an army of helpful stewards. From the raised observation deck beneath a glass bubble I gazed for hours over expansive fields of silken wheat, until after a while the landscape roughened slightly, and dark green copses began to appear. Two deer came leaping from the woods, gave the passing train a quick startled glance, then cleared a fence before running for cover. The flat earth began to roll and checkered fields were replaced by prairie ranches. Beyond the small town of Biggar the land levelled out again before erupting in confusion after Unity into a motley of lakes and grassy moors and birch copses. Much of the land was well farmed – cattle bowed their heads to the grass, and rolls of hay were tucked against the fences – but there were few signs of habitation. A few hours later the train crawled into Edmonton through a mess of sprawling stockyards, refineries, cattle lots and fertilizer plants, radio masts, and concrete football stadiums.

I had been to Edmonton some years before in the depths of January. At that time of year it had been hard to appreciate the city's attractions, since no one ever emerged into the open air except to hail a taxi. As in all sizable Canadian cities, and 650,000 people inexplicably make their home here, almost all transactions can be made in sheltered malls. The main drag of the university is not a street but a long covered mall with shops and snack bars on either side. With the temperature at thirty below, there had been an unearthly quality to the plumes of steam and condensation drifting into the air from factories and generator plants. From the escarpment just south of Edmonton's main thoroughfare, Jasper Street, there had been a fine view onto this eerie frozen scene, stilled by the cold yet animated by vapour. Now, at the end of summer, the same vantage point presented a very different outlook. From the escarpment the roads zigzag down to the banks of the muddy, meandering North Saskatchewan River before rising through the wooded banks of the South Side to the other half of the city. It was September and the foliage of maple and aspen was already exhibiting every nuance of yellow-gold and red. Cycle paths probably offered the best access to the riverside greenery, but for the pedestrian the going was harder. Making my way to the Muttart Conservatory, I had to clamber over guard rails and race across highway approach roads. City planners had preserved the trench of greenery that divides Edmonton, but it survives principally in the form of traffic islands of spiky grass. Striding across them, I had to keep sidestepping faery rings of mushrooms that grew frenziedly on them all. The Conservatory itself, constructed in the form of four elegant glass pyramids, is the most striking building in Edmonton. There is little competition.

The people of Winnipeg and Regina had spoken of themselves as inhabitants of western Canada, as indeed they are. Albertans, however, claim that they are the true westerners, and there is a sense in which this is so. Manitoba and Saskatchewan, overwhelmingly rural, are the Canadian equivalent of the American Midwest. Alberta, with its huge oil reserves and large cities, is far removed from such pastoral tranquillity. It is, indeed, the Texas of Canada: rich, paranoid, aggressive, brash, and far more sophisticated than outsiders give it credit for. Alberta's most irritating affectation is that it is hard up and hard done by. The decline in oil prices and the ensuing recession certainly damaged the provincial economy, but Alberta's declarations of poverty are misplaced. For Saskatchewan, crop failure means disaster to many of its ordinary citizens; in Alberta successive years of bad harvests had ruined some farmers in the south and up at Peace River, but the damage to the provincial economy as a whole was limited. Alberta's economy is diversified: oil is vital, but so are agriculture and ranching. Alberta was happy enough when the oil crisis of the early 1970s reaped enormous fortunes for its entrepreneurs; now times are harder, and the province is taking its decline in prosperity with little grace. Joyce Fairbairn, a Liberal senator from Alberta, told me that Albertans have felt for decades that they put more into the federal economy than they ever get back, and that feeling persists as a habit of mind however much the political reality may change.

Albertans consider themselves a breed apart from other Canadians – and they certainly act that way. The oil business encourages heavy economic petting with international markets and organizations. What's best for Alberta is not necessarily what's best for Canada. Some years ago political separatism became a vocal force in the province, though it soon exposed itself as little more than a right-wing lunatic fringe; although now discredited, it suits politicians to make occasional threatening separatist noises, just to keep the rest of Canada on its toes. The oil business had its perfect political representative in the shape of the provincial premier Peter Lougheed, a gifted politician who dominated Alberta politics from the day the Conservatives took over the reins of power in 1971 until his resignation fourteen years later, when he was replaced by another rich oilman and former professional football player, Don Getty. Curiously, the aggressively capitalist Alberta Conservatives are scarcely less interventionist than all the other administrations of Canada. The loony separatists espouse a form of laissez faire, but the Tories opt for a kind of welfare capitalism. West of Winnipeg, the Liberals have been dead for twenty years now, and Trudeau's energy policies made sure they stayed that way. They still poll a quarter of the votes, but until the elections of May 1986 had never garnered enough to be elected as MPs or MLAs.

Energy policy remains a ferociously argued issue in Alberta. Like any other province, Alberta has control over its mineral rights and resources. The Fathers of Confederation astutely relegated to federal control all the powers regarded as of central concern and importance – in 1860. Mineral rights were not among them. The root of the incessant wrangling between the Liberals of Ottawa, personified by Trudeau, and the Albertans was that the federal authorities were interfering with the province's constitutional right to manage its own resources. If the provinces have control over their oil deposits, which they unquestionably do, then they should be free to dispose of their oil as they see fit. That attitude, ornery though it may have been, was fine with Ottawa as long as there was plenty of fuel to go round; but when the oil crisis developed it seemed important to Trudeau that the federal government should increase its control over energy policy. The Liberals established PetroCanada as a national petroleum company, and devised a National Energy Program that infuriated Albertans. The policy sought to promote Canadian self-sufficiency in energy and to lessen its dependence on imports, but it was seen by Albertans as an undisguised attempt to wrest greater control over energy resources from the provinces. Ottawa had no power to snatch away Alberta's oil, but the government was able to pull other economic levers: for instance, taxation changes diverted oil exploration from Alberta to the Northwest Territories, which happen to be federally governed, with the consequence that their oil revenues, such as they were, would flow directly to Ottawa.

Furthermore, Alberta was required to sell some of its oil at below world prices. This provided cheap energy for the rest of Canada – especially, as Albertans will snarlingly confirm, for industrial Ontario – but, the province alleged, it cost Alberta billions of dollars in lost revenues (which didn't prevent the province from accumulating billions of dollars in surpluses at the same time). Albertans didn't see why they should be penalized in order to subsidize industries two thousand miles away. They also saw themselves as vulnerable to world economic forces, as indeed they were, and when prices slumped, so did the Albertan economy. Unemployment was high, and the recession had bitten deeply. The day before I arrived in Edmonton the Canadian Commercial Bank, a major financial institution in western Canada, went belly up, the first large Canadian bank to do so since 1923. Some weeks later a second major western bank followed suit.

With the election of the Conservatives, Alberta began to feel more secure. Mulroney negotiated a Western Accord that deregulated oil prices, with natural gas to follow, eliminated many taxes, and removed some federal incentives on exploration in the far north. The drilling in the High Arctic tapped less oil than had been hoped, and the extraction from beneath the Beaufort Sea above the Arctic Circle was proving expensive and hazardous. This attempt to restore Alberta's fortunes was, ironically, undermined by the slump in oil prices, which might yet prove economically devastating to the province. Not only the Western Accord but Mulroney's espousal of free trade meets with widespread approval among Albertans. For farmers it holds out the hope of lower costs for the purchase of equipment. Many businessmen fear the growth of protectionism in the United States, and wish to crawl under the protectionist tent before the pegs are hammered home. How a free trade agreement will be reconciled with the province's ardently professed right to exercise sole control over its mineral resources is less clear.

Not all the lucre acquired from the oil industry went into oilmen's pockets. Lougheed established the Alberta Heritage Fund, whereby 30% of nonrenewable resource revenues were

183

banked separately. This produces an annual investment income of about $1.5 billion. Lougheed modified this provincial generosity in 1982, when the percentage was halved, and it seems likely that the Fund will soon be capped. The precise uses to which the Fund would be put were never entirely clear. Its revenues were intended to be used to strengthen and diversify the Albertan economy, but Lougheed had gradually taken to using the investment income to top up government revenues as an alternative to raising taxes. It has become, in short, a well-stuffed piggy bank, and the provincial government owns the key. One of the Fund's most notable bene-ficiaries has been the University of Alberta. Nor is there any shortage of culture in the city, which has a strong musical life and a lively theatrical fringe.

Culture or no, I still didn't care for Edmonton. The manager of the hotel where I was staying was keen for me to appreciate the wonders of the city, and after lunch one day we set off in his pick-up truck for the South Side. Russ was of Ukrainian descent, a burly man of beaming geniality. He was excited even by Edmonton's unglamorous past. Pointing to the hillock behind the Muttart Conservatory, he explained that it was a dump filled with unsold stock of tin cans formerly dispatched to the United States for pulverization until the orders dried up. He also showed me the spot where, not far from the Legislative Building, coal had been mined near the centre of town. We inspected Edmonton's older buildings, the flour mill near the river and the old post office on Whyte, all candidates for conversion into restaurants, and the block of Whyte that was being restored to its late Victorian appearance. The scheme had the usual flaw of being over-pretty, but it was undeniably an improvement over the seedy row of shops and doss houses that had preceded the restoration. Whatever the merits of the scheme, it was the most minor of retrievals. Edmonton is architecturally a dud, though the South Side is an attractive neighbourhood in which to live and the restored Hotel Macdonald will return a touch, the merest touch, of grandeur to the downtown area. A few silvery skyscrapers rise over the downtown blocks, dashing but far from visually arresting.

Russ was also proud of the city's modest but efficient subway system, which took me to the Edmonton Oilers' Training Camp. The Oilers are one of Canada's top hockey teams, largely because they are blessed with the presence of the superstar Wayne Gretzsky, he whose clay feet I had admired in Toronto. At the training camp, which is held in public, the coaches assess the complete roster of players and make their team selections for the season ahead. For three days relays of skaters, some team members of long standing, others trembling on the very lowest rung, practise while the coaches study their performance. And not only the coaches, for idle Edmontonians also gathered in the bleachers to make their own private assessments. Gretzsky was easy to spot. He is lean and boyish, and always looked utterly relaxed. He was in no danger of being dropped from the Oilers. Cognoscenti credit him with the fastest reflexes in the business, as though he carries in his head a mental map of the ice so accurate that he can always predict where the puck will be in five seconds' time. He was so laid back that during one spell of instruction from the referee he lay on the ice propped against his stick as though sprawled on a Caribbean beach. Gretzsky is a poppet, but he's not my idea of a hockey player. Mordecai Richler had been having a go at him too, but for different reasons. In the *New York Times* he had faulted Gretzsky on the grounds that he is 'incapable of genuine wit or irreverence', which seemed comparable to criticizing Richler for his lousy golf handicap. Dave Semenko looked more the part to me, with his mean, close-set eyes and his reluctance to smile; moreover his refusal, alone among all the other players on the ice that morning, to wear his helmet, showed just that degree of cocky aggression that I want from my hockey players. Square-jawed Mark Messier also matched my image of a hockey player, and he did his part by hurling offending players against the side of the rink and whacking them with his stick. A few weeks later Messier mistook two parked cars for hockey players and smashed his Porsche into both of them. Another Oiler, Dave Hunter, found a different use for his car, a Volvo, which he stopped in the middle of the road at 3 a.m. in order to admire the act of fellatio being performed on him at the time. The cops were too embarrassed to arrest a man slouching towards ecstasy, but they did nab him for drunken driving.

I'd now experienced some of the best sport that hockey had to offer: I'd seen the Toronto Stingers Peewees almost score a goal, and I'd laid eyes on Gretzsky as he sprawled elegantly on the ice. Not only that, but I'd sat just yards away from the mentally retarded boy who fetches the iced water for the players and who features with Gretzsky in public service advertisements on Canadian television. The bustling presence of the ungainly lad, and his evident joy in making himself useful by serving the team, was touching testimony to the possibility of integrating severe mental handicap into even the most high-pressured of occupations.

The presence of the Oilers was a feather in the city's cap, but it pales in comparison with Edmonton's leading tourist attraction. Not a museum, not a zoo, but a shopping mall. The West Edmonton Mall is The Largest in the Universe. In your shameful ignorance you may have supposed, as I did, that California had carried off that prize, but the West Edmonton Mall, with 5 million square feet of space, is twice the size of its closest competitor, the Del Amo Fashion Centre in Torrence, California. Phase III of the mall had been completed just before I arrived, and I had missed the opening party. Not that I'd been invited, though that would scarcely have mattered. What difference does one extra person make when the guest list contains 10,000 names? It must have been quite a party, with 700 entertainers, half a million helium balloons and, to eat, a ton of Alaskan king crab, 60 pounds of caviar (price tag: $71,040), 15,000 pastries, and comparable quantities of champagne, beer, and fruit. Feeding the 10,000 hungry guests had cost a million dollars.

The mall is more than a place to buy tights and groceries, and it would be no idle jest to claim it is now the social centre of Alberta. The 800 shops and forty restaurants are a trifle. What makes the mall special is that it incorporates under its roof a three-acre lake containing a full-scale model of a Spanish galleon, performing dolphins, forty sharks, more submarines than the Canadian navy possesses, a 360-room hotel, three aviaries containing 2000 birds, an enormous amusement park and water park, and a miniature golf course. You can shop along Europa Boulevard, a tributary shopping arcade with false façades that supposedly resembles a Parisian shopping street, and Bourbon Street, loosely modelled on the New Orleans original, decorated with wrought-iron street lamps and filled with twenty-three night clubs. This inspired vulgarity is the creation of four former Iranian carpet dealers. I present the showbiz kings of sunny Edmonton, Alberta – the Ghermezian Brothers! The two without hair are Eskandar and Bahman, the two with thinning hair are Raphael and Nader, and down there in the electronic golf cart which can be rented to make your shopping expedition effortless is Poppa Jacob the patriarch. If they are smiling, that is to be expected. Not only have they built this fantastical place – on opening night Nader was as over-whelmed as his guests, declaring: 'I cannot believe myself what we have built' – but they appear to have had little difficulty persuading other people to finance their venture. Canadian banks and finance houses are often criticized for their reluctance to advance venture capital. A people who hold the world record for the percentage of personal wealth invested in savings banks don't like to throw their money around. The Ghermezians borrowed almost a billion dollars, some of it in the form of government grants and tax concessions, to finance the mall's construction, and by the time Phase III was opened about $150 million had been repaid. The 300 sub-contractors and outfitters who constructed the mall have also done nicely out of the project.

The gamble seems to be paying off, since the average sales recorded by the shops within the mall have been gratifyingly high. The mall's dual function – shopping and entertainment – must surely explain its success. Not for nothing do the Ghermezians spend more money promoting the mall than the province of Alberta spends promoting tourism. Those who come to shop also drop dollars at the restaurants and amusement parks; those who come to West Edmonton for a day of fun with the family – not such a laughable notion to anyone who knows what else the city has to offer in the way of entertainment – will find it hard to avoid a purchase or two. I went there to laugh, but emerged with a leather jacket and mooseskin gloves. I even paid for them. And though I didn't care for an $8 submarine ride, I marvelled at the tanks of exotic fish ranged along the upper level of the shopping arcades. How, I wondered, could I contrive a spillage of the tank containing the red-bellied piranhas into the milk-shake dispenser at Macdonalds'? Caged animals were for sale at the Puppy and Kitten Centre, and to celebrate the opening of Phase III, bunnies were 'on special' at $15.99. The food at the mall was as international as it had been at the Canadian National Exhibition in Toronto. Here there was a dazzling choice between Idaho Spuds, the Wiki Wiki Polynesian Experience (that's a new word for it), the Viet Egg Roll King, Chutty (featuring naan burger and chicken curry), and Satay Hut. This last stall offered satay with fries and pork chops. When I told the charming Bumiputra girl behing the counter that I'd never been offered satay with fries in Malaysia, she nodded sadly and said: 'Canadians are not adventurous.' No, but the Ghermezian brothers are.

17

Oil Sands and Sweetgrass

Edmonton may feel northerly, but it's only a third of the way up the province, with plenty of wilderness to go even before one reaches the border with the Northwest Territories. Up in the bush, on the banks of the Athabasca River, lies Fort McMurray, and twenty-five miles beyond the town are the vast tarry sands that contain a substantial proportion of Alberta's oil reserves. Deposits of bituminous oil sands exist in other parts of the world, such as Venezuela, but northern Alberta is the only place where these deposits are mined on a large scale, another of those mega-projects at which Canadians excel.

Fort McMurray surprised me. I'd expected a frontier outpost, but found a town of 36,000 inhabitants. Here, where the Clearwater River joins the Athabasca, there has been a settlement since the early nineteenth century, for the Clearwater is one of the few rivers in the west that actually flows westwards, which assisted early traders. Fort McMurray has become unexpectedly cosmopolitan. The two mining companies in the area, Suncor and Syncrude, began to extract the sands in the 1960s, and organized speedy recruitment. The companies engage about 6000 workers, and subcontractors and support services employ thousands more. In those days, when Canada enjoyed low unemployment rates, it was not easy to attract Canadians to Fort McMurray, which, with its protracted cold winters and short bug-infested summers, does not enjoy the loveliest of climates. Central Canadians may have given the place a wide berth, but not the Newfoundlanders, who have always had to travel in search of work; it's said that Fort McMurray is the third largest Newfoundland city. Foreigners were lured by the high rates of pay, and if you shake the town it rattles with Australians, Germans, and Dutch. Two of the Syncrude managers I met were British, though they had been in Alberta long enough to have acquired a Canadian accent and bearing. Fort McMurray, with its high proportion of technicians and managerial staff, is a solidly middle-class enclave. The housing costs are the highest in the province, and communal jollities differ not at all from those found in far larger Central Canadian cities. There's a weaving club, a parachuting club, a theatrical company, choirs, innumerable sports teams. Many executives own their own planes.

The road out to the oil sands courses through woods of birch and spruce and marshy muskeg. The sticky deposits churn some forty feet below the muskeg, sandwiched between the overburden and a limestone base. The mining technique is, in theory, simple enough: strip off the overburden, haul out the oil-rich sands, and extract and upgrade the bitumen at a processing plant to produce synthetic crude. Open-pit mining on this scale, and in such austere climatic conditions, is costly, and though the deposits are scattered over a territory the size of Belgium, only a small area is mined at present. The average amount of oil in the sands is 10.5%, though some pockets contain up to 14%. Where the oil only amounts to 6% or less of the sands, it is uneconomical to extract it. The Syncrude pit is three miles long and will, when operations are completed, be five miles across; the Suncor mine is half the size. At present Syncrude mines about 300,000 tons of oil sands each day, enough to produce 150,000 barrels of crude. Mining engineers suspect that the limestone base beneath the oil sands contains even larger deposits of oil, but no one has yet devised an economical method of extraction.

The Syncrude mine consists of level areas where the actual mining takes place, and a vast central pit, over a hundred feet deep, where the sands, once their oil has been cooked out, are returned to the landscape. The mining is done by draglines, vast machines twenty-five storeys high, their boom the length of a football field. In a single minute each dragline can claw 150 tons of material from the ground; huge bucketwheels dump the sands onto conveyor belts, which take them to the plant. Bulldozers, completely dwarfed by the draglines, clean up the mess made by the larger machine, which has a tendency to drop boulders and other debris from time to time. When part of the site has been exhausted, the dragline clumps its way elsewhere, which entails moving miles of conveyor belts too; this has to be done up to five times each year. The belts convey the sands onto hillocks called surge piles, from which they are gravity-fed onto other conveyor belts that bring them into the extractor plant, with its spaghetti of somersaulting silver pipelines. 'Conveyor belt' suggests a merry little rubber runner chortling along over gleaming ball bearings, but again the scale of this 'belt' is staggering. The day before I arrived one of the belts that takes waste out of the extractor plant had collapsed, reducing three trucks beneath to scrap metal.

After extraction the waste material is either tipped into the pit or taken out to the tailings. To ensure that none of the oily water within it leaks into the Athabasca River, fourteen miles of dikes surround the tailings pond, where water from the extraction plant is gradually clarified as impurities settle at the bottom and eventually recycled. Further quantities of bitumen can be extracted by skimming it from the waters of the huge pond. The tailings area is like a moonscape, for although it is physically possible to plant shrubs and trees on the tailings, which would certainly make them more sightly, little planting has been done, since the greenery attracts wildlife that would soon come to grief in the murky brown waters. Brightly coloured scarecrows jut from the surface to deter any waterfowl that may be tempted by the relatively warm waters, especially when the winter freeze begins. The wind was blasting across the site when I was there, whipping up a sandstorm on the heights of the tailings that forced vehicles to switch on their headlights.

This lifeless environment was an unhappy sight in the midst of the forests of northern Alberta. The mining companies claim to be deeply concerned about the health of the environment, and hundreds of acres have been replanted with seedlings. Cosmetic reparations are relatively straightforward, but other forms of pollution are less easy to control. Local Indian bands are especially worried about the effect of such vast industrial operations on their hunting and fishing domains. Syncrude does extract water from the Athabasca River in minute quantities, but its major water supply comes from its own reservoir, large enough to supply a city the size of Edmonton; and near the entrance to the plant is a power station that, according to Syncrude, produces enough energy for a city of 300,000. No water is returned to the river and five environmental stations monitor air quality. Nonetheless there was a strong whiff of sulphur in the air not just at the mine but as far away as Fort McMurray. However genuine the companies' efforts may be to protect the environment, those efforts may be insufficient, and an Indian band at Fort McKay, some miles north of the sites, has sued Suncor for allegedly polluting their water. A lawyer at Fort McMurray wryly told me that the Athabasca, because of seepage from the oil sands, was the only naturally polluted river in Canada.

Although the temperature can drop to -45°, the mining equipment is designed to function at Arctic temperatures. Nor is the site hampered by snow – the annual snowfall is a trifling two feet – and it is possible to keep the mine operating the year round. In theory. When I turned up, there was a complete shutdown, apparently for maintenance work. The draglines and conveyor belts had been stilled for a week or two, and the accident at the extractor plant the day before hadn't helped. Whether the shutdown was indeed routine or whether I was being smokescreened by Syncrude officials, I don't know, but it was no secret that the mines were experiencing some financial problems too. In 1970 Syncrude had been thrown into crisis when one of the co-owners, Atlantic Richfield, had withdrawn from the company, which then had to be bailed out by investments from three Canadian provincial governments. Expansion plans had had to be cancelled in 1982 and Syncrude was having to cut its operating costs. Some weeks later in Ottawa an MP from Alberta, Barbara Sparrow, would be telling me brightly that any decision about expanding the oil sands operations was of course up to the companies concerned, though, she added, the financial considerations included not just the price of oil but whether the provinces would be prepared to accept lower royalties than hitherto, and whether the federal government would grant tax concessions until the company's investment had been recouped.

The open pit mine proved a useful test of the degree to which I could accommodate myself to environmental devastation. By the time Syncrude and Suncor have completed their present phase of operations, over twenty square miles of wooded land will have been deracinated and stripped. Traditional modes of earning a living from the land for the local Indian population will have been altered permanently, possibly destroyed. The creation of tall tailings and a vast tailings pond that resembles a giant oil slick has further disrupted the landscape and the wildlife it once sustained. Yet given the abundance of such sparsely inhabited land in northern Canada, it would be churlish to deny to Canada on environmental grounds the economic benefits of exploiting such a resource. All ecological systems are precious, even those that seem primarily dedicated to breeding mosquitoes and horseflies, but few would claim that this flat and monotonous corner of northern Alberta is a region of outstanding natural beauty. I found myself putting aside my instinctive disquiet about such projects as I took on board the awesomeness of the undertaking. It was worth the journey just to lay eyes on those draglines, which resemble preposterously magnified Meccano models left over from a high-budget science-fiction movie. I could even take pleasure in the thought of that glutinous oil sand, that foul swampy layer of muck just below the gummy muskeg, being scooped out and transformed into something useful. Contemplating the flayed landscape refined my notions of the tolerable limits of intrusion upon the integrity of the earth we inhabit. Had the mine been situated in Shropshire or a few miles from Siena, the devastation would have been overwhelming and unacceptable. But against the rape of the muskeg I could raise only the feeblest of protests.

When I asked how many Indians were employed at the Fort McMurray mines, I was given contradictory replies. A senior official stressed that Syncrude employed more natives than any organization in Canada other than the government, but a less guarded employee said there were very few, though some were flown down from northern reserves to work four-day shifts while others formed the crews that skimmed the bitumen from the tailings pond. The minimal requirement for employment at Syncrude is a Grade 12 education, and few Indians have this qualification.

Alberta has a substantial native population, 13% of all treaty (status) Indians, though no more than 2% of the total population of the province. Their plight varies. Some, like those in northern Saskatchewan that Cynthia had mentioned, dwell wretchedly on remote northern reserves that lack proper roads and sewage systems and electricity – and employment. Others live on oil-rich reserves and royalties can amount to $500 per capita each month. This sudden manna-like shower of royalty cheques is, or can be, a mixed blessing. Well-managed reserves will use at least a proportion of those royalties for investment in community facilities or enterprises such as cottage industries that will benefit the whole band, while others squander the money on spending sprees. Inevitably a steady supply of money, whether in the form of welfare payments or royalty cheques, destroys the need to rely on traditional methods of survival. As Clifford Freeman, vice president of the Indian Association of Alberta, put it to me, 'Why chop wood when you know there's a cheque due in a couple of days?'

Until recent times it was hoped that Indians would eventually become assimilated, but that policy has failed. Indians have grown wary of schemes perceived as threatening to their integrity as distinctive native peoples. Band leaders and tribal councils are pressing for forms of self-development and self-government. Although the Department of Indian Affairs seems to be moving in the same direction, some band chiefs interpret the gradual withdrawal of direct government control – and funding – as a crafty exercise in cost-cutting. It's a tricky game for the government to play, and when documents were leaked from the Department of Indian Affairs in 1985 the anxieties seemed justified. On the other hand, it is increasingly recognized that the old system of handing out large welfare payments creates a helpless dependency on the government. Some self-development schemes are getting off the ground, and Clifford Freeman told me how his organization is encouraging remote reserves to revert to more ancient means of economic survival in the face of the white man's usurpation – by becoming suppliers, not to trappers but to oil and mining industries.

I was puzzled when Karen told me her father was a French Canadian from Québec and her mother a German descendant from Winnipeg. Swarthy and with the sagging plumpness that often comes from an over-indulgence in junk food, Karen did not look like someone who sprang from north European stock. Her parents had told her she was an adopted Indian, but it was entirely as a result of a chance conversation with an official at the Indian Affairs office where she was working that she discovered she was a Blackfoot from a Peigan band. She had experienced the discomforts of the outsider on two accounts: first, because she was so obviously an Indian in appearance, and second, because the farming folk of western Alberta, where she and her family had lived for twenty years, had never taken kindly to the presence of a French Canadian. Karen had an earnest grinding manner that made heavy demands on my attention without rewarding it sufficiently. At the same time her very lack of subtlety meant I could be sure she was talking straight. Lorne didn't have to fear giving anything away, since he was silent most of the time. He too was an Indian, from a reserve near High Prairie in northwestern Alberta. When he was eight, his parents had moved to the city, and since then he had never lived on the reserve. He was an unemployed photographer, a wry reserved young man, handsome and fit, but his bouts of inattention struck me as an arrogant touch. He was not apologetic about having left the reserve; on his infrequent return visits, he runs into his cousins, who failed even to graduate from high school and now seemed trapped within their unproductive and frustrated lives.

These two Indians were accompanying me on an outing organized by Lorne's friend Erin, who like Karen worked at Indian Affairs. On a bright chilly morning her government car purred along the highway through the dreary farmland north of Edmonton. Thirty-five miles northwest of the city we came to the Alexander Reserve. It had been established in 1889 on twenty-five square miles of dull, moderately fertile plateau land of wheat fields, copses, and hedgerows. The band consists of 738 members, 524 of whom live on the reserve. Some individual Indians have occupational rights to some areas that they farm, but the band intends to return all the land to communal ownership. At the band offices we found Fabian Lightfoot, a lean, well-groomed, dapper young man with the grand title of Community Development Officer. Though I raised an eyebrow when I heard him talking ponderously of how 'each of the seven councillors has his own portfolio of responsibilities', it soon became clear that Lightfoot was serving the band well. Although agriculture is important at Alexander, the band leaders are trying to diversify their economic base. There had been a furniture factory on the reserve but it had recently closed for lack of operating capital. It was, Lightfoot said sagely, 'a learning experience for the people of Alexander'. Natural gas had been found on the reserve but the supply was rapidly depleting, and of the original eleven wells only two are still in production. Test-drilling may soon reveal whether there are also oil reserves that will increase the band's prosperity and, Lightfoot hopes, permit investment in small businesses such as rural groceries. There are plans to develop some lakeside frontage on the reserve for recreational purposes. A recourse to law was also likely to produce additional capital for the band. In 1905 sixteen square miles of reserve lands had been sold by the government, a sale the band council believes was probably illegal. So two researchers are now investigating the land claim which, if supported by documentation, could result in a substantial financial settlement that will benefit the reserve.

Such recourse to law in the pursuit of Indian land claims has become a major industry throughout Canada. It has usually been easier for tribal organizations to negotiate with the federal than with the provincial government. In disputes with Ottawa the parties can turn to the courts for settlement more easily than in negotiations with the provinces. Alberta, industrially more developed than the other prairie provinces, takes pride in its entrepreneurial stance, and such matters as Indian claims are an irrelevance or at best a low priority. Swaggering Alberta is not known for its tender conscience. The argument is not only about control of present resources. Some Indian leaders such as Clifford Freeman argue that compensation should also be granted when native lands have been mauled or even destroyed. Surrounding many reserves are crown lands that were hunted by Indians for centuries before the crown appropriated them, and Freeman maintains that when, say, such lands are leased to lumber companies, adversely affected reserves should receive a share, perhaps 30%, of the profits. Other claims that will keep the lawyers busy for years arise where no treaties were signed with the government. One such case was current in Alberta: the Indians around Lubicon Lake signed no treaty, so the title to the oil-rich lands nearby are under dispute.

Across the road from the band offices stand the old people's home and the new Community Health Centre, which serves the surrounding community as well as the reserve. The health centre is well staffed, with a registered nurse, two community health representatives and a dental nurse. A doctor visits the reserve every two weeks, mostly to attend the elderly residents who have no means of getting to the nearest clinic, which is ten miles away. For a community of five hundred there is no lack of care. The registered nurse cheerfully admitted that she came to the reserve with a white middle-class perspective. The CHRs, who know how modern advice will be received by traditional Indians, help her to communicate with the band, for many of the old people speak only Cree. The dental nurse, who serves two reserves, told me that most of her work was educational. Regular check-ups are virtually unknown; people only make appointments when they are in extreme pain, and even then they don't always keep the appointments. Baby-bottle syndrome is common: mothers leave bottles in the mouths of their babies overnight, and for hour after hour Coke or some other sugary junk drips into the babies' mouths. By the time they are six years old, many Indian children have lost their four front teeth. The dental nurse has become so distressed by having to pull infants' front teeth that she will no longer perform the extractions and has the children sent elsewhere. The registered nurse also said that much of her work was educational: preventative medicine and prenatal instruction and nutrition took up most of her time. Preventative medicine was shown in practice at the staff lounge, which reeked of cigarettes, past and present.

The reserve's school had been run by the provincial authorities until 1982, when the band took control. At present 150 children are taught by twenty-four teachers and aides. The school also operates a 'recovery program' for twelve former dropouts who are now hoping to acquire some training in industrial arts and 'life skills'. Just a few years ago the school's performance was dismal: not a single student had graduated in a decade, the attendance rate was 60%, the dropout rate 100%, and most children over the age of twelve were on intimate terms with alcohol and drugs. In short, the reserve, and its future in the form of its large population of children, was a human disaster area. When the band took over the school, they sought a new approach and were persuaded to adopt the Anisa system, which emphasizes a holistic attitude and a 'cohesive philosophical basis'. 'We stress process as much as content,' explained the principal. 'The Anisa system lays equal stress on all aspects of the person: physical, mental, emotional, spiritual. And those values blend perfectly with traditional Indian culture.'

I tend to think that education is too important to be hampered by grandiose theories, but something was working at the Alexander school. The attendance rate has risen to 90% and in the last few years not a single teacher has left, whereas under the previous regime the turnover was continuous. The children learn the Cree language and study their own culture. Indian posters and paintings decorate the classroom walls. Four of the teachers and all the aides are Indians, although there is no hiring policy that gives natives special preference. The Monday morning assembly opens with an address from a band elder, and the first class of each day begins with the ceremonial burning of sweetgrass. All the classes I visited hummed with quiet industry as seven-year-olds scrawled into exercise books or scratched their dark heads over multiple-choice questions in their readers.

We drove off the reserve for lunch, though first we searched for the buffalo herd that is kept at Alexander. Unfortunately all 124 of the beasts were hiding in the bush that morning and all I saw was an empty paddock. We ended up at Joyce and George's Café in Onoway. The special of the day was something called a Close Denver. This turned out to be not a western variant of the Princeton Freshman but a toasted sandwich filled with a ham omelette. Karen ate a burger and fries. An extraordinary admoni-

tion was posted on the dining room wall: 'DO NOT COMB
HAIR AT TABLE. RESTROOM AVAILABLE FOR YOUR CON-
VENIENCE.' My Denver closed, we continued on our way to
another reserve, this one about fifty miles west of Edmonton. It was
the Alexis Reserve, inhabited by Stoney Indians. In terms of area,
land quality, and population, it was directly comparable to
Alexander. When we arrived, the chief was nowhere to be found.
He had gone out to lunch and hadn't returned. No one seemed to
know when or whether he was expected back. This annoyed Erin
and Karen, since this seeming capriciousness reinforced the
stereotype of Indians as unreliable. However, the chief, Howard
Mustus, had not forgotten and some minutes later he arrived at the
band office together with half the band council. They were an
unhealthy bunch. Like Karen, they were overweight, pot-bellied
and heavy in their movements. Over their faces, swarthiness and
sallowness fought for supremacy.

We sat round the table in the conference room, but it was not a
comfortable meeting. Mustus himself proved rambling and incoherent, and soon left most of the talking to his councillors. They
adopted a belligerent manner that seemed quite out of key, given
that the meeting had been set up purely as a source of information.
Not that they were unfriendly or hostile. It was more a question of
tone, and the one they adopted was pugnacious and overemphatic.
As Chief Mustus rambled on, my eyes moved slowly up the wall
behind him to a portrait of the Queen of England (and Canada),
smiling calmly down at me. The chief amazed me with the
information that on certain occasions the reserve flies the Union
Jack. (Many native peoples still regard the crown as the protector
of their rights, since original treaties were signed with the crown.)

Some years before, the Trudeau government had promulgated a
Charter of Rights, which most Canadians viewed as a positive act,
though many French Canadians feared it would undermine the
special political status within Confederation that Québec was then
seeking. The most articulate councillor, an imposing man called
Nelson who wore his tall brown hat indoors, seemed to share that
distrust. 'The way I see it, the Charter wants us all to be equal. That
sounds fine, but maybe what they really want is to turn Indians into
litte brown white men.'

'How so?'

'They want to threaten ways of life that are special to native
peoples. Like hunting and trapping. The real problem is that native
peoples have no control over their own lives.'

'That's right. I can't even make a will without the white man's approval.' (Lorne and Karen later told me that they didn't know what this speaker was talking about.)

'Perhaps the real plan,' chimed in another man at the table, his hands stroking his pot belly, 'is to get rid of us altogether. But they'll never get rid of us! We really believe in this land of ours – the little bit we've got left.'

'The white man,' the litany continued from another corner of the room, 'makes laws governing us without even consulting us! We can't even spend our own money without official permission. Some reserves around here get revenues from oil and gas, but they have no control over them. They go into a trust fund in Ottawa – and then we have to beg for the money.' (Again, this was a crude oversimplification of the actual procedure.)

'Twenty-five years ago,' added an older man, 'this reserve had no roads. I used the lake to come to school. And there wasn't no electricity on the reserve either, but all around us our white neighbours had good resources.'

In almost everything they were saying, there was a contradiction that seemed to elude them, namely, that they distrusted and disdained the interference of the white man, but at the same time they wanted, quite reasonably, to have access to the benefits of white civilization. The same contradiction appeared when someone else lamented the lack of self-employment on the reserves, and then grumbled that 'social assistance is just a small share of the country's wealth', implying they were hard done by.

Nelson talked about the education trap. 'Indian Affairs doesn't help much with education, even though it's a treaty right. If you leave the reserve you get no help, but if you want further training it's not available on the reserves and you have to leave.' On the one hand, he wanted to preserve the exclusivity of his way of life, and on the other, he wanted ready access to all the benefits of the society outside the reserve. My sympathy was dwindling. Rural peoples the world over have to face similar problems. The resources of higher education and advanced training are rarely available with ease in the boondocks. In any case, Edmonton was only an hour's drive away, though many younger Indians would have had no car of their own. The reserve, however impoverished, represents a form of security, and leaving it was perceived, it seemed, as psychologically unsettling. Nelson continued:

'Some kids leave the reserve when they're young and come back as teenagers. We've one now. She's lost her identity, she despises herself and her culture. We should be proud. White farmers round here call us drunken Indians and all that, but they forget that we helped them clear and fence their land. The whites get rich, then turn round and despise the Indians who made it possible. But we're not ashamed of our ways. We could develop some of our lakefront land for campgrounds and all that, but we don't want to open up our reserve to everybody. We have another lake with clear spring water and fine fish, but it would be spoiled if we developed the reserve.'

I noted that the Alexander band thought differently about their lakefront, and I failed to see how the Indians' exclusive right to fish on their reserve would be threatened by a campground some miles away. It seemed easier for them to reject possibilities than propose solutions. I said to Nelson: 'Nobody in this room sounds very happy with the way things are right now. What could the government do that would make a real difference to your lives?'

'Make a real difference? Kick everyone out and give us back Canada!' He laughed; then, the rhetoric over, attempted a more serious reply. 'They should allow Indian bands to have self-determination. They talk about it, but it's all talk, just a front. When the treaties were signed, bands were considered as governments, but they no longer think of us that way. We want the authority to determine our destination.'

Parliament had recently passed a bill known for short as C-31. The new act extends treaty rights to large numbers of Indians, mostly women who married out of the band and under the old rules thus forfeited their treaty rights. The old system was, at the very least, discriminatory, and the new law enfranchised many of Indian descent who had been deprived of their rights. That was not the way the council at Alexis saw it. 'We have a small land base and few economic opportunities. As Indian nations we're politically weak because of the way reserves are scattered across Canada, and because we're weak the government has been able to make changes without having to provide for what will result, for the additional burdens C-31 will make on the system. It should be left up to Indians to decide who's an Indian.'

These objections seemed not only self-serving but based on wrong information. Should, as a result of C-31, the numbers of a band be substantially increased, as will almost certainly happen, there will be a corresponding increase in governmental aid to that band. Their fears that increased band membership would place further strains on their resources appeared unfounded. I later realized the true source of this opposition, for any royalty income they may receive from oil and gas on their reserves would of course remain the same. Since royalties are often divided on a per capita basis, each individual in the band would be less well off.

Impatient with their barrage of grievances, I asked the councillors whether I could look round the reserve. Some minutes went by before one of the council and its entourage, which seemed to have all the time in the world for sitting round drinking coffee and haranguing visitors, could be persuaded to show us around. The school was in session but a teacher took me through the few rooms. There are a hundred pupils here, fifty fewer than at Alexander, but far fewer staff: there are only four teachers, one aide, and two cultural teachers. As at Alexander, stress was placed on the native culture, and all children were taught the notoriously difficult Stoney language. But unlike Alexander, there was a poor success rate for the students, and of the students who went on to high school, very few succeeded in graduating. I visited one of the farms and the cemetery, where I noted the large number of graves of those who had died in their twenties and thirties. Back at the band office Chief Mustus had posted a notice – 'Too much money has been paid out in advance, so no further payments for a while' – which suggested bad management. And more poignantly, band members were invited to sign up for a visit to the jail at Fort Saskatchewan.

I was dismayed by the Alexis reserve. Since the population and resources scarcely differed from those at Alexander, it seemed extraordinary that there should be such discrepancies between the two reserves. At Alexander Fabian Lightfoot had been unhappy about his band's unemployment rate of 28% (even though it's a vast improvement over five years ago, when it stood at 87%) but at Alexis 70% of the workforce was still unemployed. It was quite clear from my visit to Alexander, and from the candid remarks of Lightfoot and the medical workers, that there were still major problems on the reserve. It was equally clear that they were attempting to solve them. The band leaders were using the system – government funding, the training of CHRs, the legal resource of land claims – to improve their lot. Perhaps the Alexis council was doing the same, but if so they neglected to tell me about it. Instead, all I heard was a logorrheic stream of complaint, shrill with wounded pride. According to the Alexis leaders, the only conceivable explanation for their wretched condition lay first in

THE PRAIRIES

the invasion of Indian lands by the white man and second, in the
white man's reluctance to grant self-determination to bands and,
simultaneously, the white man's niggardly dispensing of social
assistance. Lightfoot had not been vain or swaggering, but he
seemed proud of his people and of their determination to improve
their lives. Chief Mustus and his council showed no pride at all.
They asserted it, and loudly, but all their arguments clearly showed
they didn't feel it. All their problems were blamed on others, and for
all the task of self-government, the council kept well concealed any
signs of being capable of it. The hard truth seemed to be that
Lightfoot was sufficiently educated to grasp what needs to be done
and how to set about it. At Alexis, that level of education seemed
lacking, and with it, a knowledge of how to exploit government
resources on offer. Knowledge brings, to some degree, power, but
ignorance, in the case of Alexis, was in a mutually destructive
embrace with lethargy and passivity. On many reserves, such as
those in northern wilderness areas far from roads and jobs and
resources, the difficulties are probably intractable. This was not
the case at Alexis, with its farms and its easy access to Edmonton.

The road out of Alexis took us along the shores of Lac Ste Anne,
past a Catholic shrine that on St Anne's feast day in July is
patronized by thousands of Indians from all over the province. The
Mass combines Catholic ceremonies with Indian rituals such as the
playing of drums and burning of sweetgrass. A few miles further on
is the little lakeside town of Alberta Beach. I had, even in the course
of a few hours, grown accustomed to the drabness of the reserves:
the rough muddy roads, the shabby prefabricated houses, the junky
old cars and battered pickup trucks, the cigarette butts filling every
ashtray. Alberta Beach was a community of neat little houses and
fenced yards, of groceries and stores selling hardware and fishing
supplies. It was prim and proper and the town museum features a
collection of a hundred bibles; but it was also, compared to the
reserve, prosperous. Not rich or flashy – far from it – for it was
impeccably middle class and undemonstratve, but self-effacingly
prosperous. I realized I was perceiving the town with a slight
sourness – its bourgeois contentment seemed too far removed from
the shabby reserve just a few miles away. I was, just briefly, seeing
the town with Indian eyes, and for a second I realized how a proud
native Canadian, whose ancestors were once masters of this vast
territory, must feel when they contemplate the thoroughness of
their displacement.

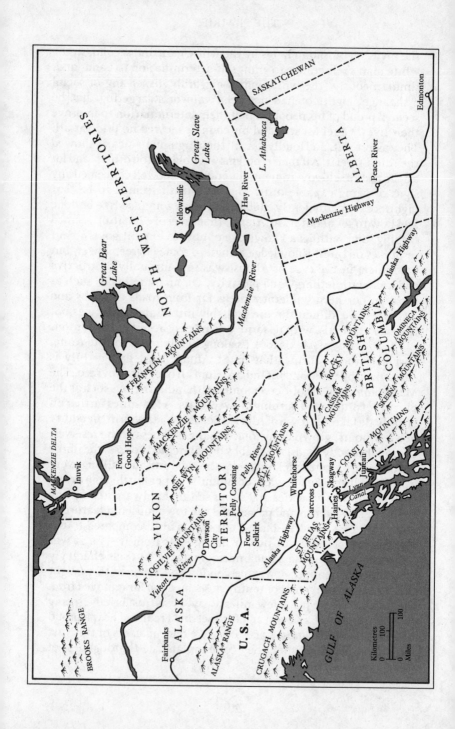

Part Six

*The Rockies
And the North*

18

The Mountain With No Name

I had intended to write a chapter about Calgary, but I must disappoint the reader. I went to Calgary, three times indeed, but there still is no chapter. To make my first assault on Calgary I took the bus down from Edmonton, and sat beside a chirpy old lady of nimble wit and bright attentiveness. I was struck by her starchy clothes and bonnet and by a lapel badge she was wearing that read 'VALU VILAJ'. I puzzled over this for some time, and eventually deduced she was a Lithuanian lay nun, if you'll excuse the expression, boldly participating in a campaign for the release of a Litvak dissident, probably a Baptist or Jehovah's Witness who had been dispatched to Siberia. After a while I shyly asked her about the motto.

'Oh that,' she laughed. 'Gee, I have a nice girl lives next door to me and she works at this supermarket that had a grand opening last week. It's called Value Village and she gave me one of the badges.'

So I had to downgrade her from wise nun to addlepate, cease our conversation, and open a less than riveting book on Alberta separatism. I looked up an hour later and found myself peering at a blizzard. It was 6 September. By the time I reached Calgary it was still snowing and three inches of slush slurped along the downtown streets. If Calgary was going to give me such a grudging welcome, I would have to leave. On arrival I bought a bus ticket to Vancouver. I had a few hours to wait, and decided to be dutiful and to see what downtown Calgary has to offer. First I needed some lunch, and slithered my way through the foggy chill towards Chinatown, a block and a half of tackiness strangled by expressways and urban renewal projects. A few secretaries from nearby City Hall darted into restaurants, and towards me stumbled a scruffy bearded man singing 'What a Day for a Daydream'. Had there been irony in the phrasing or savagery in the voice or a twinkle in the eye, I would have applauded his panache, but no, the numskull was dishing it out straight. Lunch consisted of one of those large bowls of soup cluttered with cabbage peelings, snouts of sows, verrucas of veal, vermicelli, and fatty pork chunks as red as a running sore. But nourishing. Thus fortified, I sloshed over to the Glenbow Museum, a splendid structure, full of varied exhibitions, from mineralogy to arms and armour to Buddhist Images of Asia. Best of all was a relic: another couple of inches of the rope that throttled Louis Riel. The museum was also dry and warm, which may have accounted for the high attendance that afternoon. I also enjoyed the Devonian Gardens, an entire floor of a shopping complex that has been filled with shrubs and plants in a landscape of pools and fountains and benches. Here I could sit and read another chapter on Alberta separatism.

There is much more to be said about Calgary, but not by me. I left for Vancouver Island, where it was warm and sunny.

I returned a couple of weeks later, but stayed in Calgary for no longer than it takes to rent a car. I drove out of the city in a northward direction, and was surprised to find myself on the rolling prairie. I had been told that Calgary's skyscrapers rose straight up from the prairie, but this is not so. The prairie undulates, and though the general impression is one of flatness, it is of a buckled flatness. From the crest of a wave of prairie I could look back on the city, its almost uniformly tall downtown buildings resembling skittles set up for play. And in the far distance I could see the snowy peaks of the Rockies. I turned west towards Cochrane. From the city I had phoned Brigadier Miles Smeeton of that community and introduced myself.

'Ah,' he said, 'do you want a bed for the night?'

'Actually, no.'

'Oh good. You see, my daughter's here with her family, so the house is full.'

'That's fine. I want to be in the Rockies by evening.'

'Most people who call want a bed for the night. Normally it would be easy to put you up.'

'Thanks, but I don't need a bed.'

'How about a cup of tea?'

'That would be perfect.'

The brigadier lived in what looked like a homemade house in ranching country north of Cochrane. He had attained his military rank during World War II in Burma and India, and after the war he and his wife had bought land, sight unseen, on Saltspring Island near Vancouver. They didn't spend much time there, because

Smeeton bought a forty-six foot boat and began to sail all over the world, stopping for a few months wherever the life looked good. He had had numerous adventures and was enjoying much success as an author of books recounting them. He had given up the nautical life in 1969 and during a visit to his daughter, then working at Calgary Zoo, had resolved to settle in Alberta. So he bought some acreage outside Calgary and built the house where he now lives. Much of the furniture is homemade too, and by a cunning form of recycling old agricultural implements have been fashioned into handrails and tables. This gave the house a genial, informal atmosphere, like the props room in an old music hall. Smeeton, tall and loose-limbed like a puppet in a drawer, was well suited to his house. He exuded a casual charm, like one of the more feckless characters in Anthony Powell's amble to the music of time. Indeed, with his snowy white hair and open ageing handsome looks, he bore a resemblance to the novelist. He seemed to make a merit of his slight physical infirmities, denying some and affecting others. In manner he was utterly English, with a perfection of national manner preserved by the expedient of staying away from his native island. Over the last forty years he had lived everywhere except Britain. Yet we still ate pound cake and sipped Earl Grey – or was it Lapsang? – and no doubt after I left he would have sipped a Scotch or G&T while tuning into the BBC World Service.

'I'm going to have to go down and feed the foxes.' Of course. I was growing accustomed to patting sharp-fanged predators down on the farm in Canada. 'Did you see them as you came in?'

'I saw some fences and netting. You keep foxes?'

'I raise them. These are a very rare breed, almost extinct until I got my hands on a few cubs and began raising them. When they're grown I release them onto the prairie. They're tagged so I can keep track of them, and, d'y'know, some of them are still alive out there after two years.'

He lowered his attenuated frame from the window seat where he had been reclining, and I followed him down the stairs and into the yard. He picked up a paper bag on the way and tottered vigorously towards the fence. Half a dozen small foxes, much smaller than the standard model but very alert, came charging towards him, backing away in uncertainty, probably because of my unfamiliar presence, then zooming forward again when Smeeton tossed them their supper in the form of something small, yellow, and stiff.

'What's that you're giving them?'

'Day-old chicks. Come from a local hatchery. They've got no use for male chicks, so they sell them to me by the dozen. The foxes love 'em.'

I drove down minor roads due south from Cochrane towards the Crowsnest Pass. I had asked Brigadier Smeeton about the quality of the road surface, and he had murmured something about it being a lovely drive. For the first fifty miles I crossed rolling prairie and woods in which dark spruce seemed menacing among the lighter coloured birch and aspen. At Longview I was dismayed to see a sign reading ROAD CLOSED. The diversion would add about forty miles to my journey. A workman told me the surface was a bit rough for three or four miles, but could be negotiated with care. I proceeded. There followed seventy miles of gravel road through wilderness. To my right the thick woods of the Rocky Mountains Forest Reserve nuzzled the flanks of the mountains, occasionally making way for patches of treeless heathland. Pump jacks and the neat silver thimbles of natural gas installations conducted the underground wealth of the province into pipelines. All this viewed from a car that seemed to be continuously skidding over the gravel. The road was extremely wide, so the occasional five-yard slither didn't greatly matter. What troubled me more was the cloud of dust on the horizon that signalled the approach of a fast-moving truck. I gave these vehicles as wide a berth as I could, but that didn't protect me from a bombardment of tyre-whipped grit and stone. Drivers on dirt roads are requested to slow down when other vehicles approach, since it is discourteous to throw a cocktail of buckshot grit, mud and dust into the eyes of another driver. It is also dangerous. Truck drivers seemed to take positive pleasure in speeding up when they saw me coming, and I soon learnt to reduce my speed to a crawl to cope better with ten seconds' loss of visibility.

My shoulders were aching with the tension of keeping the car under control, but eventually I came to Route 3, a road with a surface, and turned west towards the British Columbia border and the Crowsnest Pass. I passed the village of Frank and the site of the Frank Slide. One of the small hazards of the Rockies is that from time to time they collapse. On 23 April 1903 a chunk of limestone mountain 2000 feet high became detached from the rest of the peak, and when 90 million tons of rubble pummelled the valley below, that was the end of Frank. Even today the road is cut through a lake of rubble. I reached Crowsnest shortly before dusk, and the overcast skies were clearing sufficiently for me to admire the pass's encirclement by the Rockies, unfolding before me as peak after peak came into view. The suddenness with which rolling prairie gave way to Alpine landscape was astonishing. There are the shy rehearsals of foothills, to be sure, but the first true glimpse of that horseshoe of snowy peaks from Crowsnest is wonderfully dramatic.

The winding road down from Crowsnest passes through coal-mining country. I stopped for the night at Fernie. The rain thundered down all night, and it continued to pour all the next day. Three inches of water fell on Calgary, breaking a sixty-year record, and the Rockies were similarly inundated. Not, it will be appreciated, the best weather for sightseeing in the mountains. My visits to the tourist attractions of the region were, consequently, pursued doggedly rather than avidly. The Kootenay Trout Hatchery had the merit of being indoors, although the exhibits, tens of thousands of troutlets whipping about in long tanks, would probably have been equally comfortable outdoors. Eggs are stripped from female trout in well stocked lakes and fertilized at the hatchery; the orphaned trout, when they achieve a length of about three inches, are returned to the lakes. About six million fish are deposited in the lakes of British Columbia in this manner, and that's a lot of fishing and a lot of dinners.

As I approached Fort Steele I had to weave past a rockslide dislodged by the heavy rains, and it was not reassuring to note that had I passed the spot some hours earlier, my car and its occupant would have been smashed. Fort Steele, a nineteenth-century police post, was partly reconstructed, and this had been done with the usual skill of Canadians preserving their slight but heroic heritage. I made my way along the broad unpaved streets of the settlement, seeking the high ground of the ruts in a losing battle to keep my feet dry. Occasionally, as at the Windsor Hotel, I could leap onto the wooden porch for a few yards of shelter. All the elements of civilization were present at Fort Steele: the 1897 courthouse accommodated a two-cell jail; the Presbyterian church faced the Anglican church, though before the former had been built Presbyterian sermons had echoed through Coventry's Opera House next door; Shakespearean readings were given at the Anglican vicarage; and the splendidly stocked General Store had managed to stay in business until the 1950s. Perhaps it was as well to be tramping through the muddy streets in the rain: in bright sunshine, if such a thing exists in the Kootenay region, Fort Steele might have borne too close a resemblance to Toytown. On this sodden morning it looked authentic enough to me.

I drove west to Kimberley, the highest town in British Columbia, and the silliest. The entire downtown section had been idiotically transformed into – I squirm even to recall it – the Bavarian Platzl. Everything about the place was phony: the mansard roofs and exaggerated gables resting their elbows on wooden brackets, the shutters with their heart-shaped cutout designs, and flower paintings beneath the eaves of gables that rose even over the workshops of the garage. Why any community should wish to ape Berchtesgaden is mysterious enough, but what truly irritated me was that the designers had got it all wrong. Bavaria, it should not be necessary to observe, is not the same place as Switzerland. I stumbled past the Haus of Burgers and Bavarian Sports and Hardware, which looked entirely North American in its contents, and, on encountering a local resident, smarmed up to her.

'Excuse me, ma'm,' I asked, with winning charm, 'but is Kimberley a German settlement?'

'No, it's not. It's a theme town.'

'A theme town? What's that?'

'Well, Revelstoke had already called itself Alpine Town, so here in Kimberley we took a Bavarian theme. The decor's the same.'

'So I've noticed. What's the point of it, if I may ask?'

She looked rather puzzled, as though the point were obvious. 'It helps to upgrade the town.'

'Why can't Kimberley just be Kimberley, instead of Bavaria?'

'What *is* Kimberley?' We had reached the heart of the matter. 'This was a dying mining town. Now it's revived. We even have Bavarian families that have come here to run the bakery. And the Gasthaus. And the camera store.'

I thanked her and wandered along to the bakery. It did sell strudel, but it also sold doughnuts, hamburger buns, and the worst meringues I have ever tasted.

I drove on northwards. On the outskirts of Fairmont I passed the geological formations known as hoodoos, tall sandy crenellated cliffs that seemed to have strayed from the Sahara. Fairmont and other resorts along the Columbia Valley are renowned for their hot springs, but this was no weather for a warm soaking in mineral water. Windermere was aptly named, a village along a skinny wriggle of a lake that did indeed resemble its original in the Lake

District. At Invermere I passed a llama farm, an enterprise run by a former vet who had shrewdly anticipated the new craze for pet llamas that has been sweeping California. As I continued to drive up the valley the snow-flecked crests of the Purcell Mountains rose to the west.

At the top of Rogers Pass, at a height of 4500 feet, stands a comfortable hotel, where I stopped for the night. The pass is named after Major A. B. Rogers, a much loathed surveyor of notorious foul temper and stinginess. It was he who in 1881 was instructed to find a suitable pass through the Rockies for the Canadian Pacific Railway. To the railway directors it seemed possible that the best route would cut through the Selkirk Mountains, but this range was among the most formidable in all the Rockies and no one had yet managed to find a pass through these mountains. The first year of explorations proved fruitless; Rogers and his team experienced great hardships among the mountains and glaciers of the Selkirk range, and came upon no pass. But on 24 July 1882, Rogers and his team found what they were looking for. It took years for the directors of the CPR to agree that this was indeed the best route through the Rockies, but eventually the track was laid, and on 4 July, 1886, Canada was crossed for the first time by train.

Rogers' team had experienced some avalanches in the Selkirks but had not realized how prone these slopes were to snowslides. Avalanches became such a frequent occurrence that, after dozens of workmen had been buried in a particularly horrifying incident, a five-mile tunnel was dug beneath the pass to protect the trains. Even today the road over Rogers Pass – it was only paved in 1962 – burrows beneath protective snow sheds. In winter trained experts patrol the high exposed snow fields on skis and if they encounter conditions likely to lead to an avalanche, they arrange for artillery to trigger a controlled slide. Despite the hazards, once the CPR had made its decision to lay the tracks over Rogers Pass, the spectacularly beautiful spot, surrounded by high peaks and broad glaciers, became a major resort. For about forty years the Glacier House hotel attracted a fashionable clientele, until in 1929 it burnt to the ground.

The summer season is short in the Rockies. Two weeks earlier, when I had fled Calgary for the balmy air of Vancouver, I had crossed Rogers Pass in a blizzard. Now it was wet and windy and cold; there couldn't have been more than two dozen guests at the Lodge. When I told the hotel's entertainments director I wanted to climb some trails, he offered to accompany me. Derek was an engaging character, a songwriter and singer who supplemented his income by keeping hotel guests amused. The weather that morning was still poor, but an improvement over the torrential rains of the day before. A cool wind was scattering a strobe of drizzle over the mountains, but some of the clouds were beginning to lift from the peaks. We drove to the Glacier House, where we poked about among the ruins of the gutted hotel before walking up through the rain forest to Marion Lake. On either side of the path were thick clumps of devil's club, a nettle so ferocious that its ubiquitous presence in the Selkirks had almost defeated not only the hardy Major Rogers but his equally tough Indian porters.

The forest, with its formidable undergrowth and lofty trees, was, even in this dreary weather, very beautiful. It had never been logged. Until the coming of Rogers and the railway, it had been virgin territory. Not even the Indians had made any serious explorations of the Selkirks. Deer, elk and moose preferred the easier terrain of the valleys and lower slopes, and so did the Indian bands. As we climbed, Derek yelled into the woods, just to scare off any bears that might be contemplating elevenses at our expense. He admitted to me that in four summers of hiking these trails he had never encountered a bear. No grounds for complacency, though; a few days before a grizzly had polished off a young woman in nearby Yoho National Park. 'And a friend of mine once turned a corner and found himself face to face with a bear sow and her cubs. He stayed cool and darted up a tree. The sow lumbered up to the foot of the tree and howled and roared. Then my friend spotted a second cub trembling on the next branch and understood why the sow was so upset. So with the butt of his gun he poked the cub till it fell to the ground. The sow cuffed it and then the three bears headed off into the bush.'

The guidebook stated that the climb to Marion Lake would take an hour and a half, but spurred on by the cool air we halved that time. The lake proved to be a small fishless pond surrounded by bright green grasses and rushes. From the trail I could see the thrilling peak of Mt Sir Donald and the Illecillewaet glacier, like a giant lip protruding from the face of the mountains opposite. Above the lake the woods became more stunted, the vegetation subalpine. As we climbed, Derek became more cheerful – and more contemptuous of the civilization we were, however temporarily, leaving behind. He sang some of his songs, and told me that bears forage through the litter bins filled by tourists and contract cancers and all the other ailments that afflict humans. 'It's that plastic food most people eat and all the other shit down there in the cities.' I would have yelled my agreement had I the breath to do so, but the trail was relentlessly steep; and apart from the lakeside, we had encountered no level patches since setting off. The views onto the valley below and the mountains just above the line of my gaze boosted my morale. After another half hour of steep climbing, which caused even my experienced guide to pant with exertion, we reached the Alpine hut on the Abbott trail at a height of about 6000 feet. By now we had left the forest behind and were hauling our bent bodies through a subalpine tundra of rocks and heather and hardy shrubs. It was snowing. The hut was locked, so we sat on the steps munching apples and listening to the shrill whistles of marmots and looking out onto the harsh, beautiful peaks on the opposite side of the valley. Some were still covered in cloud, but others declared themselves through the swirling mists.

Derek pointed to one of them, Mt Macdonald. 'Back in the 1880s three clergymen set off to climb it. To their knowledge no one had ever done so before. They eventually made it to the summit, and as they were resting near the top, one of them spotted a rusty nail in a gully. So someone had been up there before them, and it could only have been some of the Canadian Pacific engineers who built the railway. If you go into the Alpine Club today and look up the first ascent of Mt Macdonald, you'll see that the first man to climb the mountain was Anon.'

From Glacier Park I drove east into the Columbia valley. The sun was shedding a crisp light on the peaks, which were divided from the slopes by a band of cloud above the snowline. Beyond Golden, the road enters Kicking Horse Valley, another route followed by the railway. The river, a pale green torrent the colour of young cabbage, swirled and rushed over its rocky bed. Carpets of firs swept up the flanks of the mountain ranges and thrust themselves up into steep spurs; above them was a chaos of rock and ice. I made a small detour to Emerald Lake, a ravishing bowl of deep green water encircled by snowy peaks, before pressing on towards Jasper. At the border with Alberta, the road climbs through Kicking Horse Pass, then descends towards Lake Louise. I turned north through the Banff and Jasper National Parks towards Jasper itself. To the east immensely tall castellated cliffs, like walls guarding the peaks behind, leaned back like toast in a rack. On a grassy slope above the road near Bow Lake, a solitary elk was staring across the valley, almost blending into the darkness of the woods behind but betrayed by the thicket of antlers over his large head. Much of the Columbia Icefield was obscured by mist and freezing rain as the road climbed up to the 6000-feet Sunwapta Pass. Soon after I passed the Athabasca Glacier, as thickly grey as the sullen evening sky, it grew dark.

After a night in Jasper I retraced at leisure the route of the previous evening. The sun had stopped sulking and the morning was bright and clear. On the mountain slopes yellow-leaved aspens shimmered in the sunlight, though nothing could enliven the grim dark greenery of the Engelmann spruces. To the west there was a magnificent view over the Athabasca River to Mt Fryatt and Mt Edith Cavell, and between the two an unnamed peak – 'Unnamed' – reminding me that until a hundred years ago hardly a soul had looked at, let alone explored, this stupendous landscape. At the Athabasca Falls, the broad river narrows and pounds its way through a tall rocky channel, dropping seventy feet as it goes. The walls of the little canyon lean and jut, a miniaturization of the mountains on either side, giving a craggy irregular striated outline. A bridge over the falls, permanently wetted by the spray, gives a view onto the concentrated force of the corsetted river pummelling through the cliffs.

The most accessible glacier is the Athabasca, one of six that flows off the Columbia Icefield. Over the last century the toe of the glacier has retreated a whole mile. Channels of meltwater trickled from the grubby underlip of the ice, which seems to be kicking before it a pile of muck and gravel. A few adventurous tourists, suitably equipped and booted, were venturing onto the glacier itself. Even at this tamest edge of the ice mass the surface was furrowed with millholes and crevasses. At the Interpretation Centre, a busload of Japanese tourists were scuttling out of one vehicle and piling into another, a Snowcoach that caterpillars across the bumpy glacier. I drove a mile further on to where the Wilcox Trail begins on the other side of the valley, and set off along it. The path soon climbed into the woods, where I encountered a plump ptarmigan blocking the trail. It stared at me with its red-ringed eye and fluffed its fantail pompously. I spoke to it in a reasonable tone of voice, urging upon it the expedient of removal to a safer spot. It didn't respond. I continued my argument, laying out all the reasons why it should make a run for it, and after prolonged contemplation of my logic, it consented to waddle two yards up the slope. When, an hour later, I walked back, the ptarmigan was still squatting thickly in the same spot. How trusting are our fellow creatures when we encounter them in the wild! And how stupid.

Further on, the path broke out of the woods into subalpine meadows. The springy vegetation had turned orange, russet and ochre as autumn dug in its claws; a few senile blueberries clung unhappily to their stalks; patches of snow served notice of the imminent rigours of winter. I sat on a rock that was prettily daubed with orange lichen, and looked at the great icefield sprawled between the mountains opposite. Although its movements were imperceptible, the consequences of its retreats and hesitations and forays were not. Moraines and boulders and other glacial debris littered the landscape. That the thick glaciers are still on the move, I found somewhat menacing. I walked back across the meadows and through the woods, and again encountered the dozy ptarmigan, and a very raucous chipmunk, which responded to my greeting with a concatenation of high-pitched squeaks and low clucking sounds. I pointed out that my intentions were honourable – had I wanted to eat the little chap I would already have been spitting out the fur – but he just kept on yapping at me until, bored, I walked away.

I drove on south, into a valley with a sheer rock face on either side. To the east appeared the Weeping Wall, towering castellated cliffs streaked with the tears of numerous waterfalls. Nearby a trail through subalpine forest led to a platform high over Peyto Lake, surely one of the loveliest mountainscapes in the Rockies: the valley stretches far to the north, while above the lake itself is the mass of the Peyto Glacier, as thickly white as fresh pork fat. The colour of the lake is extraordinary: suspended rock flour tints the water a pale turquoise, as if it were blue with cold. Bow Lake, a few miles further south, must be infiltrated by a different brand of rock flour, for its waters are a darker blue-green than those of Lake Peyto. Just above Bow Lake looms the Crowfoot Glacier, 150 feet thick at the snout and dented by large ice caves. It struck me as I continued to drive down this supremely panoramic road that its 200-mile length is framed on either side by long ridges, with each peak clearly visible, like fists thrust into the sky. Behind these ridges are other ranges of peaks, lined up in almost military formation. It was a landscape seemingly cut at right angles and astonishingly free of curves. Only around the lakes, as at Lake Louise, did the peaks appear to huddle round a particular spot.

When, in the late afternoon, I reached Banff, I found it packed with weekend trippers, so I returned to beautiful Calgary. I knew I was back in civilization when I turned on the car radio and heard the following advertisement: 'Your car's a BMW, your game's racket sports, your drink's Perrier.' (Pause for listener to check off the list and recognize amazingly accurate portrait of self.) 'And your furniture's Chesterfield – naturally.' I laughed out loud when I heard this, but I also shuddered. It is the job of market analysts to labour at the obvious and decide what the self-image of certain consumers is likely to be. But that such stereotyping should be flaunted as a source of pride to those who embody it was more disconcerting. Are Canadians – for this was an ad heard on a Canadian radio station, not an American one – so hideously malleable? Could a fair proportion of BMW-driving, squash-playing, Perrier-drinking executives truly be so easily induced to buy a particular brand of sofa? 'Got four legs? A snout? Curly little tail? Then you must be a pig.' The ad differed from others in that it was aimed at the well educated and highly paid, whose intelligence ought to have been insulted, but, it had been calculated, would not be.

I was disappointed. Despite the cultural invasions from south of the border, there was an upright quality to Canadians that I found maddening in some respects but admirable in others. Their lack of duplicity carried on the back of the coin a lack of irony, even a lack of humour, that was regrettable, but not contemptible. Canadians were essentially honourable. Time and again in hotel rooms across Canada I would compare the morning news shows on the various networks. The American shows were, like most programmes on network TV, an excuse for saturation bombing by advertisers; they also had no difficulty attracting to their studios the newsmaking heavyweights. 'Canada AM' was a quite different show. Its presenter spoke as though he were gargling marbles in his throat, and the show, earnest in tone, lacked a lightness of touch. It was also pleasantly short of that insufferable chumminess that elevates weathermen like the American Willard Scott to figures of almost saintly bonhomie. It was, in a word, serious, and, without any doubt, it could be dull. It was also reliable and thorough.

CBC Radio exhibits the same virtues, in even greater doses. Canadians like to knock the CBC, just as British intellectuals affect to despise the BBC, but they know how admirable it is in comparison to its commercial competitors on both sides of the border. The news reports and magazine programmes are excellent, and on Sunday morning, anywhere in Canada, I could tune in to the local CBC station and hear an hour's worth of international news and reportage. To make available that amount of information, and to present it with a high degree of sophistication, is no mean achievement. And that is why I felt so keenly disappointed when I realized, from time to time, that my slightly exalted view of the Canadians was growing out of date by the minute. The Yuppies of Toronto and Calgary were no different from the Yuppies of New York or San Francisco. No doubt they all bought Chesterfield furniture by the vanload. I had reacted with outrage when one morning the CBS Morning News was sponsored by the *National Enquirer*, a rag that doesn't even pretend to be truthful or informative; the sponsor had reminded the viewer of its product by flashing the front page of the current issue, which featured the headline 'ROCK'S LAST TRAGIC DAYS' while the AIDS-afflicted actor was still alive. That couldn't happen on Canadian television, I was convinced. But that evening, listening to the car radio in Calgary, I heard a traffic roundup in which the reporter had to abase himself by shouting the praises of Diet Pepsi at the end of each bulletin. It was a modest exhibition of how journalists can become the creatures of their sponsors, but it was Canada's relative freedom from that commercial entrapment that I would have thought was worth cherishing, and as each brick was tugged away from that edifice of good, decent, dull, honourable probity, I was saddened.

19

Ice Road to Death

Two men stood in front of me waiting for a taxi. 'Ever been up here in good weather?' yelled one of them against the whoosh of the ear-numbing wind.

'Never,' said the other. 'They don't even know what weather is in Yellowknife.'

I had flown up from Edmonton via Hay River, a settlement on the murky southern shores of the Great Slave Lake. It was 19 September and autumn was already marching across the North-west Territories. The forests of dark green spruce and jack pine were speckled with the fiercely yellow leaves of birch and aspen. When the plane landed, a man with his foot in a cast hobbled off on crutches, and five minutes later a quite different man, with the same deficiency and also on crutches, swung over the tarmac to the waiting plane. This was either a coincidence – the dullest of explanations – or, I preferred to speculate, the nub of some unfathomably brilliant smuggling or espionage scam. Towards Yellowknife, forests had thinned to the half-hearted woodlands known as taiga and were interrupted by large outcrops of pink granite, a visual reminder that Arctic tundra was not far away.

It was bitterly cold for September. Three days earlier the wind had blown over a Cessna down at the float base. My taxi into town passed a Bristol bomber stuck high on a rock near the road. This, the first wheel-based plane to land on the North Pole (in May 1967), had been sold to Yellowknife for a dollar by Wardair. Aviation has always been important to the city. From the float base, amphibious aircraft fly out to remote corners of the Territories both for recreational purposes and to supply mining camps and native settlements. Before 1961, when the road down to Hay River was completed, the only access to Yellow-knife was by plane or barge. The road is an exhausting route south. It's a thousand-mile drive, much of it over gravel, just to Edmonton, and during freeze-up and break-up, when the ferry service across the Mackenzie River can't operate, the road is closed. Buses used to attempt the journey, but after a succession of vehicles had been put out of action by the roads, the service was discontinued.

There has been a trading post at Yellowknife since 1789, but it was only in the 1930s, with the discovery of gold, that the little town began to grow. The original settlement was down along the peninsula that stretches out into the lake and leads to Latham Island, but in 1947 a new commercial district was laid out on sandier soil away from the shore. The float base still clusters around one side of Latham Island, and it is down here and along the lanes of Old Town along the peninsula linking the two sections of town that Yellowknife reveals its character. I was staying on the island at a bed and breakfast establishment run by Barb Bromley in her pleasant modern house overlooking the lake, a peaceful spot disturbed only by the rumble of planes heading out into the bay for takeoff, a friendly sound that reminded me that the Territories were less isolated than they feel. Barb was a much revered citizen, both because of her devotion to the community and because she had lived in the town far longer than most of its inhabitants. She and her husband had arrived in 1948, when Yellowknife was still very much a prospectors' town, exciting but rough at the edges. Some years later her husband was killed on a canoeing trip while retracing some of the early explorers' routes; a lake now bears his name as a memorial. It was when Yellowknife was declared the capital of the Territories in 1967 that the expansion really began. As the capital of a region larger than all Europe, it became home to teams of administrators and bureaucrats, lawyers and judges. There seemed to be three kinds of inhabitants: the old-timers such as Barb and the bush pilots, the government workers – mostly transients who would only stay for a few years – and the Indians.

Glancing at my map one morning I found the tag 'ICE ROAD TO DEATH'. This was an appropriate misreading of Detah, the village a few miles across the lake, where many of the Indians live. In the winter an ice road connects the Dogrib village with the city. Another Dogrib settlement huddles at the far end of Latham Island, out of sight of the rest of the city. Built in the 1950s, the small brightly painted houses had earned the hamlet the name of Rainbow Valley. The glamorous name couldn't disguise the dilapidation. Residents supplemented their meagre incomes and diet by drying animal skins and smoking meat in sheds behind their houses. Of the original log cabins on Latham Island few are still standing. The former Bank of Toronto cabin is now a private house, but the Wild Cat Café, founded in 1937 – an almost medieval survival in the context of Yellowknife's history – is still in business. But most of the old houses have been replaced by spacious modern houses, for the tranquil island, with its views onto the lake, is home to the town's richest residents as well as the poorest.

The future of Old Town, especially the shacks and alleys along the flats between Ragged Ass Lane (named after a former mine, not a resident) and the lake, was in doubt, for it is built on crown land to which the residents have no title. The city authorities were anxious to oust the residents from this centrally located land and to redevelop it as a marina and park. Naturally the residents were strongly resisting any move to evict them, arguing that other lands acquired by the city for development have not yet been touched. Old Town is no slum, despite the lack of running water and other amenities. Some shacks have been here so long that they have become gentrified into bijou residences, whimsically ornamented with old bathtubs and canoes filled with plants. One house is surrounded by a fence entirely constructed from old railway ties acquired from one of the gold mines. Some of the apartment buildings in the newer sections of Yellowknife were faring less well. This far north, there's a layer of permafrost some feet below the surface, frozen earth that never thaws, not even in what passes for summer. In constructing the apartment buildings, steel pilings had been driven down into the permafrost to secure the foundations. Unfortunately, the heat generated within the completed building had warmed the pilings, which in turn melted some of the permafrost, thus causing subsidence. One winter night melting underground ice flooded a car park; the waters immediately froze in the sub-zero temperatures and the cars remained half-buried in the ice until the spring thaw freed them. The harsh winters also require ingenious expedients at the town cemetery. Before the freeze-up the authorities estimate the number of deaths over the winter to come, and graves are dug in advance and shored up until needed, for when the temperature, likely as not, is thirty below, you can't dig a grave.

The Con Mine, with its 6200-feet shaft the deeper of the two gold mines in the immediate area, is on the very edge of town. The two tons of oil sands required to produce a barrel of crude at Fort McMurray seems an excellent return compared to the ton of ore needed to produce a fifth of an ounce of gold. The two mines each employ about 350 people, so mining is an important but no longer central element in the local economy. Out by the mines there was more evidence of the perpetual war waged between rock and vegetation in the North. Rough domes of bald granite lumpishly pocked the uneven plateau, and here and there, in crevices where enough soil could entrench itself without being blown away, plants and shrubs took precarious root. Berries were plentiful: cranberries and gooseberries grew abundantly throughout the region. Stands of tamarack trees added a note of charm to the dour landscape; although they resemble the ubiquitous spruce they are not in fact evergreen, and by now their leaves had turned a lovely soft yellow the colour of barleysugar. Ravens flapped noisily overhead, cawing raucously. If the polar bear is the symbol of the Territories – even car licence plates are cut in the shape of the mighty animal – then the raven symbolizes its capital. These aggressive, even sinister, birds are little loved by the executive classes of Yellowknife because of their playful habit of stealing golf balls from the course.

The most striking building in town is the Heritage Centre, a well laid out museum that commemorates the native northern cultures that the coming of the white man disrupted. The courthouse also contains some exhibits that signify official recognition of the worth of Inuit culture. There's an arresting Inuit tapestry depicting Eskimo people in their traditional roles. Animal fibres have been employed in appropriate places, so that seal hair and caribou yarn are woven within the outlines of those animals. A small display of soapstone carvings records celebrated criminal cases. In the 1950s and 1960s a certain Judge Sissons took to commissioning local carvers to portray the crimes under consideration by the court: the carvings show murders and suicides, rapes and family practices that ran foul of Canadian law. The logical rigours of white man's law, founded on the bourgeois certainties of European society, often bore no relation to other ways of social organization that were, however, entirely appropriate to a society facing conditions utterly unknown in Europe. Suicide, for instance, taboo in Western society, is to Inuit an acceptable option, since calamities affecting the food supply for the winter can force a family or tribe to make hard choices about who shall survive.

On my walks into town from Barb Bromley's – there is a feeble bus service that runs to an unknown schedule – I would pass the float base. From here many legendary bush pilots opened up the Territories, and they still play a crucial role. Many people used charter planes the way city dwellers use taxis. In the summer friends will team up to charter a plane for a fishing weekend. A 200-mile trip in a Twin Otter will cost about $1000, which split between a party of six is not an exorbitant expense – and a shorter trip to a lake forty miles away need cost a party of ten no more than $60 per head.

'Came up to Yellowknife eighteen years ago to haul fish for a month,' said Ray. 'Been here ever since.' Most conversations would open with such a statistic of residency, local longevity being a source of pride. I was sheltering one chilly afternoon in the warm fug of Ray Bart's office down at the float base. From time to time I could hear the spluttering cough of an Otter engine starting up on the water. In the corner were stacked cases of beer, from which I was invited to help myself whenever I felt like it. A lupine but inert dog guarded the battered couch on which its master sat. Cigarette smoke curled through the air, its blue ascent aided by panting fan heaters. Ray made light of the alleged dangers of his profession. Since planes must be equipped with survival gear and a minimum of ten days' rations per person, disaster is rare, strandings less so.

With the end of summer, business was slowing down. In a few weeks Ray would be taking his planes off the lake, and he and his pilots would be putting their feet up for the winter. Business had declined in recent years. 'Ten years ago you'd have had to book two weeks in advance to get a plane, but not any more.' Many companies have folded as declining commodity prices forced mining and oil companies to cut back on their operations. 'These days it's not a question of how much you make, it's how much you get to keep after you've paid the expenses. I was planning to insure two of my planes this summer. You know what the insurance company wanted? $40,000! So instead I hired some tough experienced pilots and dropped the insurance.'

I wondered about the dangers of the work. About once a year a plane simply disappears in the North. The Territories cover such a vast area that unless he can make radio contact, a pilot forced to land unexpectedly far from his flight course might never be found. Ray said that he and his pilots didn't feel scared out over the barrens. 'The way we look at it is that there's a million airports beneath us the whole time. We can always land on the water.' Many planes are also equipped with a new device that enables satellite tracking systems to locate their exact position to within 200 yards. 'If the impact of the landing is so great that your radio and all other safety equipment are inoperable, you're probably dead anyway.'

As we worked our way through a few beers, Ray began to talk of his favourite pastime – hunting. Myself, I only hunt insects, and then only when provoked, but Ray was after larger game. Caribou, for instance, which he commended not just for the sport but for the excellence of its meat, which has the merit of being immediately edible. This is not the case, he informed me, with moose, which needs to be hung for a week. The hard part for me, I suggested, would not be shooting a moose (omitting to tell him that the largest creature I'd ever slaughtered was a water bug) but lugging the carcass through the bush and back to camp. Ray told me an expert field dresser could gut and clean a moose in twenty minutes if the animal was considerate enough to breathe its last in a position that granted easy access to the appropriate viscera. Less experienced butchers may need four or five hours.

Although caribou and moose present large targets, which appeals to hunters, the drawback is that so do their pursuers. 'I was once charged by an 1800-pound moose. I managed to shoot the bull before he got too close, otherwise I'd have been in real trouble. When a bull is charging, his hooves gouge inches of soil out of the ground. That's how powerful those mothers are. I couldn't take the carcass back to camp that day, but I came back the day after and could hardly find the animal. It had just about disappeared – the wolves had eaten it.'

By way of a change, Ray can go and plug a buffalo. 'There's a herd of about 5000 up near Providence that needs to be harvested from time to time. So they sometimes allow a little hunting. It ain't easy. Moose can't see good but they have keen smell, so you have to circle them carefully. But buffalo have good hearing and they'll vanish if they see you approach. You know what I've found? If you march straight up to a buffalo you can get close enough to touch them.'

And to touch them to death.

Despite the activities of hunters, stocks of wildlife are not diminishing. Barb's son Bob, who monitors northern falcons, told me that the only species under threat was the eastern bowhead whale. Nobody knows the exact polar bear population in Arctic Canada, but it's estimated at 12,000 and about 600 are 'harvested' each year. This can be a lucrative business for remote northern communities. About fifty polar bears are 'reserved' for sports hunters, mostly from the United States. Their hunt is strictly regulated by local hunting and trapping associations, who collect a handsome fee for organizing the expeditions. The only form of bear hunting permitted is by dog sled, the expedition can last two weeks, there is no guarantee of a trophy – and the price tag is about $15,000.

Arctic game hunters are prepared to pay lavishly for northern sport, and numerous outfitters are only too happy to take their money off them. Glenn Warner lives in Yellowknife and owns and operates the Bathurst Inlet Lodge on the Arctic coast. There are quite a few hunting and fishing lodges scattered over the Arctic, but at Bathurst Inlet the object of the exercise is to study wildlife rather than kill it. Warner, a heavily built but fit looking man in his fifties, spent twenty years with the RCMP before retiring to set up the Lodge. Like Ray, he minimized the dangers of patrolling the North. 'The risks of flying solo were just part of the job. I imagine it's probably less dangerous to fly over the Arctic than to walk the streets of a big city.' Before the Warners took over Bathurst Inlet, it had been a Hudson's Bay Company outpost. The company store had closed down in 1965, and the Warners acquired the store, the factor's house, and the former church, converting them into comfortable accommodation for twenty guests. The other inhabitants of the inlet are four families of Inuit, numbering twenty-four in all. For them the changes at Bathurst have brought great benefits. During the brief summer, they are employed at the Lodge as guides. When in mid-August the Lodge closes for the season, the Inuit stay on – living in the geodesic domes the government has built for them – and survive by hunting and fishing until the Lodge reopens the following June.

Boats ferry visitors within viewing distance of falcons or golden eagles, muskox or caribou. Amateur rock hounds can spend an afternoon searching for amethysts and other Arctic gems. The guests do not hunt, but their Inuit guides do as they please in their own land, and if they need meat they will not hesitate to shoot a passing caribou, although this behaviour does upset over-sensitive guests. The Inuit are quite prepared to tolerate the lucrative two-month invasion of their inlet, but remain absolutely convinced of the superiority of their own way of life. To them, winters of almost perpetual gloom, not to mention the appalling cold and frequent storms, are not a hard life. Their culture is so powerfully organized around the need to survive in such conditions that they take the consequent way of life for granted. Warner told me that some of the older Inuit at Bathurst can recall a time when no living natives had ever seen a white. Their ancestors had encountered members of the doomed Franklin expedition in the 1840s, but thereafter no white men had come to the Inlet until the 1930s.

While Central Canadians regard Yellowknife as about as remote as Vladivostok, I was beginning to realize that the city was no more than a tassel on the immense draped landscape of the Territories. It was possible to travel a couple of thousand miles due north from Yellowknife and still be in Canadian territory. Somehow, despite my limited resources, I would have to find a way up to the Arctic.

Most Northerners now agree that the Territories are too large to be administered from Yellowknife alone. Two thousand miles of Arctic wastes separate the citizens of Inuvik from those of Frobisher Bay. The residents of Resolute or Igloolik are further from the capital than England is from North Africa. A plebiscite of 1982 had shown a slight majority in favour of dividing the NWT, and the government was funding two constitutional forums, the Western Constitutional Forum (WCF) and the Nunavut Constitutional Forum for the eastern Arctic. Their recommendations would not be binding on the government, but would indicate which courses of action would be most popular. The impetus for division comes from the east; there was less enthusiasm for the idea in the capital, though most people thought division inevitable. The sticking point had been establishing where the border between the two new provinces should run. Should it be geographical, topographical, ethnographical?

The trailing cables of television cameras and sound equipment in the United Church auditorium suggested that the first WCF hearings in Yellowknife for two years would be well attended, but fewer than a hundred people showed up. Provision made for simultaneous translation into two Indian languages proved unnecessary: almost all present were white. The Forum members sat behind a long table at the front of the hall. The chairman was a pugnacious and articulate MLA, Bob MacQuarrie. Native interests were represented by the soft-spoken but shrewd Steve Kakfwi of the Dene Nation and by the remarkably incoherent

Larry Tourangeau of the Métis Association. There was little love lost between the Indian factions. The Dene, in the eyes of many, had put a spanner in the works by rejecting the authority of both the federal and the provincial government; they sought to regain control of the resources they had lost and to press for greater political autonomy before agreeing to division. The Dene, as the largest Indian nation in the region, wanted to name the proposed new region Denendeh. No one objected. It is not every day that you get to name a territory half the size of Europe. It is also more fun to think up names than to sort out political differences.

The contributions from the floor were less than inspiring. Each speaker chose to ramble on for twenty minutes or more, following the example set by the equally garrulous WCF members. Yellow-knife MLA, Ted Richard, who was exceedingly slow of speech, was prepared to accept division but disagreed about the boundary line. He also observed that the annual federal subsidy for the NWT amounts to roughly $12,000 per resident. What will happen to that subsidy after division? There were murmurs of disquiet from the audience, as if no one had thought of this before. It had been proposed by the WCF, and generally accepted, that the boundary between the two areas should follow the treeline, which, contrary to popular belief, is more diagonal than horizontal. This troubled another speaker, who muttered that 'it don't make sense 'cos the treeline don't stay in the same place'. He was reassured by MacQuarrie that the notion of a boundary along the treeline was not to be taken too literally. Only one speaker opposed division. 'It's a case of divide and conquer!' he declaimed. No one seemed very interested. (Tentative agreement was reached by early 1987.)

I enjoy political meetings, but this one was as exciting as a box of Valium. The point at issue was of some consequence. The financial, political, economic, and cultural implications, to whites as well as natives, were considerable. An enormous chunk of the world's land surface, though admittedly much of it permanently covered by ice, was about to be carved up, and Yellowknife, with almost a quarter of the NWT's population, was represented before the Forum by a mere roomful of mostly silent or inarticulate people. Perhaps they, and the thousands of Yellow-knifers who stayed at home, were baffled by the complexities of the issue. Some of these were put to me by James Wah-Shee, an MLA from the northern arm of the Great Slave Lake. When I called on him one morning, it took him about twenty minutes to pull himself together. Just as I managed to complete a question, he would rise from behind his desk and dart out of the room to buttonhole his secretary or find his cigarettes. I had to tell him who I was three times. I suspect a projected shortfall in cigarette supply was the root of his panic, and when he had at last settled behind his desk with an ample supply of smokes, he relaxed and actually answered my questions.

He made clear, intentionally or not, how factionalism dominates the politics of the Territories. Any constitutional change would, he insisted, have to incorporate guaranteed representation for native peoples. Aboriginal rights had to be protected. The WCF had yet to agree on the forms of authority that would rule a new Denendeh. Any constitutional settlement will have to resolve jurisdictional disputes between different levels of authority. The NWT contains important mineral reserves and future decades might see fresh discoveries made beneath the permafrost. At present, since the NWT is under direct federal control, revenues from mineral rights are placed in a kind of trust fund. Should division take place and the two new territories win provincial status, all such revenues would go directly to the new provinces. Until such constitutional change takes place, there must, argued Wah-Shee, be some kind of revenue-sharing arrangement negotiated with Ottawa.

An outsider's view of the debate was offered to me by Melvyn, a young lawyer who had moved up to Yellowknife the year before. He thought it unlikely that the two forums would ever agree on the boundaries, which would probably have to be decided by a commission from Ottawa – 'the worst possible solution, since Ottawa regards the North as a remote colony'. The area under dispute is the oil-rich Mackenzie Delta around Inuvik near the Alaska border. The WCF considers that for geographical reasons it makes sense for the Mackenzie Delta to be in Denendeh. The eastern Arctic argues that because the Delta shares an Inuit culture with the people of Baffin Island, it should be incorporated into Nunavut. This argument struck Melvyn as worthless. If the primary justification for division is the remoteness of the east from the capital, then it is clearly illogical to incorporate the even more distant Mackenzie Delta into the eastern region. The debate illustrates the lengths to which people will go to argue for a point of principle when a few oilfields are at stake.

Another problem was raised by the language issue. The NCF

wanted Inuktitut recognized as an official Nunavut language, in courts, schools, and government offices. Inuktitut was indeed spoken by some 13,000 people, about 30% of the entire NWT population, but there are six different dialects and the problems of translation would be immense. Inuktitut and six Indian languages have already been designated as 'official aboriginal languages' and there are circumstances when they may be employed in the courts. For obvious reasons, this is rarely done.

Some weeks later I presented to a refreshingly acerbic journalist called Tim my impression that complex issues were being put into the hands of politicians whose primary loyalties were factional. On average the intellectual quality of the discussion I had heard at the WCF meeting would have discredited a school debating society. Perhaps I shouldn't have been surprised. After all, the NWT had a total population of no more than 50,000, and why should such a tiny population base foster a large number of gifted politicians? 'You're right,' said Tim. 'Because of the size of the Territories, its politicians have a great deal of power, but the truth is most of them couldn't even run a paper route.'

When the meeting was over, I set off for Latham Island. The two-mile walk hadn't bothered me earlier in the evening, but the temperature had dropped sharply. I tried hitching, without success, and walked hesitantly through the dark, for there were patches of the road near the Old Town that were feebly lit. Dogs barked in the distance as they sniffed my approach, and I prayed that they were securely tethered. I crossed the causeway onto the island and took the road over the rocky hillock in the direction of Barb's house. It was a brief but steep climb through the darkness. The wind was slapping the rock so hard that once or twice I had to stop and crouch for fear of being blown over. The cables strung above the side of the road swayed alarmingly, like a children's swing in full flight, and the wind whined, high-pitched and shrill, through the wires. From a cabin chimney, red embers glowed intensely as they were whisked into the night. I felt a fear out of proportion to the foulness of the weather, for I was in no real danger.

It was the harshness of the immediate environs that unsettled me: the hard grey granite on either side, and the frigid waters of the lake, as dark as Marmite, a few yards beyond. A hundred steps in either direction and I would be in the wilderness. In the North the boundaries between civilization and raw wilderness are frighteningly thin. I recalled that the average annual temperature for Yellowknife is −5° centigrade. At this moment it was warmer than that, just above zero perhaps, though the wind chill factor made it feel much colder. If it was like this in September, I'd stay away for the winter months. In the North even car tyres can freeze – a condition known as 'square tyres' because the flattened area at the bottom of the tyre is frozen into a bone-shaking angle. Other parts of the car were equally likely to freeze up. There are three remedies when the temperatures plunge: an oil and engine block heater, a warm blanket around the battery, and an inside heater. Plug that lot in, and within two hours the car should start with ease.

I dug my chin into my chest and stumbled on against the shrieking wind. Only a lunatic, I was convinced, would come to live in a place where such a night constituted above-average weather. Yellowknife was indeed notoriously full of dropouts of various kinds but your social dislocation had to be extreme to keep you here. Either that, or somebody, most likely the government, was paying you handsomely for your endurance. On the other hand, only a lunatic would choose to *walk* to Latham Island on a night when the wind was like a hammer from the Arctic. It was John Ruskin who wrote in 1860 to his friend Pauline Trevelyan: 'The state these Arctic Regions are kept in seems to me a declaration from Heaven that we are not wanted there.'

Nevertheless, I still wanted to lay eyes on some Arctic settlements. One morning I phoned Bob Engle, the president of Northwest Territorial Airways. Would it be possible, I mused, for me to go along just for the ride on a cargo flight up north? No, it would not, he replied, pointing out that, first, any passengers on cargo flights had to be connected with the cargo, and, second, that any special arrangements had to be made weeks, not hours, in advance. I apologized for troubling him and was about to hang up when he asked me to 'hold' for a minute. When he returned to the phone, he said: 'I've been checking the payload on one of our afternoon flights, and if you can get to the airport in an hour we'll take you to Frobisher Bay and bring you back tonight.'

I did have an imminent lunch appointment with the lawyer John Bayly and his wife Christine. I dashed over to their office. 'I hate to do this,' I explained, 'but I'm going to have to stand you up for lunch, as I'm going to Frobisher Bay for the afternoon and have to leave immediately.'

'It's fifteen hundred miles to Frobisher from here!'

'That's why I'm going. Bob Engle has offered me space on a cargo plane.'

'You certainly can't go dressed like that,' said Christine, gazing in horror at my nifty leather blouson and Jermyn Street shoes. 'You'll freeze. Those planes aren't even heated. We'll have to get you back to the house and get you some clothes.'

'But I have to be at the airport in forty minutes.'

'Our house is near the airport. Let's go. We'll get you there in time. We'll have lunch together another day.'

I suspect the kind Baylys were amusing themselves at my expense by kitting me out in the most ludicrous Arctic gear: a heavy cable stitch sweater that seemed to have done recent duty as a dog blanket, mittens large enough to crawl into, a sagging knee-length parka, fur-lined boots, a woolly hat. This was no time, they scolded me, to be worrying about modishness; it was a question of surviving many hours at 25,000 feet over the Arctic tundra. They rushed me to the airport, where I made contact with an airline official. It was then that I learnt that Bob Engle had given me a free round trip on a scheduled flight, not a cargo plane. My fellow passengers were neatly dressed in suits and elegant parkas. I, however, looked like Nansen.

We flew in a Lockheed Electra, its roomy interior as plush as beige plastic can be. Thick cushiony layers of the stuff on the roof and beneath the overhead racks made me think I was flying in a padded cell. The first stop was Rankin Inlet, 700 miles due east on the northwest shore of Hudson's Bay. As we approached the Bay over the treeless tundra, the ratio of water to land increased. Countless lakes and ponds were pitted into the grey rock; soil and vegetation, where it existed at all, had with the coming of autumn taken on the colour of rust. The plane wheeled over the bay before coming in to land, and the waters were a deep green, except when the sun struck them from a different angle, changing the colour to a shimmering grey satin. To the east the sky was a perfect pale blue, but to the west there was a pulpy mass of thick grey cloud from which curtains of rain were falling.

Rankin Inlet looked as if it had been built yesterday. Knots of prefab houses sported bright yellow roofs, as cheerfully painted as children's building blocks. Waiting for some of the passengers were three Inuit women, with pretty round faces and straight or braided jet-black hair. Two were wearing *amauti*, loose Inuit parkas with decoratively coloured hems and bands and fur-lined hoods large enough to accommodate a baby, which these did. When their husbands emerged, they all climbed onto fat-wheeled all-terrain tricycles and roared off into town. On the terminal steps I struck up a conversation with one of my fellow passengers. She was on her way home to Frobisher Bay (now renamed Iqaluit). Sinikka was a smartly dressed Finnish woman who didn't correspond to my image of a typical Arctic resident, and I asked her how she was enjoying life on Baffin Island. She told me her life was exceptionally busy. With her work as a librarian, and various committees, and a range of social and recreational activities, she found it easy to fill her days, even those long depressing winter days when there's no more than four hours of daylight. It was the same story I'd heard from everyone who lived in a remote community. Was there truly no one in the North who was bored or hated the place?

'But I'm a newcomer to the Arctic. You should talk to my husband. He's an Inuit.'

So I did. Jens was a trim man of obvious energy, his lively presence only slightly modified by the studious cut of his mandarin goatee beard. He was a Greenlander by birth but his Inuit allegiance seemed more powerful than any national identity. He worked for the Canadian government (so, I would guess, did everyone on that flight, since who else could afford the thousand-dollar fare?), selecting Inuit who could be trained to take managerial positions with the government. At present only 3% of government jobs in the North are filled by Inuit.

'Many Inuit never leave their islands or bays except on hunting or fishing trips. I'm lucky. I've travelled all over the world. I must be one of the very few people to have visited almost every Inuit settlement in the world except for those in Siberia. We're spread out, but we do have a cohesive culture. We speak one language – though there are many dialects. Name one other ethnic group that considers its home to be a territory of three million square miles spread across half the world! When the sun sets over Siberia, it's rising over Greenland, and it's all Inuit land between the two. Compared to most Inuit I'm something of a big shot, I guess, but when I come home to Frobisher I realize that sitting on international committees doesn't count for a thing back home. That's humbling, and it's good to be humbled that way.'

When I asked Jens whether his relative sophistication put a barrier between him and, say, Inuit families such as those Glenn Warner had told me about at Bathurst Inlet, he looked at me with some surprise. 'Not at all. I still go out hunting when I'm home. Just a few weeks ago I went out with a friend from Frobisher into the interior of Baffin Island. We shot four caribou. We field-dressed them and then we each carried two of them back to camp on our backs.'

'Two caribou? On your backs?'

'They weigh about 175 pounds, I guess. The hard part is not the weight but that once you set off with such a load you mustn't make any stops. We carried those caribou for seven hours without a break. If you do stop, you lose your momentum and may not be able to get the load off the ground again. That was only half the journey. From camp there was another hundred miles by boat.

'Inuit are taught that nothing comes easy. We expect hardships and we know how to deal with them. Even in winter, if a storm blows up when we're out on the ice, we'll immediately make a shelter and sit out the storm. We're used to snow and ice and isolation. Sometimes I've travelled two or three hundred miles on a hunting trip, and I'll be standing on a hilltop in the High Arctic and I know there isn't another soul around for hundreds of miles. There is just space and silence. Perhaps a snowy owl will fly overhead to remind me that there are other creatures on this earth besides me, but that's all. Standing there reminds me that I'm a mere speck of existence. Inuit have those kinds of experiences all the time. That's what gives us such certainty about the existence of a spiritual dimension. That's what our carvings are all about. They're not just representational. They're deeply connected with the spirit world.'

Sinikka said she had been struck by the strength of Inuit communal as well as religious feeling. 'There are three thousand people in Frobisher Bay, and we have good stores and services. But when Jens returned the other week with his caribou, the first thing he did was give half the meat away to families in need.'

We landed in Frobisher – how refreshing it was to see the outline of hills and mountains after the flat plateaux of Alberta and the Great Slave Lake – at 8 p.m. local time. The small airport was jammed. Jens moved swiftly round the crowded hall, shaking hands with just about everybody there, greeting them in Inuktitut, a language that, with its characteristic clicking ks, sounds like a clockmaker's workshop. Jens was not the only person who seemed to know everybody. Judging from the hubbub of greetings and embraces, this could have been a family reunion. But then the Arctic is like that. Hundreds, even thousands of miles, may separate communities, but since the total population is so minute it is hardly surprising that the entire Territories feels and acts more like a village than a sub-continent larger than India. There was only one discordant note. Gerry, a passenger sitting in front of me, had been quietly tippling from his private supply of whisky all the way from Yellowknife. When we landed at Frobisher, Gerry was too drunk to stand, and he made a belated but rather dashing entrance into the terminal in a wheelchair. He tried to make it out of the terminal on his own but as he stumbled through the exit doors, I heard him cry 'Holy shit!' as he lost his balance and fell flat on his face.

From the cabin of a Lockheed Electra and a couple of airports, I hadn't experienced much of the Arctic, though I'd had a panoramic view of plenty of it, but at least I'd escaped from Yellowknife for a day, stood on Baffin Island, spoken to a few Inuit, and been instructed on how to gut a caribou. Jens may have thought nothing of hiking a hundred miles in the middle of winter, but I was differently constituted and took a taxi back to the cosiness of Latham Island.

John Bayly's address was Bayly Burrow, which made him sound like a furry little chap out of a Beatrix Potter book. The house, tucked away behind granite cliffs on the shore of the lake a few miles out of town, was a former log cabin, adapted into a comfortable and warm home. It was guarded by sixteen sled dogs, all chained up on the slope beneath the cliff, all yapping rowdily as we arrived in the pickup. John and Christine, Torontonians originally, failed to observe local etiquette by informing me how long they had lived in Yellowknife, but I guessed about twelve years.

'When I graduated from law school and told my friends I was thinking of starting a practice up north,' remarked John, 'everybody thought I meant Georgian Bay. Of course even Yellowknife isn't really the North.'

'That's true,' I nodded, thinking fondly of my thirty-minute stopover in Frobisher Bay, which I intended in future to expand in the manner of oral legend into at least a day or two.

'In fact the only difference between Yellowknife and Edmonton is that there are a few more mornings up here each winter when your car won't start.'

Three other guests had come to the Burrow to snuffle up some of the Baylys' hoard of nuts. There was a farmer called Wayne, who had grown wheat somewhere near Peace River in northwest Alberta, and Iris, the only black person I'd seen in the Territories, and a young man called Chris who had just returned from three months in the bush.

'Alone?'

'Yes.'

'For three months? May I ask why?'

'To clear the head. To contemplate.'

'I think I could do that in twenty minutes with ease. Was it worth it?'

'I guess so. I've done it before. You get visitors. Indians on a fishing trip mostly. And birds. After a while the birds and animals get used to having you around. By the time I packed up my tent and moved back to town, the whiskeyjacks were confident enough to snatch mosquitoes from underneath the brim of my hat.'

The bush in summer is full of solitude freaks, men and women who like Chris go out to cleanse their souls, observe the changes of nature, and live a pure simple life. Then in September they come back to town and look for a job to get them through the winter. *Humani nihil a me alienum puto*, to be sure, but I do find this kind of thing perplexing.

John sat us all down at the table and asked us to join hands while he said grace. I found myself clasping the sticky hands of two Bayly children. Their father, intoning, had the puffed-out chest of a baritone; he exuded robust cheerfulness, while Christine bore an uncanny resemblance to a Stalinist trade union official of my acquaintance. On arrival, I had flung their Scott Expedition relics back into the closet and dog basket as they asked me whether I had enjoyed my day trip to the other side of Canada. I told them how I felt the Arctic was shrinking on acquaintance into a village, and how conscious I was of a subtle snobbery attached to Northerners' personal familiarity with the most remote outposts. Even well travelled Jens had appeared apologetic when he mentioned that the only Canadian Inuit settlement he hadn't visited was Grise Fjord, some 700 miles north of the Arctic Circle. And I had caught John and others referring knowingly to tiny communities they had once had occasion to visit.

John admitted there was some truth in this. 'We get very dependent on human contact, even in a big place like Yellowknife. Some years ago they decided to introduce mail deliveries here, and Canada Post was amazed by the opposition to the idea. That's because for many people driving down to the post office every morning is a social event; it gives them a chance to see their friends and catch up on the news.'

There is no such thing as a free lunch. No sooner had we gulped down our coffee than John marched all his guests into the scrubby garden. The previous owner of the Burrow had flown in some good-quality soil, which, sheltered by the cliff, hadn't blown away and was still used for vegiculture. While the children fed about fifty pounds of chow to the yowling yappydogs – in the winter the Baylys run dog sled teams – John and I applied our boots to our spades and uprooted potatoes, which were shaken free of their clinging soil by Chris and Wayne, then wheeled away in trugs by assorted children. As we toiled, John asked me whether I'd seen the Northern Lights a few nights earlier. I'd missed them, to my keen disappointment, for the immense skies over the vast lake would have provided the perfect screen for the show. To my surprise the other guests began to discuss whether they had *heard* the Lights, which, some say, emit a kind of crackling sound. Wayne was sceptical, but both John and Iris insisted they had heard them.

When the spell of hard labour was over, Christine rewarded us with tea and I had a chance to talk to John about his work as an Indian land claims lawyer. The new Canadian constitution, I gathered, is clearly going to provide a bonanza for lawyers. According to the constitution, aboriginal rights are recognized, but there is no agreement as to what they consist of. To some bands 'rights' means land and resources, to others self-government. The whole situation is complicated in the North because many Indian nations never signed treaties with the government. This can be an advantage in that both sides can now start with a clean slate when they begin negotiations. Other nations that did sign treaties now dispute their implications. Such treaties were, some bands (and their lawyers) argue, peace treaties that permitted non-native settlement on Indian lands but did not assign any rights over resources to the white man. Such an interpretation is, predictably, contested by federal governments, which regard the signing of a treaty as the relinquishing of rights. John, who represented various bands, said he found the work fascinating, 'but it's not easy when your client is fifteen thousand people'.

Melvyn, the newly arrived lawyer who had been so sceptical about the proposed constitutional changes, had, like John and Christine, been drawn to the North by the challenges of dealing with cases that would rarely come the way of a city lawyer in central Canada. He too had contacts with local Indians, not as a land claims specialist but as a criminal lawyer. He had been surprised by the vast cultural gap that yawned between native and non-native in Yellowknife and the Territories. Not only is there little social contact between the two groups, but there is, despite the relative poverty of the Indians, considerable resent-ment among whites that, in their view, Indians have had so much handed to them on a plate, and with such discouraging results. In Melvyn's view, the two ways of looking at the world, Indian and white, were so much at variance that he could see no way to bridge the gap. He confirmed the widely held view that alcohol was the cause of endless social problems. He had spent countless hours in court dealing with cases of sexual assault, almost all sparked off by overindulgence in alcohol, and recalled a recent case when a man went on a murderous bender after drinking a few bottles of mouthwash. The RCMP estimates that 95% of crime in the North is alcohol-related. I was astonished to learn by ploughing through government statistics that in 1983 30% of all deaths in the NWT were caused by 'accidents' and suicide.

'Whites get drunk too, very drunk. But most whites can exercise some control over their drinking. Indians, it seems, are incapable of leaving anything in the bottle once it's been opened. It's not only drink that's the problem either. Over in Frobisher they have a serious drugs problem too.'

John Bayly, with his busy law practice and dog sled teams, fitted well into brawny Yellowknife. Melvyn, though he didn't say as much, was evidently less at home there. What he missed was the CBC Stereo channel on the radio; for classical music he was dependent on his record collection. He and his wife no longer had access to their friends. Air fares were so high that they could afford relatively few forays out of the NWT to visit family and friends, who in turn could not afford to come and see them. Apartments and houses were so hard to come by in Yellowknife that even a well-paid lawyer was living in the depressingly decorated tube of a trailer. Nor was the work as satisfying as he would have wished. It was varied, certainly, but, with its succession of domestic crimes, it rarely challenged his intellect. It was only a matter of time, I sensed, before Melvyn bought his family one-way tickets to mainstream Canada.

I had my own ticket out of Yellowknife, and one crisp morning I boarded the very plane that, a plaque informed me, had carried the Pope on one leg of his journey across Canada. I put my trust in the papal aura, and an hour later was back in Edmonton.

20

First Take a Potato

Although Whitehorse, tucked into the northwest corner of Canada near the Alaskan border, is almost as far north as Yellowknife, there is a cosiness to the city unlike anything one experiences at Yellowknife. From Bayly's Burrow, walk five yards from the lot and you're in scrubby granitic wilderness, flat, harsh, unyielding, with emptiness and a terrifying silence pressing in from all sides. In Whitehorse the back yards open onto forests and mountains. Much of the Yukon, indeed, although it touches Mackenzie Bay in the Arctic, is well within the treeline and despite winter temperatures as low as those in the Territories, the immediate environment is less hostile. The woods harbour game that is plentiful and various, while lakes teem with fish as large as sheep.

At 5.30 in the morning, when the bus from Edmonton pulled into Whitehorse, there were signs of life in the town, even a line of taxis ready to take the handful of visitors to the hotels. The long, long journey past the Peace River settlements, Canada's most northerly prairie, and up the partly gravelled Alaska Highway for 913 miles, through endless wooded mountains and alongside countless stony river beds and beneath the snowy shoulders of aggressive peaks, had encouraged the notion that I was approaching the edge of the frontier. At the lodge at Summit, where wolf skins were draped over moose antlers, hunters in lumberjack shirts and unlaced hiking boots had been discussing a grizzly one of them had sniffed earlier that day. There, high in the Rockies, I felt exhilarated by the wild mountains all around, though at dusk they became more threatening as the snowy peaks took on the colour of asbestos tailings and folded into the gloom. Yellowknife is the end of the road, but Whitehorse is merely the entry point into the Yukon. Even during the Gold Rush of 1898, most prospectors hurried a further 330 miles north to Dawson City. Whitehorse had been a bustling town four decades before Yellowknife was even a collection of miners' shacks.

There was a time when the Yukon was positively tropical, when sabre-toothed tigers stalked through the ferns, while most of North America was petrified beneath a mile-deep sheet of ice. That was, of course, 40,000 years ago, and things have changed. Even so, the Yukon was far from unexplored during the nineteenth century. Whaling ships stopped along its Arctic shoreline, and prospectors were sluicing away decades before the Gold Rush. Five Indian tribes also populated the region. Tlingit Indians had control over the passes that led from the coast to the interior; they had a trade monopoly with the bands of the interior and, like most monopolists, vigorously exploited their exclusive access to the market. When Robert Campbell, a factor from the Hudson's Bay Company, set up an outpost at Fort Selkirk, he offered the bands of the interior far better terms than those they received from the Tlingit, whose leaders retaliated by burning Fort Selkirk to the ground.

By the end of the century there was a good deal more traffic in the Yukon. Prospectors were queueing up to travel north. Most would arrive at Skagway, Alaska, and, laden down with mining equipment, families and household possessions, climb the fearsome Chilkoot Pass and hike to Lake Bennett; from there boats would transport them to Whitehorse and the gold fields. Inevitably Whitehorse prospered as a communications rather than as a mining centre. At the height of the Gold Rush the population of the Yukon was double that of today. Between 1866 and 1955 a total of 250 handsome black and white sternwheelers such as the S.S. *Klondike*, now dry-docked near the Yukon River as a museum, would make the two-day journey to Dawson with thirty passengers and freight. Once the gold rush subsided, Whitehorse became a sleepy little town of a few hundred inhabitants. Some of the early buildings still survive: the log house of 1900 that used to be the Anglican cathedral, and some curious two- and three-storey log cabins with separate living quarters on each floor. In 1942 Franklin Roosevelt authorized the construction of the Alaska Highway. Apparently no one troubled to inform the residents of Whitehorse that a 1400-mile road would pass through their town, and one morning the residents awoke to find they had been joined by 10,000 soldiers, part of the enormous workforce required to construct this extraordinary wilderness highway in a trifling eight months.

One of the most charming buildings in town, the MacBride Museum, has a sod roof from which a healthy growth of grass still sprouts. Among the displays is the first container wagon used on the railway that used to cross the White Pass from Skagway to Whitehorse. Containerization, the people of Yukon insist, was a local invention, and the exhibit is here to prove it. Next to the main library stands the government building, which some locals, who don't care for its bluntly contemporary style, refer to as the Library Annex. I rather liked it. The legislative chamber inside is in Scandinavian style, cool, modern, and bland. The bright swirling tapestry behind the Speaker's chair is an imaginative touch that makes nonsense of the former Speaker's grumble that the chamber resembles a discotheque. Some of the downtown blocks, especially those dotted with hotels and bars (no shortage of those in Whitehorse), have been tarted up to resemble façades of the 1890s rather than the 1950s. When I pointed out that restoration was all very well but fakery was another matter, a local booster calmly told me, 'We're trying to get Whitehorse to look the way the tourists expect.' (Which reminds me of my long cherished scheme to build a theme park called Londonland on the perimeter of Heathrow, so as to save tourists the trouble of actually coming in to the city.)

I was given a minder named George. This was not a tribute to my supposed importance as a visitor, and I rather suspect George took on the role because he expected to have more fun chaperoning me round town than sitting behind his desk in the Tourism Department writing policy studies. I could not accuse George of neglecting me. By 8.30 he was at my hotel, and by my side he stayed all day and well into the evening. The high point of George's life had been his years at Sandhurst. Indeed, so British was George in dress and accent that I was startled to learn that he was born and raised in Ontario. With his burly build, his neat moustache, his passion for telling long stories about japes in his army days, and his devotion to scouting, he was indistinguishable from any retired colonel in the Home Counties. He exhibited another facet of that extreme Anglophilia so common in certain corners of Canada, though probably something of a rarity in the Yukon.

George was standing in the lobby of the Edgewater Hotel as I ran down the stairs after an invigorating two hours' sleep. We took a leisurely tour of the town – a place of sites rather than sights – and out a few miles to Miles Canyon, which the explorer Frederick Schwatka had described as a 'narrow chute of corrugated rock'; here rapids had once clattered between cliffs of volcanic basalt. In the nineteenth century new arrivals used to play a game of chicken when they approached the White Horse rapids, which Schwatka considered 'a veritable horseshoe of boiling cascades'. The faint-hearted would walk the mile or so along the canyon rim, while the suicidal stayed on the boats and were either dashed to a bruising death or emerged breathless and smiling at the other end. With the completion of the White Pass railway in 1900, the rapids could be avoided altogether. A hydroelectric plant was built nearby in the 1950s, since when the water level of Miles Canyon has risen by twenty-five feet, thus calming its flow. Near the reservoir, also just outside town, is a fish ladder, an intriguing little aqueduct built for the Chinook salmon that come swimming up the river for 2000 miles on the world's longest salmon run. The fish, some of which weigh up to sixty pounds, had been and gone – August is their estimated time of arrival.

The original blocks of the town soon filled up after the soldiers arrived, and suburbs, with such predictable names as Riverdale, were built. The latest section had been built in the 1970s when it was assumed that the Alaska pipeline would enrich Whitehorse. It didn't, and many local land speculators and builders got their fingers burnt. George passed swiftly along the edge of the Indian quarter, which, even from a distance, did not look at all salubrious. When I asked to see it, George put me off, but eventually I persuaded him to drive through. I could see why he'd tried to keep me away. Why a large proportion of the Indians of Whitehorse should live in such conditions he could not, or would not, explain. Nor why the streets were unpaved and the shacks, complete with outhouses that could be no pleasure to frequent in mid-winter, in such deplorable condition. George assured me that this slum would soon vanish, for the Indians were being moved to a new subdivision, indeed to one of those very housing developments intended for the pipeline workers who had never materialized.

There are no Indian reserves in the Yukon, so natives share the same space as the whites. The land area of the Yukon Territory is 186,000 square miles, and the entire population of 25,000 is probably no more than the human contents of Selfridge's on a busy day. Yet until recently the Territory itself controlled no more than 5% of that land; the remainder is under federal control. Not surprisingly, I heard the same grumbles about Ottawa's colonialist treatment of the Yukon that I'd heard in the Northwest Territories. The former mayor of Whitehorse, Flo Whyard – 'I'm the former Flo Whyard,' she introduced herself to me, 'the former editor of the *Whitehorse Star*, the former minister of health, the former mayor of Whitehorse' – told me that it would be a long time before the Yukon had provincial status, or even a greater degree of self-government.

'Alberta waited twenty-five years after it became a province before it won ownership of its land and resources. We're going through the same slow process, but there's no point becoming a province until you control the land, which we don't. Incidentally, when I was younger I was taught that the Yukon was 206,000 square miles in size. After further surveys, the figure was changed to 186,000. What I want to know is how the hell did we lose 20,000 square miles? Anyhow, there's a strong feeling here that the land is our own. Any day I want I can drive into the forests and cut some firewood – it's crown land, it belongs to us. Sometimes the forest comes to see us too. A few times a year bears wander into town, mostly scavenger bears that have to be shot. If people had any idea what comes walking through their back yards some nights . . .'

This land is policed by a hundred RCMP officers – that's 2000 square miles each, and no one-man detachments are permitted. As in the NWT, there is a high proportion of alcohol-related offences. Liquor laws are liberal, and bars also function as off licences. The inference I drew after a few days in Whitehorse was confirmed by government statistics: the Yukon has the highest per capita rate of liquor consumption in Canada. Policing the Yukon, long a haven for determined individualists (known affectionately in Whitehorse as 'our colourful five percent') is an acquired taste. All officers in the North are volunteers for a minimum of three years. After that period many leave for less demanding postings. Distance rather than climate is the greatest obstacle to their work. One sergeant I spoke to told me he had once had to drive 400 miles just to investigate an accident. Officers in remote detachments are obliged to resolve situations on their own. They can try phoning headquarters in Whitehorse or summoning reinforcements, but it could be hours or days before help arrives. Apart from alcohol-related crimes, infringements of hunting regulations occupied the energies of the Mounties. Although, with the exception of moose, wildlife stocks are stable, the RCMP and the courts take a dim view of such infringements. A man who shot an untagged moose ended up paying $1600 for the privilege. (At Flo Whyard's I met a woman whose husband is a former minister for renewable resources. He now lived in British

Columbia and was in Whitehorse to visit friends and had, she told me, been slightly miffed to have to apply to his old department and cough up $75 for a nonresident's licence.) Once in a while people go missing in the bush, a problem which also comes at the police in reverse, so to speak, when unidentified bodies poke their feet out from the wilderness. The sergeant was diplomatic when I asked about Indians and crime. Indian customs and tribal practice that are technical infractions of Canadian law are often overlooked.

'Such as growing pot?'

'No.'

We were just about the only customers in the Monte Carlo that evening, but we made enough noise to convince passersby that the restaurant was full. George had organized a small dinner to further my northern education. He had invited Doug, a gold prospector and trapper and, it soon became clear, one of the colourful five percent. Doug had brought along a girlfriend, Jan, who was about thirty years his junior. Like George, they were both from central Canada. Jan had come to the Yukon nine years earlier in the wake of a marriage, while Doug, born in Montréal, had ended up in Whitehorse after twenty-three years in the air force. He was an impish man, accepting his position as the centre of attention as though it were his due, and taking full advantage of the generosity of our host. ('If the government's paying, I'll have another brandy. Make it a double.') I asked Doug how he had earned his living in Whitehorse.

'I got into real estate. Didn't know the first thing about it, of course, but in those days there wasn't anybody else around selling real estate, so I made a fortune. Then I started building custom homes in Riverdale, but one of my partners was no good, and the business went belly up. I wasn't too smart in those days. The company wasn't incorporated, so after it went under all my assets were seized. A week later I couldn't even afford a cup of coffee. So I started up again, and six months later I was making money again. A couple of years later my wife died. That made me stop and think about my life and where it was headed, and I decided to do what I'd always wanted to do: go into the bush and work a trapline.'

Indeed, he was leaving for the bush the next morning. It would take six hours by road and canoe to reach his camp, and he invited me to join him. I would have done, had there been time. But my journey through Canada was marked by the calendar as definitively as a chessboard is governed by squares, and it was impossible to delay my departure from the Yukon for that long. Out in the bush Doug pans for gold, working the gravel bars along the creeks in the old way, extracting the flecks by absorbing them into mercury.

'And how do you get the gold out of the mercury?'

'Well, the best method is to take a potato.'

I looked at George to see whether my leg, not for the first time that evening, was being pulled. My cultural interpreter confirmed that Doug was on the level for once.

'You take the potato and hollow it out,' explained Doug, 'and then you put into it the mercury amalgam. You heat it in a fire for hours, and after a while the potato absorbs the mercury and you're left with a button of gold. You take out the gold, put it in your pocket, and then boil the potato to get the mercury back.'

When he has acquired enough gold by this laborious method, he sells it. 'It's still legal to sell gold privately for cash. It's one of the few good ways left to screw the government. Folks from the east think we're dull, stupid. We're not. We're just crooked. In Ontario they screw the government but they try to keep quiet about it. Here we like to yell it from the rooftops. We just smile about it, us and the government.'

Doug is no freak pursuing a private eccentricity. Gold-panning is still common in the Yukon, even though a century has gone by since the fortune-making discoveries at Klondike and Bonanza. Later I would meet a businessman who was also about to vanish into the bush to nurse his creek.

'It's gold fever,' said Doug. 'Hasn't changed. People come up here in the summer, and they pan for the fun of it. They find a few flecks, and the next year they're back, and the year after. They're convinced they'll strike it rich. They sell their homes, sell their wives, their kids, anything just so they can keep on panning. They're not likely to make a fortune, but they're stuck on the idea of supporting themselves by mining and panning. And, like I say, it's still a good way to screw the government.'

'How do you do that?'

'You only pay tax on gold when it leaves the Yukon. So instead many miners keep their gold in the bank as collateral.'

'A panner will never tell you how well he's doing,' said George. 'If you ask him how he's doing, he'll say "Okay" and you interpret that according to his tone of voice.'

'How're you doing, Doug?' I ventured.

'Makin' expenses,' he shrugged.

When in November the snow begins to fall, Doug transfers his attentions from the gravel bars to the trapline, a misleading term, since it refers to an area rather than to an actual line like a piece of string. Some Yukon traplines measure fifty miles square. Since trapping is a traditional Indian means of survival, natives are not allowed to sell or even bequeath their lines to non-natives; nevertheless a number of hardy whites, such as Doug, do have traplines which they tend through the winter months. Bouncing through the woods on a snowmobile, Doug sets his traps, first scouting for the appropriate game tracks before deciding precisely where the traps should be set. There are different ways to execute the unfortunate animals. Some opt for traps that break the animal's neck, but Doug considers these too dangerous. He told of a man who accidentally caught his hands in such a trap; since the trap can only be released by using one's feet, he was unable to free himself and froze to death. Other trappers, including most Indians, favour leg-hold traps, cruel but effective. These maim but do not kill the animal, which must be shot when the trapper returns about three days after setting it.

'Once you've shot the animal,' Doug continued with dispassionate relish, 'you case-skin it – easy, it's like pulling off a sweater – and spray it with Raid to get rid of the bugs. You take the skins back to the cabin and thaw them out, and after the winter you send the skins to some big city to be auctioned. The Japs buy their furs in Vancouver, Europeans prefer Toronto or Winnipeg.'

'What do they fetch?'

'Canadian sable – that's the same as marten – fetches between one and two hundred, lynx from five hundred to a thousand, and wolverine slightly less.'

Doug insisted that trappers were sensitive to natural cycles, that without their harvesting of certain animals, other species would be endangered. In short, trapping is, even if fortuitously, an act of conservation, which makes one wonder how furry animals ever managed to struggle along during the millennia when man wasn't around to hunt them. Northerners are as defensive about trapping as Newfoundlanders are about sealing. Dave Porter, the statuesque Minister of Tourism and Renewable Resources in the Yukon, later told me that animal rights organizations and Greenpeace pose a serious threat to aboriginal lifestyles. 'Animal rights campaigners base their arguments on direct emotional appeals, but here in the North we're not talking about animal rights but human rights, the rights of communities that can only subsist by hunting and trapping. In the Arctic many communities have been impoverished, almost wiped out, by the collapse of sealing. I know it's hard to draw a line between hunting for subsistence and hunting for commercial exploitation, but if the demand for furs does collapse – and I don't believe it ever will – then a lot of people up here, mostly natives, will not be able to survive. The irony is that the noisiest Greenpeace activists are often the same people who are most supportive of aboriginal rights!' (A few weeks later the North's counter-effort succeeded, and Greenpeace UK called off its anti-fur campaign.)

I asked Doug whether it was lonely in the bush during those winter months. He shook his head. 'There are other people around. There are the Bradleys at Pelly Crossing. Interesting people, the Bradleys, they're the only commercial farmers in the Yukon. They've got three hundred acres and about eighty head of cattle. Then there's another family out in Kirkman Creek beyond Selkirk maybe a hundred miles or more. Their kids are educated by correspondence courses. It's weird: those kids know a hell of a lot, they even read Gibbon for the fun of it. Problem is that socially they're poorly adjusted, not used to being around other people. And there's the Pelly Crossing Indians. They know about the gold in the hills, but can't be bothered to get it. The thing about Indians is that they live too much in the present. If they catch a few salmon, they'll stop everything and have a party and get stewed as newts.'

In that respect there was nothing that the native peoples could teach our party. Even before the meal, we had exhausted the Monte Carlo's supply of Dry Sack, George's favoured tipple, and now there was a postprandial crisis as the restaurant ran out of the Drambuie stocked solely for Doug's benefit. He made an effortless switch to brandy.

I asked my companions whom they truly admired in Canadian life, past or present. 'Who are the Canadian heroes?'

'There aren't many of us left,' said Doug.

'Riel?' offered Jan, but her liberal-minded bubble soon burst as Doug and George wrinkled their noses at the suggestion. Canadians are not fond of governments, but even less fond of revolutionaries.

'Robert Campbell,' Doug said firmly. 'After the Indians destroyed Fort Selkirk, he walked back to Minnesota to report to his superiors.' (A heroic act, indeed, involving a 3000-mile trek on snowshoes through largely uninhabited territory.)

'Trudeau's a hero,' said Jan.

'He is?'

'He must be, because everyone hated him so much.'

'There won't be Canadians much longer anyway,' grumbled Doug. 'Before too long we'll just be part of the United States. I don't like it but it's bound to happen. Still, it's too bad, and true Canadians will fight it.'

'No,' said George, 'true Canadians will talk about fighting it.'

'As you can see,' Jan said, turning to me, 'people up here are very opinionated –'

'Especially about things we know nothing about,' nodded Doug.

'And that's what I like about it. There's not much pressure to conform, no social demands, no snobbery. Life isn't dull here. With people like Doug around, how could it be?'

'And if you want to see something really exciting,' said Doug, helping Jan into her coat, 'follow us home.'

Fresh snow dusted the mountains overnight. In the crisp light, Whitehorse was looking spruce and brisk. After coffee with a local bush pilot brought along by George, I spent two hours on my own. I enjoyed the novelty of having my hair cut, for the first time in my life, by a woman. As my locks fell around me, she told me that she would soon be going off to New Zealand for her holiday. The idea seemed daft, until I recalled that Whitehorse, hundreds of miles west of California, is not that far from New Zealand, which would also be enjoying its summer while the people of the Yukon were enduring their interminable winter.

I then strolled towards the courthouse to call on a prominent lawyer, a man of silver-haired elegance and a mind as cool as his appearance. I told him about my raucous evening with Doug. I had genuinely enjoyed it, but had also wearied of all that talk about screwing the government and how lazy the Indians were. All these rugged individualists I was meeting ended up by saying the same things. Both Doug and the businessmen who are weekend gold-panners the way suburban men are weekend gardeners may relish the challenges of life in the bush, but when they tire of it they can load up the canoe and be back in their comfortable Whitehorse houses by dusk. The lawyer, Charlie, confirmed that many people who come to live in the Yukon are escaping from problems elsewhere, whether financial or marital or even criminal. With a measure of guts and resourcefulness, it is not too difficult to carve out a new life in the Yukon, and those who succeed often develop independent but conservative attitudes. Although Doug's remarks about Indians were mild enough, Charlie, after twenty years in Whitehorse, detected a strong streak of racism in many white residents' feelings about the natives, though it is rarely voiced. Many whites come north with a positive attitude towards Indians, but soon come to realize that it is very difficult to employ them in the organized professions. The ensuing lack of contact between whites and Indians, except at the most menial level, helps to foster stereotypical attitudes. Nor does a rekindled sense of obligation towards native peoples fit the whites' cherished notions of independence. Other whites are blatantly contemptuous of the native peoples and brazenly exploit them, by selling them, for instance, secondhand cars on the point of terminal collapse.

Nor does the cultural organization of Indian bands encourage natives to participate in the white man's world. Working for whites in, say, an office job may require a change in daily habits that will strike other band members as standoffish. Putting the demands of the workplace before the tribal customs of the band can and does, according to Charlie, lead to the ostracizing of integrated Indians, and not all of them can take the pressure. As a lawyer he frequently encountered the same problems that Melvyn had spoken of in Yellowknife. Canadian law is often at odds with Indian customs, and the primary difficulty is in knowing what those customs are in the first place. In some bands, it is customary for an aunt to care for infants, so as to give the parents time to hunt and fish; in other bands, grandparents rear the children. Courts and child welfare agencies may discern neglect where there is in fact none; absent parents are sometimes brought to court and punished even though their children, within the context of Indian life, are being well cared for.

All the stereotypes about lazy Indians were shaken by Dave Porter, the Minister of Tourism, himself a native. Tall, bearded, powerfully built, a cigarette glowing permanently like an additional finger, he spoke forcefully about Indian land claims. His forthright manner was almost intimidating, until I noticed that his shoelaces were undone, at which point I warmed to him. There are no Indian reserves in the Yukon and bands are represented by the federally assisted Council of Yukon Indians, which supposedly ensures that all the bands are represented in negotiations with the authorities. Settlements should, Porter told me, include the ceding of lands to native peoples, compensation for past use of Indian lands, and power-sharing arrangements in such matters as wildlife management. Porter felt that initial hostility from whites to these claims has now dissipated; a sufficient number of other settlements has been reached for wary whites to see that their own rights are not threatened by land claims. I recalled something Robert Fulford, the editor of *Saturday Night*, had said to me: 'I don't know much about land claims, but I do feel that were a Martian to land here, he would be astonished that the natives of this country don't own their own land. It seems self-evident, yet governments and lumber companies laugh at the idea.'

(My well-informed journalist friend Tim, who had derided the abilities of NWT politicians, was more blistering in his appraisal of land claims negotiations. 'The Yukon,' he told me, 'arranged a deal that gave natives 5% of the land and a cool 80 million dollars. Great. But the Indian leaders started thinking, and realized this meant the end of the gravy train for them. Once a settlement was reached, they reckoned, there would be no more federal grants to Indian organizations, and their leaders would be out of a job. So the twelve band chiefs obligingly pointed out that they hadn't been consulted when the deal was struck between the government and the Council of Yukon Indians, and after a good squabble the deal was turned down. But Crombie in Ottawa cut off the gravy train anyway. There was much gnashing of teeth, because it had paid for expensive clothes for Marxist-Leninist tribal council leaders and, of course, for the fat fees the lawyers and consultants had been raking in for years. Now the ball is back in the chiefs' court. Yukon politicians are, I'd have to say, marginally less incompetent than their counterparts in the NWT. In fact the government leader Tony Penikett is extremely bright, and how could I fault a man who once wrote the screenplay for a film called *The Mad Trapper of Red River*?')

Porter, who had obligingly taken a break from an evidently tedious Cabinet meeting to talk to me, had to return to his colleagues, and I hurried down to the lobby to meet George. The hall was cheerfully decorated with paintings by Yukon artists. I particularly admired some brightly coloured canvases, somewhat stylized in manner, depicting small human figures scurrying about against a backdrop of lurid and dominating mountains. Heavily outlined in black, like the leading in stained glass, the forms of these paintings stressed the power of the landscape and, rather like the wispy figures in a Lowry painting, placed the bustle of the animate beneath the overpowering shadow of the environment, the industrial north in the case of Lowry, the mountainous north in the case of this artist, Ted Harrison.

When George told me the artist's name, I recognized it as that of a painter Shannie Duff had told me to look up. A phone call and a short drive later I was sitting in the painter's studio drinking tea and munching on home-made biscuits. Harrison, whose prominent belly testified to an excessive consumption of his wife's delicious biscuits, was a transplanted Geordie from Durham, and his wife Nicky was a Glaswegian – and how. The Harrisons lacked the civility of Canadians, but instead exhibited the warmth of North Britons, welcoming me to their home as though I were an old friend. Ted was short and scruffy, his clothes suitably flecked with paint, and such was his modesty that he spent more time showing me the work of other artists he admired than his own canvases. After long spells as a teacher in Malaysia and New Zealand, Ted returned to Britain, 'but I found it too crowded, couldn't stand the queues', so he moved to northern Alberta; 'it was too flat and isolated for us', so he took a teaching job at Carcross fifty miles south of Whitehorse until five years ago, when he took a year's leave to paint. Ever since he has been successful enough to be self-supporting. The Harrisons clearly loved the North; the long winters they regard not as a protracted and unwelcome interlude but as an opportunity to savour what Ted in one of his books calls 'the precious gift of time'. The vistas of the Yukon, in all the seasons of the year, glowed from his lively paintings, and after decades of wandering the world, the Harrisons seemed at perfect ease in their latest home.

Flo Whyard, 'the former Flo', had, on the other hand, always been at home in the North, and was able to peer astutely into the future of the Territory, which, in economic terms at any rate, looks grim. Flo hadn't always lived in Whitehorse, and thirty-five years ago she had run the Yellowknife radio station on a volunteer basis. 'I worked eighteen hours a day at it, but it was worth it. If the town didn't have it, we'd do it – it was that simple. It's not that different in the Yukon. I was mayor of this town because I was prepared to do the job. In the North the population is so small that we need anyone who is willing to do something for the community, no matter where they come from.'

In her view, the economy of the Yukon zoomed up and down like a yoyo. After the Gold Rush subsided, there was a spate of copper mining, and in the 1940s the Alaska Highway construction brought prosperity; after the army moved out, the Cyprus Anvil mine was started up in Faro (though it is typical of the Canadian economy that the mine was jointly owned by companies from Germany and the United States), and in 1982 it closed. She regretted the decision not to build the Alaska pipeline through Whitehorse. 'I'm not scared of pipelines – we've already got oil lines from Skagway. The Alaska pipeline would have given us cheap natural gas to heat our homes, not to mention 150 jobs for the town. I'd rather have the pipeline than more handouts from Ottawa.' Even the oil exploration hundreds of miles north in the Beaufort Sea was benefitting Whitehorse, since the oil companies did much of their recruitment in the town. Unlike other towns in the North, Whitehorse has good communications, especially roads. 'In the future employers will be drawn to Whitehorse because we have excellent hydro power, a stable government, good labour relations. Unfortunately we're too dependent on external investment, because Canadians never put their money where their mouth is.'

'Why's that?'

'We're so timid, I guess.'

Like Yellowknife, Whitehorse is a government town, and a full 20% of the workforce consists of civil servants. Mining had once been the leading industry, but the last decade had seen numerous closures; in consequence the rail link to Skagway had also been discontinued. When the Cyprus Anvil mine closed, the population of what was then the Yukon's second largest town, Faro, dropped from 2000 to 70. The Yukon contains 30% of Canada's mineral resources, but present mineral prices are too low to justify the high cost of extraction and transportation. The slump inevitably affects its periphery, and suppliers and bush pilots are also having difficulty making ends meet. The official unemployment level is 20%, and with the cost of living some 30% higher than elsewhere in Canada, the Yukon is not a good place to be jobless. Mining has been supplanted by tourism as the leading industry, and the Yukon benefits from being the doormat to Alaska. But the tourist season is short, from late May to mid-September.

The Yukon is a long way from the rest of Canada, and feels it. On the map Vancouver, the city with which the Yukon has the strongest economic ties, looks like a reasonable journey down the coast, but by road it is 1700 miles away. I asked Flo whether Yukon people shared the Newfoundlanders' sense that they weren't part of Canada at all.

'No, we know we're part of Canada. Most folks have come here from other provinces. But just now and again we have to give the rest of Canada a hard kick just to remind them we're here. The ignorance of the North shown by the rest of the country does appal me. I was once talking to a deputy minister in Ottawa, and when I mentioned the proportion of native peoples living in the Yukon he told me my figures were wrong. We argued about it, and I happened to be right. What annoyed me was that the man I was talking to was in charge of the federal government's policy towards the entire North.'

Charlie too had lamented that the rest of Canada showed no interest in the North. 'Despite the best intentions and efforts of the CBC and our one national newspaper, the *Globe and Mail*, this country still isn't united and most of Canada doesn't know or care about us.'

Their view had received the most direct confirmation just a few days earlier, when the Canadian Press wire service had announced it was closing its office in Yellowknife on the grounds that the Canadian newspapers it served simply weren't sufficiently interested in stories about the North.

As I got up to go, I asked Flo about the large horseshoe magnet that dangled from a string near her chair.

'That's a little device invented by my husband Jim. With my old bones I can't bend easily to pick up my knitting needles when I drop them, so now I can use this magnet to get them back.'

On my last day in Whitehorse, George invited me to the weekly Rotary Club lunch as his guest. It was not an occasion I enjoyed. The middle-class elite of the town was present, the businessmen and government officials, the police chief, the property men. The food was abysmal, the level of conversation not much better, and the pleasantries mostly offensive. There was an AIDS joke and an Ethiopian famine joke, and stale quips about the northern climate, on the lines of: How many seasons are there in the Yukon? Two, fall and winter. Alternative answer: two, this winter and last winter. The national anthem, 'O Canada', was sung in a communal squirm, and a number of loyal citizens were none too sure of the words. The occasion was elevated by a brief talk by an overseas exchange student. Illustrated by slides, it was an introduction to the tourist attractions of his native New Zealand.

After lunch I packed my bags. Shortly after my arrival in

Whitehorse George had asked me where I was going next. To Skagway, I told him, to catch the ferry to Vancouver. And how, he asked me, was I proposing to get from Whitehorse to Skagway? By bus, I replied, at which point he informed me that the bus service had stopped weeks before in early September. To my great relief, George found in my predicament the means both to come to my rescue and to extend his absence from the office desk: he offered to drive me to Skagway. For this I was deeply grateful, since my budget did not extend to the chartering of planes. We set off at three, heading for Carcross to the south of Whitehorse. We passed Emerald Lake, one of those beautiful splashes of frigid water coloured pale turquoise by decomposed shells suspended in the water. Shortly before Carcross there's a miniature desert, formed by a sandy lake bed almost bare of vegetation, which is deterred from taking root by the strong winds that whip the dunes.

Carcross was formerly the descriptively named settlement of Caribou Crossing. Neatly spread along the shore of Lake Bennett, it had evolved into a pleasant little village with 150 inhabitants, its centre composed of a green and white Anglican chapel, another dry-docked sternwheeler, the SS *Tutshi*, the rundown Caribou Hotel painted a stern grey, and the cheerfully pink Matthew Watson General Store. Opposite the store stood the railway depot, now defunct. The hotel was once famous for its parrot Polly, who had been left there while her owners went on holiday. Their steamer sank, the passengers were all drowned, and Polly, orphaned, was invited to stay on as the guest of the hotel, which she did until her death in the 1970s. The old bird was notorious for her foul language and intemperate boozing, and when she croaked her last, she was buried in consecrated ground with full honours, which in this case meant the presence of TV cameras. It was not revealed until after the obsequies that a post mortem had established that Polly had in fact been male.

Emerging from the General Store, I saw walking slowly towards me the man I had come to Carcross to see, Johnnie Johns. A short dapper man in a stetson, Johnnie was an Indian guide, then in his eighty-eighth year. Apart from his slightly stiff movements when walking, there was nothing in his gestures, speech, or vellum-smooth face to betray his great age. He first took up this line of work in 1917, he told me (though George warned me that Johnnie had a tendency to make up dates as he went along). I was surprised to learn how many sophisticated hunting expeditions were taking place in the Yukon over fifty years ago. Johnnie recalled a 73-day hunt in 1921 and an Austrian count who in 1933 had employed Johnnie to take him trophy hunting continuously for four months. When the Alaska Highway was being built, Johnnie was hired to blaze the trail.

'I went ahead on foot, using local trappers to advise me in advance where the bad patches were, the muskeg and the swamps. I had to make the road crooked, so the Japs couldn't bomb it easily from the Aleutian Islands. But I also pushed the road past a few good fishing lakes.'

Johnnie groped in his pocket for yellowing brochures, which he thrust into my hand as he said, boastfully: 'Then I became an outfitter – after I finished the Alaska Highway. Did a lot of trapping too, using dog teams, as they could go where the snowmobiles couldn't. And I was the first outfitter in the Yukon to use bush planes to take hunting parties into the remote bush. See? Here's a picture of me in my plane. That was in nineteen fifty something. Another thing I did: when Polly died, I read the oration at the funeral, dressed in my ceremonial robes. It was on television too.'

'And what do you do now? Don't suppose you still take hunting parties into the bush?'

'No, I'm involved in land claims. And I live here by the lake. My daughter's nearby.'

'Pretty spot.'

'Sure is. And when it's hot I drive up to the mountains or take the boat out onto the lake. I can't find no better place to live.'

It was certainly beautiful, and the landscape became even more breathtaking, savage rather than picturesque, as George drove up towards the White Pass through a treeless region strewn with rocky hillocks and dark ponds. We drew closer to the snowy coastal mountains, whitened by glaciers extending their swollen lips over the edges of the icefields. Near the top of the pass, we drove between sharp-toothed peaks, their rocky sides gnarled and pitted like an old mastiff's belly.

Descending the pass we drove through the US customs post into Alaska. Skagway itself was a lively little town, catering to the small but steady tourist trade brought here by ferries and cruise ships. As in Whitehorse, some façades had been faked to conform to tourists' expectations, but a few of the old hotels were genuine enough, including the oldest in Alaska, the Golden North Hotel, where we were staying. The rooms were named after venerable citizens of the town, which had known prosperous days; indeed, its city hall had long been the only stone building in Alaska. My room was named after 'Ma' Pulham, George's after Ferdie de Gruyter, and family photographs and other mementoes of eighty years ago decorated the walls. A careful study of the righteous frozen features made me gasp with relief that I hadn't been consigned through some hideous accident of birth to live in such a place at such a time. (Not that the people of Skagway were averse to pleasure. As a stepping-off point for prospectors, the town was famous for its plentiful supply of whores, and their wooden cabins, called 'cribs' and now converted into souvenir stalls, still stand on the sidewalks.) My room was as grim as the Pulhams, but it was full of character. There was a brass bed, huge and lumpish dressers, a radiator like a sousaphone. The landing outside was decorated with flock wallpaper, and open bibles stood on chests of drawers flanked by porcelain pitchers and backed by gilt-framed mirrors. The bathtubs had claws.

The ferry I would be taking in the morning was the last southbound service of the year. Within a couple of days, Skagway would have closed up for the winter. But now there were still a few bars open, and two restaurants, and after a dinner of scallops George invited me to his room, as uncomfortable as mine, for a generous nightcap. George was easily persuaded not to get up, at 6 a.m. for the sole purpose of seeing me off, and so I said goodbye to my most obliging and assiduous of guides.

The MV *Matanuska* steamed out of Skagway at 8.15 and an hour later made its first stop at Haines, a journey of fourteen miles by sea but 350 miles by road. The sky was cloudy but the peaks on either side of the green waters of the Lynn Canal were clear. For the next two days there would be a dazzling succession of views of the coastal mountains, broad glaciers and vertiginous rock. Most of the passengers, and the ferry was far from crowded, stayed put in the observation lounge, where amateur naturalists kept their field glasses trained on the horizon for signs of wildlife. We were not disappointed. Orcas poked their shiny backs through the waters, and at dusk we were besieged by porpoises impersonating basketball players. The passengers were mostly retired American couples composed of shuffle-footed, box-tummied old men and their ebullient wives. A lifetime of insurance brokerage had reduced these specimens of American manhood to a state of barely animated somnolence, but their womenfolk, large-boned, bright of hair and tooth, were exultant at their release from house and home. While their husbands had been exhausting themselves in the pursuit of a good income, their wives had conserved their energies for such jaunts as this. They were in command, and their wizened, unprotesting husbands followed them meekly as they tottered through the cafeteria queues, staggering under the weight of trays laden with fried foods, or initiated protracted games of cards. Some husbands retreated from this onslaught of female energy by cringing behind day-old newspapers or heavy binoculars. A few, very few, of these couples would circle the deck after meals, but most remained slumped in their chairs.

The ferry was part of the Alaska Marine Highway System, an efficient service primarily designed to link the otherwise isolated fishing communities of the Alaskan coast. The American ferry made no stops at Canadian ports, but it did follow the Inside Passage, a sea route that weaved its way between the large islands along the spectacular coastline of Alaska and British Columbia. The stop at Juneau gave me time for an hour's stroll. It was the eve of the municipal elections and the town was in a tizzy. Had I been eligible to vote I would have had a hard time choosing from such an *embarras de richesse*. Would I have marked my X against the name of unemployed Betty 'Belle Blue' Breck whose principal campaign issue was 'lawfulness', as though the opposite were under serious consideration by her opposition. Or perhaps my vote would have gone to dear loyal Peggy Garrison who wouldn't reveal her age but told the press she was running because 'Juneau has been good to my husband and I'. Ernest Polley, bearded, took a more intellectual line, declaring that he longed for a 'genuine shot at impacting those things I want to impact'. I admired his sense of purpose, but couldn't vote for anyone who garottes the English language in my presence. No, I think I'd have voted for Rich Poor, whose name alone so skilfully appeals to the entire electorate. Nor was this a mere quirk of fortune. His campaign utterances implied the same desire to unite opposites: 'I'm really concerned about the Capital City and we have a low coming up.'

I conducted an experiment in Juneau. I wrote and posted a letter to England. During the previous months I had had numerous occasions to use Canada Post and had not been satisfied with the results. A letter sent from Montréal to New York to inform friends when I would be arriving at their home arrived two weeks later, long after I had. When I was told at the Edmonton post office that there were no letters for me, I said I knew for a fact that two letters had been posted over two weeks earlier from New York. The clerk seemed most surprised at my assumption that they should have arrived by then. When I complained about this unacceptable level of service, I was challenged to prove that it was the fault of Canada Post, since my correspondents were writing from England or the United States, which might also, in theory, be at fault. Hence my experiment. I had posted a letter home from White-horse two days earlier. Eighteen months have gone by and it has still not arrived. The letter from Juneau, Alaska, was in London five days later. Letters from London to Vancouver either never arrived or took on average three weeks to do so. Canada Post, and its complacency, are a national disgrace.

At lunchtime on the second day we stopped at Ketchikan, a lively island town dominated by the roar of float planes and the thrumbling of fishing vessels and pleasure craft. Near the docks a creek tumbles into the sound, and the waters were thick with the small salmon known as 'humpies'. They were attempting to negotiate the rocks and make their way upstream, but their progress was impeded by the activities of two small boys. One clutched a length of copper tubing, the other a rock, and between them they clubbed to death a fair number of the fish. The slaughter was a slow business; humpies, their bodies gashed and heads pounded in, still squirmed in the bloodied water until yet another cluster of blows provided the *coup de grâce*.

The third day found us cruising through the waters of Queen Charlotte Sound, past innumerable small islands ringed with barnacle-brown rocks like hatbands. Soon we could see the northern coastline of Vancouver Island swelling against the horizon. Binocular-wielding passengers spotted a pair of bald eagles flapping over the island. Approaching the port of Campbell River, the tides and currents in the sound formed so many whirlpools that the surface of the water took on the rippling sheen of black marbling. That night a full moon sequined the water, and the mountains on both island and mainland were silhouetted against the luminous sky.

After dinner that last day at sea, I wandered into the bar where a Californian and his German wife were engaging in conversation a pleasant inoffensive couple from Missouri. The Californian had 'been in the military' and proceeded to impart his predictable views to the Missouri couple. His jaw worked furiously as he revved up his indignation and stoked his certainties. South Africa, he declared, 'was the only stable place in Africa', while the rest of the continent had 'gone down the toobs'. His wife waldheimed, assuring the couple that Germans had not known of the dreadful things that went on under Hitler. The couple were too polite to take issue with her, though their dipped eyes and slack assent suggested they were not happy at being conscripted into her version of history. The military man spoke of the Tet offensive, how 'we had the VC beat', but 'they' wouldn't let us 'go in there and finish them off'. The dull murderous litany spouted from his mouth – 'I know what those people are like . . . they breed like rats . . .' – and I suddenly longed to be back in Canada.

Part Seven

The Pacific Coast

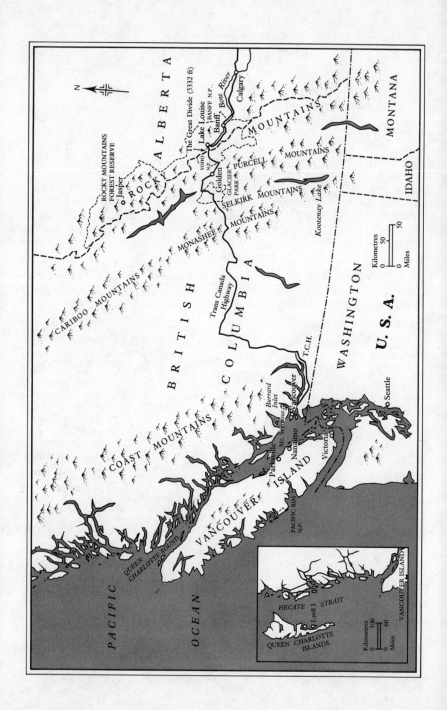

21

Trouble in Paradise

Local wits proclaim that in British Columbia you don't tan, you rust. I was fortunate: during most of my stay in the province eastern Canadians dismiss as Lotusland, the weather was dry and sunny. British Columbians are thrilled by their climate to the same degree that other Canadians are envious of it. That so sodden a climate should be so envied accurately indicates how abysmal the weather is elsewhere in Canada. The west coast may be drenched but it's rarely cold. Even in winter, snow is something you watch on the CBC Evening News, while in summer British Columbia rarely experiences the sweltering heat of the prairies.

I revelled in Vancouver because I too could leave my hotel confident that I wouldn't need my scarf and gloves that day. I was sitting one lunchtime on the terrace of a restaurant at Prospect Point in Stanley Park. It is the great treasure of the city, apart from its romantic location at the foot of some formidable mountains, that an entire 1000 acres, shaped like a nail on the thumb of downtown Vancouver, is and has always been a magnificent park. The workers at Fort McMurray had mock-heroically named a few square feet of garden adjoining the vapour-ridden plant Stanley Park, but I was now sitting in the original, looking across Burrard Inlet towards the Lions Gate suspension bridge, one of twenty that link the different parts of the city. Below me, in the glades of the park, were rose gardens and totem poles, a cricket pitch and an aquarium, and a five-mile sea wall that ringed most of the park and provided a pathway along which cyclists could run down joggers. In the warm sunshine I was picking happily at some fresh salmon and sipping a very acceptable glass of flowery local white wine. Nobody works very hard in Vancouver, and I could quite see why.

Vancouver itself is no more beautiful than any other North American city. It is an urban newcomer, founded 120 years ago and not incorporated until twenty years later when its economic future was guaranteed by its selection as the western terminus of the Canadian Pacific railway. Before that decision was made, it had wiggled its hips at the United States, and there are many in British Columbia who still feel more strongly drawn to the American West Coast than to the Canadian East. The quality of its architecture is a notch above that of Calgary or Winnipeg, but downtown Vancouver is as briskly and unexcitingly commercial as a dozen other cities. Nor does the proximity of mountains make the city itself any lovelier. You can see the Alps from Milan, but that doesn't do much for Milan itself. No, Vancouver is beautiful from *outside* Vancouver. From Prospect Point or from Burnaby Mountain, from which there are spectacular views not only onto the city but eastwards, to where Burrard Inlet and Indian Arm wriggle towards the open sea and where the lush wooded slopes of Mount Seymour rise from the waterside. Sailing boats dot the waters – a quarter of all Vancouver families own a boat – and pack the numerous marinas interspersed with the beaches, grain elevators, docks and fish-packing plants along Vancouver's ninety-nine miles of waterfront. From the shore the compact of mountains and water looks marvellous, and from the mountains the shimmering city on its peninsula looks dignified and spruce.

Adjoining the commercial downtown area is the thoroughly residential West End. Originally an older district of stately houses, its character has changed greatly over the past thirty years, for all but a handful of those houses have been replaced by apartment blocks. This is unusual for a Canadian city, where the standard layout is a downtown core of skyscrapers and a skid row encircled by older suburbs of simple frame houses within an outer ring of grander landscaped suburbia. Here in Vancouver, in contrast, is a malnourished graft of midtown Manhattan, albeit with the top few dozen storeys shaved off. The West End is handy for young city workers, but the Vancouver rich prefer to live in North and West Vancouver on the opposite side of Burrard Inlet along the slopes of Grouse Mountain. Winding roads curl along the shoulder of the mountainside through the development known as British Prop-erties. Predictably, the Union Jack flutters from a few flagpoles. The slopes are filled with lovely gardens, woods, and shrubberies, but with the amount of moisture that routinely tumbles from the Pacific sky, you don't have to work hard to make things grow here. At the foot of the slopes, near the Capilano River and the Lions Gate Bridge, is an Indian reserve. This is no slum, for the reserve includes a luxury hotel and shopping mall. There's a salmon hatchery here, and when the fish are released to begin their run up the river, Indian boys stand on the banks and enjoy their exclusive right to spear them as they pass.

The credit for such architectural distinction as Vancouver possesses goes mostly to one man, Arthur Erickson. The spectacular downtown Law Courts that he designed opened in 1979. Along the length of the building a glass roof supported with tubular struts slides down towards the street like a ski slope on Grouse Mountain; beneath that roof is a vast triangular space overlooked by buttressed concrete terraces protruding from each storey. The presence of potted trees, flowing ivy and comfortable furniture suggests the grand hotel more than the rigour of the law. Gowned barristers and suited lawyers lean over the terraces and enjoy a quick smoke while the court is in recess. Erickson also designed Simon Fraser University at the top of Burnaby Mountain. Its uncompromising concrete squares sprawl lazily along the mountainside, their severity tempered by beautifully tended gardens and covered walkways that protect the students from downpours. The charm of the structure is that although as a university it must enclose its functions within its walls, it does not appear to do so and, again as in a hotel, the interior seems to flow outdoors onto terraces, courtyards and gardens. A less grandiose example of Erickson's skill can be found off Marine Drive near the University of British Columbia. Here he has built the capacious Museum of Anthropology to house one of the best collections of its kind in the world.

Indian culture was effectively destroyed across the breadth of North America, but surely the most heartrending crippling of an indigenous American civilization occurred here on the west coast of Canada. For most northern bands, survival was always a struggle, but here in the west the natural world was at its most bountiful. Salmon jumped into the hands of anyone straddling a stream during the run; magnificent forests teemed with game and made possible the construction of villages more permanent than the tepees and huts of the more nomadic interior bands. The more rooted coastal Indians were able to develop a highly sophisticated and ceremonious culture. It did not, alas, accord with Christian missionaries' ideas of what was good for them. The first contacts with the white man must have been exhilarating, for the newcomers, in return for furs, gave the Indians tools and other useful objects. The art of carving flourished as never before: this was the great age of the totem pole, some funerary in purpose, others heraldic, while many served no other purpose than to support the roof of a house. But soon Christianity was doing its usual wrecking job on paganism, and encouraged the stiff-necked bureaucrats who administered and regulated Confederation to outlaw the central tribal ceremony of potlatch, the ritual exchange of gifts that bestowed honour and nobility on the most munificent donor. The artistic tradition most spectacularly exemplified by the poles of the Haida bands and the masks of the Kwakiutl began to fall apart once the ceremonies that nurtured it were outlawed. Those artistic glories, with a few exceptions such as the standing poles on the distant Queen Charlotte Islands, are now confined to museums. The most conspicuous artifacts are of course the great poles, those complex conglomerations of images and references to the spirit world too baffling for any but the expert to decipher; but scarcely less marvellous are the wealth of smaller objects – the combs, pipes, baskets, raven rattles, and masks – that lent grace and beauty both to the ceremonial and the quotidian. Native art is not extinct, but it has been transformed. The root stock was virtually destroyed, and we are left with a graft in which, as in the work of contemporary sculptors such as Bill Reid, the two cultures, maimed Haida and ascendant Canadian, find a powerful and forward-looking expression.

A Canadian artist very much aware of the Haida heritage was Emily Carr, who often painted the totem poles abandoned in the rainforests of the Queen Charlotte Islands. At the Vancouver Art Gallery there's a large collection of her work, all expressionist swirls and Van Gogh-like skies, thickly coloured atmospherics rather than visual precision. But her paintings are not views of the forests, but depictions from within the forests, and their emotional power outweighs their technical deficiencies. Upstairs the displays of contemporary British Columbian art seemed refreshingly sophisticated after the tired clichés and tourist pap I'd been exposed to in Québec. I chanced upon a show of the work of Gathie Falk, a mixture of exuberant waterscapes, sculptural paintings resembling large quilts, and delightful ceramics including a row of hanging cabbages and a line-up of eighteen pairs of red shoes. All that bright-eyed playfulness and splashy energy seemed, to my unaccustomed eye, thoroughly British Columbian, messages from a relaxed and carefree world.

From the Art Gallery I walked east towards the silvery-skinned Canada Pavilion, with its distinctive roofline resembling a row of five tents (it's supposed to resemble the superstructure of a liner, but doesn't); the largest of the Expo 86 pavilions, it is slung out over the water along an old pier. Close by lies Gastown, an old district near the waterfront, now a major tourist attraction. This former skid row was restored in 1971, and now skid row has moved a few blocks away. Gastown is rather worse than most of the other urban reconstructions I'd seen across Canada. In Montréal and Québec, for instance, the basic material – whether seventeenth century houses or nineteenth century warehouses – is of some interest, whereas the Gastown buildings lack such distinction. So the emphasis has been put on street furniture: brick paving, clusters of globular bulbs on the lampposts, an ingenious steam clock, pretty little courtyards. There's a Gift Village and a shop that sells 'creative sandwiches', but for my lunch I walked a few blocks further on into Chinatown. Many of its 30,000 residents are descended from the workers who helped build the CP railway in the 1880s. Here jewellery shops and emporia are almost as thick on the ground as they are in Singapore. There's also a cultural centre, the offices of the *Chinese Times*, and dozens of restaurants. A block away, on Powell Street, is a tiny Japanese neighbourhood. There isn't much of it, but it's there.

Even with seven months to go before the opening of the World Exposition known as Expo 86, its publicity machine was in high gear. Its logo was everywhere, even on the paper cups in which coffee is dished out on the coastal ferries. A 173-acre site along one side of the aquatic cul-de-sac known as False Creek was being transformed into a series of pavilions, monorail tracks, and fairground rides. A leaning hockey stick, rising 150 feet into the sky, marked the rail terminal. Some pavilions were of imaginative design: the Northwest Territories pavilion resembled an iceberg; Alberta and Saskatchewan were incorporating grain elevator motifs into theirs.

I heard much criticism of Expo on the grounds that with the provincial economy in poor shape, this was no time for such an indulgence. Until a few years ago BC was booming; people flocked here not only from all over Canada, but from Europe and the Far East. Then the recession came to the United States and the housing industry slumped; this in turn maimed the Canadian lumber industry. BC is excessively dependent on the lumber industry for its economic health. Mining is the other major industry, but low prices have kept it in the doldrums. In 1982 there were twenty-nine mines in operation; two years later only half were still active. Wage levels are high, which may deter businessmen from moving their factories here. Still, there are indications that the economy is diversifying. Financial services, especially to other countries on the Pacific Rim, are becoming increasingly important, as is film-making. Many business people saw an expansion of these Pacific markets, especially Japan and China, as the most likely way to reverse the economic decline.

It's said that you can always tell when an election is in the offing in BC because the government starts building a new dam or lowers ferry fares and paves roads. Expo, its critics suggest, was intended to draw attention away from economic problems and give the people a source of pride that would later be gratefully reflected in the form of votes. My friend Tim, who could always be relied on to put the cynical point of view, insisted that Expo 'was the biggest boondoggle in years. It was dreamt up by the government in better times as a kind of giant party for British Columbia. But this isn't the right time for a party. Any economic benefits will be strictly short term. It's all been a stirring saga of bad management. At the beginning they hired, as Canadians are wont to do, executives from the States. That posed a political problem – using taxpayers' dough to pay Americans to run our affairs may be standard procedure, but it looked bad, so they hired Canadians instead. So many people were fired that figures of dignitaries who appeared in a giant mural had to be blacked out and replaced – rather like the Russians doctoring photographs after their leader dies.'

Yet the number of those who visited Expo far exceeded expectations, and any financial losses were probably outweighed by the promotional benefits to the city as a whole. Like Montréal after Expo 67, Vancouver can now claim to be an increasingly international city.

It is the theory of the journalist Allan Fotheringham that British Columbians are as loony as they are because they don't wear hats. It is certainly true that they don't wear hats – hardly a baseball cap in sight, thank God – and equally true that provincial politics are bizarre and eccentric, and I suppose there must be a causal relationship between the two. Certainly Fotheringham's theory deserves serious consideration. For decades provincial govern-ment has been the preserve of the Social Credit Party (Socreds) under Messrs Bennett. W. A. C. Bennett spent a fifth of a century as premier, and his son Bill governed the province for years, eventually retiring in 1986. A previous incumbent adopted the name Amor de Cosmos, thus setting the tone for BC politics until the present day. The current premier also stepped out of a Star Wars sequel, as his name, Bill Vander Zalm, confirms. Socred ideology does not differ substantially from that of Reagan or Thatcher. Great stress is laid on accepting new economic realities. For British Columbians, such adjustments have entailed extremely savage cuts in spending on social services and education. Welfare payments as well as funds for a variety of social programmes have been slashed, union powers emasculated, rent controls abolished, child abuse investigation teams disbanded, and legislation was introduced to enable civil servants to be fired without cause.

'The trouble is,' said Tim, 'that the cuts were made on ideological grounds. The economy was certainly in poor shape, but butchering social programmes wasn't going to solve anything. Ironically, some of the changes proved more expensive to administer than the programmes they replaced. What's more, government spending rose 12% at the same time that they were tightening the screws on us. Megaprojects doubled the debt load. Not just Expo but the delicious ineptitude of the coalfields at Tumbler Ridge in the northeast. The silly buggers sank the coal shaft in the wrong place. The whole project is going to cost 3 billion, with the province contributing a billion in infrastructure, and now they'll have to spend another $300 million to move the shaft. What's so crazy is that we already have large coalfields in the southeast producing coal we can't sell. By opening up another coalfield, all we're doing is increasing the competition within the province itself. When the Japs heard what we were doing they roared with laughter – and made us cut our coal prices by ten dollars a tonne. The truth is the province is close to bankruptcy. To turn around the debts of BC Hydro alone would mean increasing energy charges by about 30%. That would be politically unpopular, so the Socreds simply do nothing. It'll catch up with them one day, or more likely with their successors, since their chances of winning the next election don't look too good.

'I don't see the economy picking up for some time yet. It's not that we're inefficient producers. We can sell lumber to the States much more cheaply than they can cut it down themselves. Unfortunately the world doesn't need all that wood. New industries aren't going to flock here, not just because of high wages but because we're so far away from major markets. We're a primary resource economy. We cut wood but we don't make furniture. We mine ore, but we ship it overseas. And now the rest of the world is finding that many of those resources are available more cheaply elsewhere.

'But let's look on the bright side. It's hard to think of a government anywhere that has provided its people with such entertainment over the years. Not long ago a minister left office and the very next day he hired a hooker. Swell. But McClelland paid with his credit card. Unfortunately the escort service from which he rented the girl was being wiretapped, so the voucher was traced to his office. The poor bastard didn't do anything wrong, but it was certainly dumb. Then another minister turned in his first-class plane tickets, bought economy-class seats, and pocketed the difference. Now that was dumb and wrong. It was discovered in a delightful way. An NDP member, Alex Macdonald, asked a question in the legislature about Pacific Western Airlines. He was alluding to allegations that PWA had been distributing Socred pamphlets for free. But Bennett thought Macdonald was referring to the minister cashing in his air tickets, which nobody knew about until then. So he had to fire Davis. The NDP jokes that Macdonald went duck shooting and brought down a 747.'

Tim's forecast proved false, for in 1986 the Socreds were returned to power with a large majority, and will doubtless continue to appal and to entertain the electorate for years to come.

Since almost half the workforce is unionized, trade unionism is a powerful force in BC, and there is considerable anti-union feeling, a sentiment the government shares and fosters. A British acquaintance, long resident in Vancouver, told me that many unions 'are run, I'm sad to say, by ex-Brits, who, having fucked up their own country, have come here to do the same to us. Not that I approve of everything Bennett is doing with regard to the unions. But he wants to smash them, there's no doubt about that.'

An official at the BC Federation of Labour admitted that wage levels in the province were the highest in Canada – just – but he also pointed out that the minimum wage was the lowest. 'Wage are high because the cost of living is high. Three-quarters of Vancouver residents are outsiders and they're prepared to pay a lot to live here. But if you're out of work, life can be tough in such an expensive city. Every week three thousand people line up outside the downtown food bank.'

He was particularly concerned about the state of the lumber industry. So are many British Columbians. One morning I idly switched on the television and found my eardrums quivering through an outburst of verbal savagery delivered in a Glaswegian accent. The voice and the rhetoric belonged to Jack Webster, the host of a chat show. He doesn't pull his punches and I found his programme compulsive watching. His influence is great, and no Canadian politician visiting Vancouver ever turns down an invitation to be bellowed at by Webster. His bark may be worse than his bite, but it's quite a bark, irascible, curmudgeonly, and invigoratingly rude. He was particularly incensed that morning by environmentalists who were objecting to logging on Lyell Island in the Queen Charlottes. The argument is simple enough. The environmentalists cite Lyell Island as a magnificent specimen of coastal rainforest that must be preserved from further logging; the loggers argue that this fastidiousness will cost eighty men their jobs. Webster's sympathies were entirely on the side of the loggers, and he scorned the environmentalists as Mercedes-driving sub-urbanites and airy-fairy bleeding hearts. It was all very enter-taining, though such a sustained level of bluster can be wearying after a while. A more serious threat to the environment developed a few days later, when the go-ahead was given to start logging the remote Stein Valley, wilderness up to now, but about to be despoiled. My own sympathies were with the environmentalists, and they would be reinforced when, a few days later, I travelled around Vancouver Island and saw how hideously logging and forest fires have scarred the island. A Business Council official had assured me that logging in wilderness areas was acceptable because of its 'invisibility'. He must be blind.

'There wouldn't be so many fires,' said the union organizer, 'if the industry weren't so atrociously mismanaged. The government has sold off fire-fighting equipment and got rid of many of the people experienced at getting fires under control. This year half a million acres burnt to the ground. Any replanting is inadequate. Because the lumber companies lease the forests from the crown and pay stumpage fees, they argue that the Feds are responsible for replanting. While the Feds say that the lease obliges the com-panies to manage the forests and that includes replanting. It's because the companies haven't replanted on the lower lands that they are so eager to log virgin forest on the islands and in places like the Stein Valley. The companies believe in keeping the forests healthy – until they've chopped them down, and then they walk away.'

It was ingenious of the early settlers to position the provincial capital on an island. No wonder the government has always been eccentric; the legislature and Cabinet are anchored two miles offshore. This relative isolation has enabled Victoria to retain its charm, though its much vaunted Britishness is overstated. Much of that Britishness is an invention, in the form of red doubledeckers, horse-drawn charabancs owned by Tally Ho Sightseeing, and an English village containing replicas of Anne Hathaway's cottage and the Old Curiosity Shop. High teas are offered all over town, though the famous afternoon tea at the Empress Hotel didn't seem quite authentic to me. Do we English really eat fruit salad with our tea? Not at my club. But the local newspaper is called the *Times Colonist*, and instead of the ghastly euphemisms for old people's homes – retirement homes, sunset communities, whatever – found all over North America, one such institution in Victoria proudly sniffed across its nameplate that it was a home 'for retired ladies and gentlemen'. British accents were to be heard on the streets, and the tourists in the lounge of the Empress Hotel were interspersed with ladies convincingly clad in cardigans, tweed skirts, and sensible shoes. Whether they were British Columbians of British lineage or newly retired arrivals from the Home Counties of England there was no way of telling.

The pulse of the town beats most rapidly around the harbour. Grandiose buildings loom against the horizon: the brown and cream turrets of the Maritime Museum, and, set back against an immense lawn, the huge Parliament Buildings. The British imperialists clearly believed that the population and size of the territory to be governed need bear no relationship to the size of the building in which the administration would make its laws, for these Parliament Buildings would be better suited to Bombay than to this dippy little island town. At night the rooflines and green cupolas are strung with fairy lights, which may not be quite appropriate to so pompous a structure, but do match the daintiness of the rest of the town. Along the downtown streets baskets overflowing with flowers dangled from cinqueglobed lampposts. The Victorians exhibit the same passion for gardening as their British ancestors, and for the same reason: it rains much of the time. There's a cricket pitch in Beacon Hill Park, but a more Canadian note is struck at Thunderbird Park, which contains a fine collection of totem poles, though some are reproductions. The most splendid gardens are a few miles north of town at the Butchart Gardens, which are almost brash in their splashy colourfulness. Additional sparkle is given to Victoria by the movement within the harbour, a constant bustle of seaplanes, ferries to Seattle, and ocean-going yachts. One of the waterfront lanes, Wharf Street, where, incidentally, Emily Carr was born in 1871, is lined with tastefully restored warehouses and commercial buildings, and along Yates and Johnson old houses have been painted startling shades of lilac and yellow, which may also be in questionable taste but does seem quite fitting. Within the nineteenth century Market Square, renovated in 1974, is a courtyard overlooked by wooden walkways filled with plants and giving access to shops and restaurants. The shops, as is customary in such developments, sell items that nobody needs: quilts, wooden boxes, kites. The kite shop was trying to stimulate business by holding a peculiarly limited sale: 'HONEY-MOONERS 10% OFF'. The door was wedged open by a queue of eager newlyweds clutching their sheets.

I was given a nocturnal tour of Victoria by one of the few social workers who has managed to hang on to her job – a quarter of her colleagues had been given the push. Marion came from New Brunswick, and had been a fellow guest over tea at Louise Hill's. She had in tow a friend called Mary, another typical Victorian in that she came from New Orleans. They whisked me off to a pub called Spinnakers. Ontario and Newfoundland are full of pubs, and it's not hard in Canada to find the gassier varieties of British beer. But here there were no fewer than four varieties of real ale on tap, and good cheap food. Tucked away on the far side of the harbour, it was off the tourist track and the customers were the after-work crowd from downtown offices. Marion told me that Victoria had been transformed in the last ten years. When she first came here you couldn't order a meal after eight. Now it's bursting with restaurants. 'Still an awful lot of old people, though. It's not for nothing that they say Victoria is full of the newly wed and the nearly dead. Most people who live here never leave the town, let alone the island. Talk about provincial.'

We moved on to another watering hole, the Bastion, a downtown basement bar of extreme seediness, where the smell of beer and piss were indistinguishable. My guides were accommodating my wish to see the 'real' Victoria, not the genteel capital of the tourist brochures. The Bastion was certainly real: there was a real sailor struggling to remain on his feet, dozens of real drunks who kept 'accidentally' bumping into my companions, and an intoxicatingly real smell of marijuana. When we were on our second pitcher of beer, Mary leaned over to ask me if I had any good antidotes. For what? I asked, since her health appeared in no immediate danger. Then Marion gave me a nimble kick under the table: 'She means anecdotes.' There was a great deal of one-way traffic trailing into the men's lavatory, which excited Marion's curiosity, and the women dispatched me into the house of urine to investigate further. Lurking about in lavatories in the company of sailors pissing on their shoes is not my idea of fun, so my visit was brief. My researches established that the principal activity in the lavatory, other than ridding the body of waste matter, was not a homosexual orgy but innocuous dope-peddling.

'Don't you love this place?' sighed Mary.

'Wonderful.'

The next day I set off to explore the island. The road climbed rapidly through the hills, since Vancouver Island is mountainous for much of its 280-mile length. From 1150 feet up at Malahat Summit there was a spectacular view onto the Saanich Inlet, which resembled a lake entirely enclosed by steep wooded hills. Much of the coastline is speared by these long narrow inlets and sheltered bays. I came to Cowichan Bay, a fishing village in harness with many resort hotels. Just beyond the village the paved road became a dirt road after it crossed a wooden bridge into the Cowichan Indian reserve. The squalor of the reserve seemed startling after the prosperous neatness of the fishing villages and Victoria itself. There were as many mobile homes as houses, most of them shielded by three or four battered old cars. In the village centre, some forty or fifty Indians stood around, leaning against their pickup trucks, chatting and drinking beer.

As in the Yukon, the federal government didn't sign treaties with all the Indians of British Columbia; hence the native peoples can convincingly assert that they have not relinquished any of their rights. No single organization represents the combined interests of the various Indian nations; instead each has its own pressure group seeking to establish title. The coastal nations are quite distinct from one another – in the 1770s Captain Cook recorded no fewer than four hundred languages in use among the coastal Indians – and the amount of well-publicized disagreement between the tribes is less surprising than the degree of unity among them. When British Columbia entered Confederation in 1871, the federal government accepted the responsibility for crown lands. The provincial government argues that it is accordingly absolved from any responsibility for negotiating with the

Indians. Indeed the BC Attorney-General simply if controversially asserts that aboriginal rights don't exist. The province cites an old court ruling to support its argument, but it seems probable that the ruling will soon be overturned and that Indian bands will win title and compensation from both levels of government. It would be sensible to negotiate a deal before this happens, but, as Tim put it, 'there's no political will in BC to hand over millions to a bunch of thirty-year-old Haidas.' For ten years negotiations have been stalled because Ottawa argues that the province must contribute to any settlement, a view to which the Socreds do not subscribe. While the two levels of government argue back and forth, the frustration of the Indians, who are caught in the middle, grows. The argument is just one, and a very important, instance of the murkiness of the distinctions between levels of responsibility spelt out by the acts of Confederation and the constitution itself. (A more absurd example is the fact that most salmon stocks are a federal responsibility, with the exception of steelheads, which are a provincial responsibility. Were the fish consulted?)

As in other parts of Canada, the basis of any settlement will not be cash alone. The indigenous economic base of most Indian nations has been taken away from them – some Indians have been prosecuted for selling fish and timber from 'their' lands – and where lands have been commercially exploited by, say, lumber companies, the Indians have rarely received any economic benefit, let alone compensation. Any settlement will need to devise an economic and political structure that will free natives from the dependency to which they have been reduced.

The Tory government has not been slow to alter the way native organizations are funded. One of David Crombie's aides later told me: 'Our policy is to fund bands directly. One danger of funding these umbrella organizations is that some of them have used the money to gain leverage over individual bands. We're not against self-government, but it can't happen overnight. The concept has to be tailored according to the differences between the bands. Some are sophisticated, with good education and resources; others are in a desperate state. In BC the Squamish in Vancouver have a prosperous reserve, but in the North conditions are completely different. If you ask me how those remote bands are going to survive, I don't have the answer. It's up to those bands to make the decisions about their future. It depends a good deal on the leadership. Ed Johns in northern BC has led his band well and set up timber-related industries and farms. Over in Fort Good Hope a band that originally opposed the laying of a pipeline through their lands on the grounds that it would only provide jobs for whites, have changed their mind. They've negotiated with the oil company and are now working out a deal that will guarantee the band's participation in management and monitoring. So the situation isn't all bad even in the bush. What's clear is that the new constitution establishes once and for all that the aboriginal peoples have entrenched property rights. The problem in BC is that these rights are accepted in principle but that the province claims to lack the resources to reach or honour any settlement.'

The paper-mill town of Nanaimo boasts 'the largest amount of retail shopping space per capita of any city on the continent'. From here the ferry crosses to Gabriola Island. Most of the Gulf Islands scattered like loose change between Vancouver Island and the mainland are populated. They were once inhabited by Indians, fishermen and a handful of artists and eccentrics who enjoyed their unspoiled and relatively primitive seclusion. There was an invasion in the 1960s by hippies who wanted to grow dope and chant mantras in peace but more recently island properties have been bought up by the well-to-do. The islands maintain a mixed population of old-time residents, ageing hippies, commuters, Indians, summer residents, crafts enthusiasts, and the very rich. On a bus ride over the Rockies I heard a passenger chatting to the driver about the islands where they had their homes, Gabriola and Mayne. Their conversation hinged on such touchy topics as land speculation, the size of subdivisions, and how the erratic water supply was threatened by the burgeoning summer population. On the Gabriola ferry the ads on the noticeboard painted a fair portrait of the residents of Gabriola: there were houses for rent, classes in fitness training and in Kundalini and Hatha Yoga, a recruitment poster for the Cooperative Preschool Association ('Learn & Grow With Your Child' – an alarming concept, for I envisaged dozens of totally ignorant dwarf-like parents mastering their two times table in company with their offspring), and services such as tree-felling and wood-stove installation.

The island itself is certainly lovely, with its abundance of magnificent trees, the cliffs tufted with woods that Malcolm Lowry described as 'mere broken bottles guarding the rim', and wooden houses perched on stilts. With a permanent population of 2800 (doubled in summer) spread over twenty square miles, this lush green island seems idyllic, but the Irish landlord of the White Hart Pub told me there was an unemployment rate of 24% here. I asked him how the islanders supported themselves.

'Well, everyone's a carpenter. And the rest are either retired or unemployed – those are the two major occupations on Gabriola.'

Further up the coast, I came upon the Nanoose Peace Camp, a modest group of three tepees. On the opposite side of Nanoose Bay is a small naval base, where American ships are serviced by the Canadian armed forces. The peace camp was objecting to the use of Canadian facilities and waters to provide a testing range for American underwater weaponry. The protesters were particularly concerned by the frequent visits made by huge American nuclear-powered submarines, which may be carrying nuclear weapons, a possibility that neither government will confirm or deny. In a way it seemed a futile protest, given the very close but longstanding reciprocal links between the defence establishments of both countries, yet I could share the sense of violation that the protesters were registering as they saw these beautiful waters invaded by instruments of war and destruction. Walking back to my car from the shore, I passed a flourishing stand of blackberry bushes, which provided me with my lunch.

In the little town of Parkville I paused for spiritual refreshment at the Pentecostal Assembly Church, where the pastor, Harold Rowledge, dressed in his best three-piece suit, was addressing a congregation of forty. By his side sat the organist who, with her white face, black hat, and unyielding severity of expression, could have been a double for the late Queen Mary. A member of the congregation rose heavily to his feet and, couching prejudice in the form of prayer, hoped that teachers who had been influenced by 'humanism and the philosophy of the world' – dangerous stuff for a teacher, the world – would return to the way of Christ. After other worshippers had had their say, the pastor brought the proceedings to an end by announcing a baby shower for Lorinda Lynn, and on that happy note I went on my way.

I felt almost assaulted by the beauty of the island, which is so complete in its blending of elements: the mildness of the climate, the clarity of the sky, the tranquil bays, and, overwhelmingly, the fecundity of nature. At Bathtrevor Beach Provincial Park, which even on a weekend was almost deserted, I stepped from woods of tall elegant pine onto a broad shallow beach with wonderful views onto some of the smaller Gulf Islands nearby, while behind them there was a jagged backdrop of the coastal mountains flecked with snow that glinted in the sun. I finished my bag of blackberries beside the canyons at Little Qualicum Falls while the scents of the aromatic pinewoods wafted around me. A deer ran into a glade a few yards from where I was sitting, gave me a glance, and bounded on. A magnificent road alongside Cameron Lake was bordered by towering conifers. At Cathedral Grove, massive Douglas fir and red cedar rise in almost parallel lines over 200 feet into the air. Lower down the almost horizontal branches of young hemlock trees reach towards each other like outstretched hands. At ground level ferns flopped over the forest floor, and fat olive-green slugs nestled between ridges of ancient bark. Some of these trees were 800 years old, but the majority had been here for a mere 300 years. There was an immense stillness in the forest, no wind to rustle the branches, no children yelling their way through hide-and-seek games, just a sombre, almost sacred silence.

As I continued east along the shore of sprat-shaped Sproat Lake towards the thinly populated west coast of Vancouver Island, the landscape filled me with gloom. For mile after mile I passed huge tracts of burnt forest, with nothing remaining but charred spiky slivers of trunks, like black and grey pick-up sticks, some standing naked and leafless, others tumbled down gullies and propped against boulders. It had been a particularly devastating summer; unexpectedly hot weather had increased the risk of fire, and fires there had been, dozens of them, many raging simultaneously, while the overstretched fire fighters struggled, often in vain, to bring them under control. Here, above the lake and along the Kennedy River valley, they had failed, and where there had once been stately coniferous forests there were now exposed hillsides as bare and grey as the shaved shanks of a dog.

I eventually came to the Pacific Rim, a national park that stretches for miles along the beaches of the west coast. Sea lions frequent rocky offshore islets; a wealth of rare birds nest in the forests while delicate crustaceans lurk in the rockpools. It was a warm afternoon, uncharacteristic for the Pacific Rim, which can be wild and windswept as gales come roaring in over the ocean. As I walked along a trail towards South Beach, I saw garter snakes wriggling under the salmonberry bushes as I approached. On the beach itself there was a rotting saline smell of seaweed, and the hard grey sands were cluttered with driftwood worn smooth as tusks, though perhaps Malcolm Lowry was nearer the mark when he compared them to the lashed bones of dinosaurs. From the horizon a slow steady parade of Pacific breakers came rolling towards me; below the high-tide mark dark grey rocks, encrusted with barnacle and sponge, looked sinister against the paler sands. Fringing the beaches are stands of Sitka spruce that shelter the remaining rainforest of the interior. It is not easy to stroll through those forests, for the path is frequently blocked by fallen trees, shrubs, and patches of swamp. Some trails pass through areas of rainforest, and boardwalks make the passage easier. Along the drier patches the path, on top of layers of decayed vegetal growth, is as springy and soft as a deep pile carpet. These marvellous forests – or the few that are left after a century of felling by avaricious lumber companies – are cool and quiet, a rich tangle of vegetation, gigantic trees, blowsy shrubs, parasitic ferns, and branch moss like baize or green velvet. Cathedral Grove, by contrast, is considerate to visitors, with plenty of space elbowed clear by the branches of the immense trees. The rainforests of Pacific Rim are entirely different – primeval, unaccommodating to humans. It was hard to realize that this deep forest, with its fat moist smells, its teeming insect life, its sickly looking clusters of puffballs and fungi, and its stillness, was only a few hundred yards away from the point where beneath vast and turbulent skies the rolling waters of the Pacific first touch the broad battered beaches of the American continent.

I returned to Vancouver briefly before heading back east. I was staying on Howe Street, not the most stylish of addresses, but convenient. Parallel to Howe ran Granville, which for half its length was a pedestrian precinct lined with department stores. Further south it became distinctly seedy. Some other streets parallel to Granville were less gaudy, and played host to an interesting mixture of commercial and residential developments, secondhand bookshops, cheap hotels, chic nightclubs such as The Edge, interior design studios, junk shops, old frame houses. On Richards, one such house was festooned with models of barns and windmills, all placed on brackets and ledges; the effect was as fussy as a Tyrolean hat stuck with badges. A crudely lettered sign along the front of the house justified the romper room ornament in the following language: 'I'D RATHER BE HAPPY IN MY CRAZY WORLD THAN BE SANE AND SAD.' I'm all for loonies, but looniness conjoined with pomposity is an insufferable combination.

In the evening I walked up Granville to a cinema, queued for forty minutes to see the only film of the summer not aimed at the adolescent, the retarded, or the sedated, but failed to get in. I took a stroll down some of the side streets and found myself almost besieged by hookers. The concentration was far greater than in Toronto, where they hadn't been exactly thin on the ground. Some were evidently stoned and should have been at home nursing a mug of hot chocolate rather than peddling their young bodies so that their favourite pusher could get his BMW resprayed. One block contained a gaggle of transvestites, their flesh pressed by corsetry into an approximation of cleavage which they exposed daringly above their décolletage. These lads were aggressive, and needed to be, for louts in passing cars would roll down the windows and scream obscenities at them, which the transvestites would return with a few colourful coinages of their own. I noticed that all the transvestites were tall. True, they aided nature by tottering about on stiletto heels, though most would have been six feet tall just in their pantyhose. I inquired of a hustler standing nearby why this should be the case, but he couldn't enlighten me. He did make one or two other suggestions, which I politely declined, at which point a mate of his came running up crying, 'Take us both! Take us both!'

Back on Granville, I pushed open the door of a bar. A woman wearing not very much was cavorting saucily on a stage to the accompaniment of badly amplified music. I was turning on my heel when the manager, reading my mind, bawled: 'No cover! Come on in!' The beer wasn't marked up either, so I decided to go in and enjoy the show. Quite a few women were in the bar too – some of them hookers taking a breather or gargling mouthwash in the ladies', but not all. Nor were the lights dimmed to the level of Ireland's Newgrange burial chamber. Although the customers, as is usual in such establishments, were not encouraged to touch the strippers, there seemed no prohibition on gropes in the opposite direction. Three sailors seated near me were amiably drunk, and the strippers ragged them by clasping their hands around the men's necks or by grabbing the men by the hands, then pulling them up towards the stage and pressing the beery male lips briefly against their rolling breasts. Then, as punishment for the daring they'd been forced into, the men were roughly pushed away. A similar ritual took place during another act, when a stripper yanked the T-shirt off a man's torso, rubbed it all over her body, and then scrunched it into his face. They loved it.

This was harmless enough, but what was going on out on the streets was not. Vancouver is notorious across Canada for rampant prostitution. Moreover, most of the kids on the streets were exactly that: children, many of them runaways, some as young as fourteen, some hooked on drugs and driven to prostitution to support their habit, others in thrall to the pimps, who were almost as ubiquitous as the hookers. Nor was the problem limited to downtown Vancouver, for a couple of months earlier about a hundred whores, obliged by police action to abandon a particular neighbourhood, had moved en masse into Mount Pleasant, a smart middle-class district behind False Creek. Young stock-brokers and boutique owners and their families had moved into elegant $1500-a-month flats with terraces and courtyards, and now they couldn't step out of their front door without being besieged by importunate hookers or tripping over a pander or two shooting up in their garden and stomping on the dahlias. The city had tut-tutted the rash of prostitution downtown, but now that it had moved into the Yuppies' own fortress the residents were none too pleased by the new services on offer in their neighbourhood. But what could be done? Prostitution is not illegal, so there were no grounds for arrest as long as the gals didn't importune too brazenly. There is a warehouse district adjacent to Mount Pleasant, but the hookers were reluctant to ply their trade in a district that was so utterly deserted at night. There were quite enough beatings and deaths and disappearances already, thank you very much. Pressure was being exerted by local politicians on Ottawa, where Liberals in particular were being accused of dragging their feet when it came to drafting legislation to deal with a problem that affected every city.

The next day I turned my face to the east. I was sorry to be going. British Columbia may be beset by problems, economic and political, but it's an enjoyable corner of the world, far from the Presbyterian restraints of Ontario and the climatic constraints of the rest of Canada. Its residents, though accused of apeing Californians, secretly aspire to be Tahitians.

Over a valedictory cup of coffee I said to Tim: 'A friend from New York who came out here some years ago told me BC was full of blond girls with backpacks and unshaven legs who keep saying "Ever neat". But it hasn't been like that at all, though I did meet an Albertan whose favourite expression was "Holy spit!"'

'Come back in the summer and I'll dig out a few for you at a beach party. You haven't been here long enough to appreciate the true hedonism of Vancouver. My life is devoted to exposing the ills of the province, but I wouldn't live anywhere else. Of course there's more to BC than Vancouver, as you know. The other half of the population consists of beer-swilling woodsmen in the north and of old bats in twin sets and pearls in Victoria, and the one thing that unites them is that they loathe Vancouver – but that doesn't bother us. We know how to enjoy life. In winter even the unemployed are out on the ski slopes, which are twenty minutes away from the city. In the summer we're all in our boats or on the beaches. We don't overwork – much of the work available is seasonal anyhow. There's a lot of dope grown here – joint for the road? – and we're happy to go our own way. The restaurants are good, plenty of night life, beautiful women, great dope. Fact is, we don't give a shit about what happens on the other side of the Rockies. Most of the people here have escaped from there, and would just as soon not think about the rest of Canada ever again. Our links are with the west coast, not the east. For our vacations we fly to Hawaii or Palm Springs, not Cape Breton. Tomorrow, while I'm sitting on my patio in the sunshine, you'll be chugging your way into a blizzard, I expect. *Bon voyage.*'

Tim was absolutely right. I boarded the train at lunchtime and squeezed myself into what Via Rail coyly calls a 'roomette', which turned out to be a cosy cell, well if tightly equipped with a broad seat, pillows, good reading lights, a sink and lavatory, drinking water, and a shoe rack. The train tiptoed through the Vancouver suburbs and then hugged the west side of the Fraser Canyon. From the window I could have thrown myself over precipices into the seething khaki waters of the river. The track had been cut through fearsome black rock. I had read accounts of the extreme hardships undergone by the navvies who pushed the railway through these hundred of miles of mountain wilderness, but it was awesome to lay eyes on the terrain that had to be traversed. The human cost had been considerable, and every ten miles or so we would pass a tiny cemetery, with plain crosses poking above the tall grass. Whether these were the graves of local people or of navvies, mostly Chinese, killed a century ago there was no way to tell. Landslides had caused almost vertical piles of scree to tumble down to the valley floor. Geological savagery was exposed at China Bar, where stratified layers of rock seemed jaggedly carved from the face of the cliff. Elsewhere the cliffs were as flaked and brittle as *mille-feuille*. The autumn colours of aspen and sumac were muted by the leaden skies, and as the train crept along the gorges it was as though we were crawling beneath an army blanket.

280

With a few tugs and heaves, I converted my seat into a comfortable bed, and slept well through the night until woken by the realization that we were not moving. We had made an avalanche-free trip through Glacier Park and were now at Golden. The porter informed me there was a freight train derailment up ahead; in going off the rails, the train had torn up some track which would have to be relaid before we could proceed. A loud cheer ran down the train like a fuse when, eight hours later, we haltingly began to move again. We soon came to the appropriately named Cathedral, where the cliffs loomed a thousand feet and more above the valley floor, and a glacier lip leered between craggy buttresses. Slowly, almost gingerly, the train made the ascent to the Kicking Horse Pass. I positioned myself in the observation car to have the best view of this ancient but still overwhelming example of railway building. The track wound around the hefty shoulders of high ranges, their peaks flanked by glaciers. Where it had been impossible to skirt the mountains, spiral tunnels had been built through the rock. Towards the top, snow lay thickly over slopes with a northern exposure, boughs of spruce and pine sagged whitely towards the ground. Ponds and tarns were already filmed with ice. Fellow passengers, maps and guides on their laps, identified the very spot at which we crossed the Great Divide. We were now 5332 feet above sea level. With equal slowness a freight train crawled up the pass towards us, its wagons pulled by no fewer than four engines.

Towards Lake Louise, the snow lay heavily on the ground, transforming the boulders strewn in the creeks into giant white acorns. Around Banff there were localized blizzards. Through the grey swirling light the Bow River appeared the colour of steel as it wound between the whitened banks. Moving parallel to the track for a spell, a pickup festooned with icicles was crunching its way down an unploughed lane. It was still only early October but when we arrived in Calgary that evening, the temperature was −5° and a harsh wind was tearing across the city from the rangelands. The storm was the merest knock on the door before the true arrival of winter turned the handle and opened it, but it was a demonstration that nothing in Canada ever takes precedence over the relentless march of the seasons.

Part Eight

Ottawa

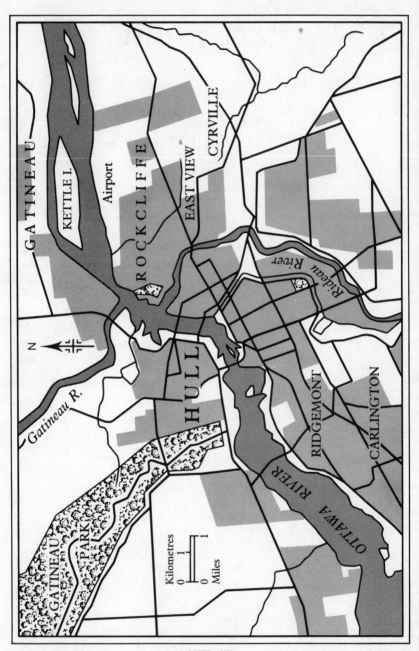

OTTAWA

22

Will the Real Canada Please Stand Up?

I first set foot in Ottawa in 1965, when I went to stay with Joe Savage and his family: his father, a prominent lawyer, and his stepmother Sylvia, who greeted me at the door wearing the skimpiest of cut-off jeans and black fish-net stockings. Round her ankle was a gold chain with the word 'SEXY' engraved across it. She embraced me fervently, though we had never met before. She was clutching – it was mid-morning – a tumbler of Scotch. Whenever the liquor level fell low enough to expose the ice, Sylvia would thrust it high in the air and shout 'Emergency!', at which point Joe was trained to trot over with the decanter and top her up. Joe couldn't stand her, this round-faced emotional woman of forty who dressed like a whore, but she took no notice and behaved as though he could do none other than love her dearly. Mr Savage was subdued at lunch. He was a bit tired, he told me. He and Sylvia had gone to a party the night before. Anxious to complete work on a complicated brief, he had gone home at midnight. She had followed two hours later, and as she walked in the door she had cooed: 'Darling, I've brought a few people back with me.' He had counted them as they filed through the door. 'I didn't mind the numbers,' he told me; 'it was when I asked them what they'd like to drink that I ran into difficulties. Ever tried to keep eighty-five drinks orders in your head? They finally left at six this morning.' Sylvia beamed, for she delighted in the role of gracious hostess. To end the lunch she served cantaloupe melon, then placed half a dozen liqueur bottles on the table. I was enrolled in a culinary experiment, as she sliced my portion of melon in two, and poured over one half Cointreau, and over the other crème de menthe. After lunch she led me into the garage, where two Cadillacs stood side by side. An acquaintance had stopped by a few weeks earlier to cadge a cup of coffee from Sylvia. She told him he could only have his coffee if in exchange he gave

285

her a pale blue Caddy. He agreed. She poured his coffee, and a few days ago the Cadillac, in the correct shade of blue, had been delivered.

That evening Sylvia changed into a sarong. Her toenails were painted black and around her neck she wore a heavy gold chain, to which was attached a watch at least four inches in diameter that swung bruisingly from breast to breast. Various teenagers were hanging about in the den – nobody seemed to know who they were –and Sylvia sent out for thirty-five hamburgers. At this point the teenagers left. Six of us munched our way through as many burgers as we could stomach. After supper Joe took me to see Bob Hope's show at the fairgrounds, and we returned at midnight to find Sylvia languidly sprawled along a chaise longue, her bare shoulders warmed by a mink wrap. Asleep across her thighs was her black spaniel, Baby, who was at least ten years old. To entertain us, she played a record of Martin Luther King's 'I have a dream' speech. We all sobbed. Joe then retaliated by playing both sides of an LP of Churchill's greatest speeches. At 4.30 I went to bed. My hostess woke me six hours later by tickling me all over. I came downstairs for a late breakfast to find Sylvia affectionately pouring a glass of whisky over Joe's head.

So when I think of Ottawa, I think not of bureaucrats and politicians but of exuberant Sylvia, who single-handed contradicted all the Canadian stereotypes. That she could flourish there seemed to modify the city's reputation for dullness. Then, as now, there were few capital cities as maligned as Ottawa, for the capital of Canada is singled out for almost universal loathing by the subjects over whom it rules. Canadians regard government as something alien to them, and speak of people who 'work for the government' as though it were an organization that had no connection with their lives. This hostility also reflects the ceaseless warring between provincial and federal levels of government, but it also has something to do with the insignificance of the town itself. The location has a slight strategic importance as the confluence of the Ottawa, Rideau and Gatineau rivers, but its status as a capital city is almost accidental. It was Queen Victoria who, required to choose a capital for Canada in 1857, more or less picked the name out of a hat and that was that. Its critics seem aggrieved that so marginal a town as Ottawa should be able to shape the lives of Canadians who live thousands of miles away.

It is easy to see why Canadian mandarins become entrenched in Ottawa, for the system of government, modelled on the British, does not encourage the game of musical chairs among civil servants that takes place whenever an American administration changes. Moreover, Ottawa is as pleasant a city as you'll find in central Canada. As in the case of Vancouver, its charm lies in its location more than its architecture. The rivers coil around the city, and separate it from the town of Hull in Québec. Waterfalls and rapids, and the sight of chained logs floating down the Gatineau, lend variety to the riverscape; and the recreation-conscious Ottawans take pride in the hundred miles of cycling and jogging paths along the landscaped riverbanks, as well as the ease of access to the ski slopes of the Gatineau hills a few miles away. There is greenery within Ottawa too, much of it provided by a 1200-acre experimental farm that lies within the city limits and is traversed by Winding Lane (French: Ruelle Winding).

Without the presence of the government, Ottawa would be no more than a river junction. Even now it's a small town, spared the bland suburbia of larger North American cities. There is hardly any industry, with the exception of some hi-tech outfits on the outskirts, and the air is clean. Its airport is little more than a few sheds, and in the departure lounge, as in the airport at Frobisher Bay, everybody seemed to know everybody else. Behind me two civil servants from the fisheries department wondered aloud whether they would have to testify at forthcoming hearings investigating the scandal of the tainted tuna, and a few minutes later a government minister, David Crombie, smiling and nodding at friends and associates, came tearing through the departure lounge in hurried pursuit of the shuttle to Toronto. Because the city is small, its establishment huddles together. Most of the eighty embassies, the rich lawyers, the mandarins, and some of the politicians have colonized the most attractive corner of the city, the district of Rockcliffe overlooking the Ottawa River. Here, secure behind guarded gates on Sussex Drive, stands the prime minister's residence, though it is upstaged by Rideau Hall, the residence of the governor-general. This top-heavy classical mansion is set within a lovely park stacked with maples that were looking their brightly coloured best in the October sunshine. Winding roads twist confusingly through Rockcliffe and give the impression that the enclave is larger than it actually is. Black squirrels leap about, preparing their hoards for the winter. One local resident, infuriated by the damage the squirrels do to his garden, has set a trap for them. When he comes home from work, any squirrels unfortunate enough to be inside it are liquidated. This is illegal, but since all his neighbours share the benefit provided by this one-man assassination squad, they keep mum.

Rockcliffe is a very tranquil place, and rowdiness is provided across the bridge in Hull. Dreary government offices crowd the downtown area, but there is plenty of room left for dance halls, restaurants, and bars licensed to stay open until 3 a.m. Hull is both a government town and a paper-mill town, and combines the staidness of the one with the working-class brashness of the other. Ottawa too has a good supply of restaurants, especially along Elgin Street and at Byward Market, a few renovated blocks of pleasant brick and stone buildings where fruit and flower markets still operate. By strolling down some of the residential streets that cross Elgin, I gained strange glimpses of Ottawan life. In a lighted window sat a woman exhibiting not her body but her mind, for held up high for passersby to admire was a copy of *Cahiers du Cinéma*. A few doors away an uncurtained window allowed me to view a hallway beatifically dominated by a portrait of the Maharishi. With a high concentration of lawyers and administrators, all well paid, there is no lack of cultural or intellectual life in town. The educational level is high, and the most common failing of those who run Canada from Ottawa is that ideas interest them more than people. It was just such an accusation that was often levelled, with some justification, at Pierre Trudeau, and I was to hear it again within Ottawa itself. Not far from Parliament is Ottawa's newest cultural monument, the National Museum of – well, no one is yet sure. Originally known as the National Museum of Man, the building is nameless until a special committee of experts (who else?) alights on a truly non-sexist name. Suggestions from the public include National Museum of Herstory and History, National Museum of Men, Women and Gays, and National Museum of Others, any one of which is sure to pull in the crowds.

The Parliament Buildings are the most conspicuous landmark in Ottawa. Their swaggering neo-Gothic grandeur is a fitting embodiment of this vast country, as is the dour stone of the buildings, so chillingly reminiscent of a Scots theological college. The green copper roofs, the one element that adds a little sparkle to the pomposity, are almost upstaged by the equally grand structure next door, the baronial Château Laurier hotel, with no fewer than three storeys of dormers jutting from the steep pitched roof. Beside the Parliament is a statue of Sir John A. Macdonald, inaccurately portrayed as clutching spectacles rather than a whisky bottle. Beneath the plinth on which he stands is a seated figure that I at first mistook for Queen Victoria. Closer inspection revealed that her gown was sliding off her left shoulder to expose the upper regions of a ripe left breast and, a titillating touch, that her right nipple was erect. Unlikely, then, to be the puddingy Empress, and in making an attribution I plump for a personification of Britannia. There are still vestiges of Anglophilia in Ottawa, though they are less pronounced than in, say, Fredericton or even Toronto. At a newsstand a current issue of *Private Eye* touched edges with *Royal Monthly*, and I wondered who would buy either. For Ottawa is a remarkably French city, and not only because Québec is just across the river. Since all federal workers must be bilingual, most of them are French Canadians, for it is still more common to find French Canadians who are fluent in English than Anglophones who speak perfect French.

I was particularly surprised, since every doorman in Ottawa is bilingual, to encounter an MP from Québec whose English was poor. I met other MPs from the West and from Ontario, and I suspect their French was no better, and possibly worse, than her English. If Members of Parliament from one country have difficulty understanding one another, it is not surprising that regional and factional interests within Canada should have remained so divisive for so long. The situation is changing, as ambitious politicians recognize. It's arguable that part of Mulroney's electoral appeal is his fluency in both languages. The Canadian Parliament reflects, as parliaments are supposed to do, wide differences in background as well as ideology. It is refreshing to find that socialism is not a dirty word in Canada, although the New Democratic Party (NDP) trails behind the two major parties. However, the NDP leader, Ed Broadbent, is, the polls affirm, the best of the three party leaders. I asked Steven Langdon, an NDP MP, why socialism enjoyed good parliamentary representation in Canada, while south of the border it remained an unthinkable political option. He attributed it in part to the strength of trade unionism within Canada, where 40% of the workforce is unionized. The NDP also benefited from the influx of radicals from the United States in the 1960s, as well as from Canada's own radical socialist tradition that remains strong in the prairie provinces. In the United States, Langdon argued (in a thin quavery voice that made me fear he was about to burst into tears at any moment),

1960s radicalism eventually fizzled out because there were no political structures, other than the broad church of the Democratic Party, to which they could attach themselves. In Canada the NDP offered just such a political structure. Not that the NDP is a doctrinaire party. In style and structure it resembles the British Liberal Party, with its roots in specific communities, and a lively youthful populism as the basis of its appeal.

The autumn of 1985 was a good season for the NDP, and for the Liberals too. The previous year John Turner, the Liberal leader, had suffered a crushing defeat at the hands of Brian Mulroney. But the end of the summer had found the Mulroney team committing gaffe after gaffe; every time it managed to clamber out of one hole, it dug itself another that was even deeper.

First, there was the issue of Canadian sovereignty in the Arctic. The United States had sent an icebreaker through the Northwest Passage without troubling to ask the Canadians for permission, since the Americans claim the waters are international. Embarrassed by the Americans' disregard for its claim to sovereignty over the waters, the Canadian government feebly announced that the American icebreaker was 'authorized' by them to make the journey. Although the row was about symbol rather than substance, the Americans' presumption was humiliating for the Mulroney government, which floundered for two months before declaring that either the Americans should negotiate a deal that respects Canadian sovereignty or the matter would be taken to the World Court. (A political commentator in Ottawa suggested to me that the two-month delay was only partly lack of resolution. 'The voyage took place in August, when everybody's out of town. The government had to wait till the bureaucrats were back from their vacations before anything specific could be done.')

Even more embarrassing was Tunagate, the scandal that led to the resignation of the fisheries minister, John Fraser. A million cans of New Brunswick tuna had been examined by federal inspectors and found wanting, or in the words of the inspectors, 'rancid and decomposed'. Myself, I have difficulty telling rancid tuna from acceptable tuna, but not so the inspectors, and not so the Canadian armed forces, who were fed some of the stuff, failed to identify it as tuna, and declared it 'unfit for human consumption'. The inspectors' report was, however, overruled by Mr Fraser, who asserted that the revolting stuff posed no health hazard. The row simmered delightfully for a few weeks, as ministers blithely contradicted one another.

The most serious political row of the season focused on the collapse of two Alberta banks, which despite a history of ill-judged loans, had been bailed out by the government earlier in the year. One had been given an infusion of $225 million, no mean sum. In volatile Alberta it doubtless seemed prudent to rescue the banks rather than let them collapse with political as well as economic consequences damaging to the government. After the banks failed, the government agreed to pay out about a billion dollars, even to large depositors who had been lured by high interest rates. This too was a controversial decision, since it set a precedent absolving depositors from the consequences of a risk-laden decision. However, since many of the large depositors were western companies and pension funds, it would have been politically awkward to let them suffer losses of millions of dollars.

And there was much more. John Crosbie, the minister of justice, had first implied that the Prime Minister's Office had dealt with some of the above matters incompetently, and then implausibly denied that he had done so. The able and popular communications minister, Marcel Masse, had honourably stepped down from office while allegations of financial irregularities in his campaign spending were investigated (he was exonerated). The environment minister, Suzanne Blais-Grenier, pronounced that the US government's refusal to take further action to reduce levels of acid rain dumped over Canada was fine with her. This was just one example of this minister's extraordinary ineptitude, and her front-bench career would soon come to an end. And in the spring the industry minister Sinclair Stevens, ensnared by conflict-of- interest allegations, also threw in the towel. All in all, it was a lousy season for the Tories, whose popularity was plummeting.

Mulroney himself, though personable, was increasingly perceived as vague and aimless in his leadership, unwilling to make or incapable of making the decisive policy changes he had promised the electorate. Like a shadow puppet, he was beginning to seem more image than substance.

With so many well-publicized difficulties confronting the government, it was hard to speak to Conservative MPs without raising questions that would embarrass them. Barbara Sparrow, from Calgary, proved endearingly adept at dealing with such questions. She simply agreed with everything I said, even if I was contradicting something she herself had just said to me. When I asked about government ineptitude, she perked up. 'Stephen, you're absolutely right. But in fairness I should say that the government doesn't always get a fair shake in the press.'

'The newspapers can hardly be blamed if with every day that passes ministers keep contradicting each other.'

'Well, Stephen, that's a very good point and I'm glad you raised it. All I'm saying is that not enough is written about our positive achievements. Such as lower mortgages, interest rates, lower inflation, provincial accords.' And she delivered, personally, just to me, a five-minute campaign speech, which concluded: 'And we're looking forward not to free trade, but to freer trade. Nothing's going to impinge on our sovereignty, there'll be no trade-off of social programmes, but at the end of it all we'll have great positive things to look forward to. In five or six years.'

Monique Tardif, a Tory MP from Québec, took a similar line. We had an excellent rapport. I would ask her a question and she would reply at length on another topic altogether. To my interesting musing on why the New Right didn't have much impact on Canadian politics, she replied with an excellent speech on cooperation between federal and provincial governments. It was as if we were speaking two different languages, and as a matter of fact we were. I had a better answer to my question from Reg Stackhouse, another Tory, who, as the former principal of the University of Toronto theological college, must have felt entirely at home in the Parliament Buildings. A stern man, who sat throughout our talk with his hands folded in his lap, he reminded me that Canada was not a clone of Britain or the United States, and that neither of the major parties was rigorously ideological. 'Because of the size of the country, the parties have to be comprehensive in their approach rather than doctrinaire. If the government is too radical in its policies, it can kiss the Atlantic provinces goodbye at the next election.'

I asked him about the recent embarrassments for the government. Didn't it worry him that they allowed the opposition to exploit the seeming incompetence of the government?

'Exploit it?'

'Take advantage of it, if you prefer.'

'Aren't you making some bold assumptions? Perhaps what you describe as incompetence is merely inexperience.'

'Perhaps. Well, we needn't dwell on this matter. I have other questions –'

'I see you wish to change the subject. I'd rather you didn't. I'd rather you thought more carefully about what you just said.'

'All I meant to say is that ministers contradicting each other and resigning at the rate of one a week doesn't look good. I don't think that's a controversial statement.'

'Doesn't look good? Perhaps we should ask: Is it good? rather than Does it look good?'

I appreciated the rigour and fine morality of his distinctions, but I hadn't come for a tutorial in moral philosophy. But he wouldn't let go, and proposed certain 'models' to explain why Mulroney hadn't been told about Tunagate. Of all the possibilities, Stackhouse favoured the theory that the prime minister hadn't wanted to be told about political embarrassments for fear of being implicated. Not that Stackhouse was happy about this explanation, since he feared that a policy cultivating ignorance could eventually destroy Mulroney's credibility. 'Honesty,' he told me severely, 'is always the best policy.'

I thought Stackhouse, who, as a man of God, favours the reinstatement of capital punishment, a bit of a brute, but rather liked him in spite of it. His moralistic nit-picking was not all pedantry. Party discipline, he informed me, is probably tighter in Canada than in Britain. 'But freedom is ours to take. We shouldn't expect it to be implemented from above.'

Canada is spared the absurdities of a House of Lords, though it does have an upper chamber in the form of a Senate. Its 102 members are appointed by the prime minister, who is expected to behave like a gentleman and not restrict his favours to members of his own party. Inevitably prime ministers usually exercise their powers of patronage in ways advantageous to their own political interests. Yet the Senate does contain a few members who have distinguished themselves in other walks of life such as business or medicine. It has also become a favourite resting place for former ministers and provincial premiers. The Senate can initiate legislation, though its principal power is one of veto. This sounds more impressive that it is in practice, since it would be highly imprudent for the appointed Senate to throw out legislation passed by the elected House. Instead the Senate aims to improve legislation and introduce regional perspectives that may be lacking in the Commons. There is talk of reform, and the opposition – both the Liberals now and the Tories formerly – favours an elected Senate. It's unlikely to come about, since no government, whatever its political complexion, is eager to introduce reforms that would increase the powers of a second chamber. Sedate, benign, and far from threatening, the Senate as presently constituted suits the government, any government, just fine. Nevertheless the system is in urgent need of reform. The two most populous provinces, Ontario and Québec, decide the outcome of any general election. What happens west of Thunder Bay is electorally largely irrelevant. Power resides in central Canada just as it always has done, and there is a strong case for ensuring better regional representation within the Senate. Meanwhile the smaller provinces' complaint that their voices are rarely heard in Ottawa is not stilled.

Tension between the provinces and the federal government is nothing new. It has been a feature of Canadian politics since the birth of the country. Nor is the problem likely to go away. Canadian provinces are far more powerful, especially in economic matters, than their counterparts south of the border, the American states. If the provinces, like medieval baronies, flex their muscles, and why should they not, they are bound to clash with the central government, which by its very nature cannot take the parochial view embodied by all the provincial governments. Indeed it is the function of a confederation such as Canada to pit the two authorities against one another so as to impede any attempts at domination by one side or the other. Whether an uneasy balance can be achieved, or whether perpetual warring between two branches of government is worth the candle, are interesting debating points, though the outcome is largely irrelevant. Confederation is here to stay. The provinces probably do have more power than is compatible with political stability, but there is nothing that can be done about it now. And it's worth recalling, as they storm and rage against Ottawa, that many provincial governments would collapse without generous infusions of funds, sometimes amounting to half of all their revenues, from the federal government. Newfoundlanders may, many of them, rue the day that the province voted, oh so narrowly, to join Confederation – opponents wore black armbands in the streets of St John's when the result was announced – but no one believes the clock can be turned back.

Perhaps the Canadian provinces would be more tolerant of the interests of their fellow provinces if they knew more about them. But the size of the country militates against such familiarity. So does the rootedness of Canadian society, which is far less mobile than that of the United States. Newfoundlanders are prepared to travel thousands of miles in search of work – it's an old pattern taking a modern form – and malcontents from all over the nation will head north to begin a new life, but mobility remains less of a tradition here than south of the border. French Canadians tend to stay put in Québec or New Brunswick, Nova Scotians, murmuring Gaelic curses, like to remain in the coves of the Atlantic coast. Internal travel in Canada is expensive. Families that move, in particular to the North, may well be unable to afford to change their minds later.

As I wandered about Canada I often asked what the following people would have in common if thrust into the same room and forced to make conversation: a Newfoundland fisherman, a Toronto banker, a Dene trapper, and a Vancouver restaurateur. The answer, most people agreed, was not much. They could all talk about hockey, and perhaps they could debate the merits of rival beers, and they could certainly grumble about iniquitous Ottawa, but that would be it. From this one might deduce that the question of Canadian identity, which is said to vex the nation, is deeply problematic. I take a different view. National identity is indeed tenuous and exists primarily in terms of a contemplation of Canada's relation to its mighty neighbour, the United States. Regional identity, on the other hand, is far from weak. Canadians may indeed have a dimmed sense of national wholeness, but their sense of local rootedness is, if anything, overdeveloped. In part it is a matter of ethnic descent – it is easier for Acadians to identify with fellow Acadians than with Presbyterian bankers or Ukrainian undertakers – and in part it is simply a matter of geography. But it also reflects the inherent tension of the politics of Confederation to which I alluded earlier. Since the interests of the whole – that is, of the nation, which appears to tug less forcefully at the patriotic heartstrings than does the locality – require provincial sacrifices, a sense of grievance at the provincial level is inescapable.

Canadians probably do feel a quasi-mystical sense of unity when they consider their collective relation to the land, a feeling which can be shared by no other nation with the possible exception of the Russians, but on a more practical level political and cultural unity seem elusive. The CBC, especially the excellent radio network, should be a unifying force, but there is evidence to suggest that, if anything, it has reinforced the divisions within the country. The immediacy of television can show more graphically than any other medium how remote the concerns of one part of the country are from those of another. The passionate invective of the Parti Québécois must have seemed as alien to the oilmen and ranchers of Alberta as a Loyalist march through the streets of Belfast; and the water-skiing secretaries of Vancouver might be inhabiting a different world from the Inuit and the fishermen of the Labrador coast. The edges of the country have always been drawn southwards rather than east or west: Maritimers have more in common with New Englanders than with Albertans, Vancouverites share more with Oregonians than with Manitobans. Call a strike in Europe and a nation grinds to a halt; down tools in British Columbia and it could be weeks before the rest of Canada even hears about it. Politics too is regional. True, there are national parties, but Conservative provincial premiers are almost as likely to clash with a Conservative prime minister as with a Liberal one. Some provinces – BC is the obvious example – are dominated by parties that are mercifully *sui generis*. Similarly, economic policy is provincially rooted, and one of the stumbling blocks along the path to free trade is that it is far from certain that the federal government has the power to conclude any agreement unless the provinces, every one of them, concur.

Canadian nationalists argue passionately that Canada is already a 'branch plant economy' and no one can dispute that its economy is utterly dominated by the United States. Yet I found little evidence that Canadians deplore this state of affairs as much as the nationalists feel they should. In part this is a reflection of Canadian passivity, but equally it suggests that Canadians do not see economic issues in nationalist terms. They do not consciously buy Canadian products in preference to American ones, nor do they seem to care much who owns the company they work for. A linking of hands with the American economy, even if it poses some unspecifiable threat to national self-esteem, seems to be accepted as a reasonable price to pay for a very high standard of living. The evidence that Canada is, and has long been, living beyond its means is the size of the national debt, which, in per capita terms, exceeds that of the United States. Within a few years one third of every dollar of revenue taken by the government will be spent serving that debt. No doubt the spending cuts and increased taxes announced in the budget of spring 1986 are in part an attempt to address this problem. Canada, of course, has vast natural resources, though the world seems reluctant to purchase them at prices that justify the cost of extraction. It also has a weak manufacturing sector. As mentioned before, a copybook example is the exporting of lumber by BC and the importing of furniture. Many manufacturing industries that do exist, such as those producing shoes and textiles in Québec, are propped up by tariffs and hefty import duties on foreign goods. Were it not for tariffs and subsidies it seems obvious that the steel industry of Nova Scotia and the shoe industry of Québec, and no doubt many others, would be defunct. Again, the needs of the regions take precedence over the needs of the nation. Much is made of the new hi-tech industries being developed in Ontario, and of the Pacific Rim service industries growing in Vancouver, but their significance in terms of the overall economy, and for that matter their longevity, may not be as great as has been claimed.

It was Robert Fulford who observed to me – and the analogy strikes me as brilliantly appropriate – that Canada is like the Roman Empire, a group of distant and far-flung outposts. (Only it is surely a Roman Empire without a Rome.) One might suppose that a confederation of such diverse regions, with their potent factional-ism and entrenched vested interests, would be a hopelessly divisive system. Yet Canada, for all the separatist murmurings and mud-slinging, is not an especially unstable or unhappy nation. The ship creaks noisily, but its timbers show no sign of cracking. It is Robert Fulford, again, who has offered the most likely explanation for this strange state of affairs. 'The curious fact,' he has written, 'is that in order to qualify as Canadians we are not required to be loyal, even in theory, to the idea of Canada. . . . We understand, without having to articulate it, that it is as Canadian to resist Ottawa as to support it.' That, surely, is the strength of Canada, that its uneasy Confederation admits conflict. There is room enough within the baggy political system of the country for dissension, which can be bitter indeed in Canada, to be expressed without threatening the survival of the nation. Sometimes Canada, if one can speak of such a collectivity, has sailed perilously close to the wind. The arrogance of the English-speaking minority in Québec certainly drove a majority of that province's population to a state of near insurrection. And yet Canada survives, like an awkward bouquet composed of thorny roses, hard-edged ferns, and prickly weeds that yet smells sweetly.

Nevertheless, Canada is not at ease with itself. And the source of that unease is its proximity to the United States.

I had conversations with two distinguished Canadian academics that illustrated startlingly different attitudes to the United States.

Robin Mathews is a professor of English at Carleton University, and he lives in Ottawa a few doors away from the Existence Consciousness Bliss Bookshop, poor fellow. He told me the following story. An acquaintance at Simon Fraser University in Vancouver suggested they attempt an academic exchange. Since Robin Mathews is a full professor and outranked his friend in Vancouver, Simon Fraser would, on paper at any rate, be getting the better deal. The English faculty at Simon Fraser rejected the proposal on the grounds that Professor Mathews held 'dangerous' views on literature and cultural nationalism. The faculty stoutly proclaimed that they had no wish to provide a platform for views they considered 'intolerable'. The professors at Simon Fraser are, one might suppose, entitled to their opinion, however wounding it might be to the professor from Ottawa. What galled Robin Mathews, however, was not the mere fact of rejection but the background of those who spurned him.

'Of the thirty-six members of the English faculty at Simon Fraser, eighteen come from the United States, four from other non-Canadian countries, and the chairman has lived in Canada for twenty years but retains his American citizenship. It amuses me, just, that the chairman, who is after all a guest of Canada, should oppose a Canadian appointment to a Canadian university on such grounds.'

Mathews is not an uncontroversial figure. He made himself unpopular many years ago by pressing for the introduction of more Canadian material into courses and for the hiring of Canadians to posts at Canadian universities.

'All I was arguing for is that 80% of the faculty should be Canadian. That's far more generous to outsiders than most other universities in the world. British universities have only 3% foreign appointments, the French just about none. The problem in this country is that Canadians feel they can't have a brilliant university if it's staffed with Canadians. University appointments here, the vast majority of them, used to be made on the old boy network. In the 1970s we succeeded in getting them to advertise in Canada before looking abroad. Of course they get round such requirements by advertising, say, for a person with qualifications that are only held by one particular foreigner. Hence no Canadian application can succeed, and it's discovered that, surprise surprise, only Dr Schmidt from Cologne fits the bill.

'There's a happy ending to the story. PEN International was alerted, and letters of protest came pouring in from Margaret Atwood, David Suzuki, Ed Broadbent, and many others. And I've just heard that I've been invited to be visiting professor at Simon Fraser. Should be an interesting year. . . . The fact is that I'm tired of being patronized by Americans, who are invited to our country and then have the presumption to tell us which attitudes are acceptable to them. The trouble is that imperial powers, whether British or American, find it next to impossible to slough off their supposed superiority. Immigrants from so-called minor nations don't behave in this sort of way when they come to Canada.'

Robin Mathews resists the Americanization of Canada. It is fashionable nowadays in Canada to be scornful of such national-ism. 'You can't manufacture Canadian culture like cornflakes,' I was often told. This is perfectly true, but such measures as the legislation withdrawing tax breaks for advertisers in magazines that were not Canadian-owned and that did not have a high measure of Canadian content, were successful in stimulating Canadian publishing at the expense of American magazines. Nor would the likes of Arnold Spohr regret that they were required to hire primarily Canadians, and to nurture native talent, in order to stock companies of the performing arts.

No such obligation applies to the game of baseball, which Canadians embrace passionately. Unfortunately they are no good at it. True, the Toronto Blue Jays did extremely well during the months of my visit, and such was the excitement in the country that schools and offices, and even the stock exchange, more or less closed down for the afternoon during a crucial playoff. Why Canadians should be such frenetic fans of a team that contains not a single Canadian player is a mystery to me. When, before a Blue Jays game against the Yankees in New York, one Mary O'Dowd rose in the stadium to sing 'O Canada' it transpired that the young American chanteuse was familiar neither with the words nor the melody. Uproar! Jimmy Breslin, interviewed about all this on CBC, bravely neglected to pander to Canadian sensitivity and soundly berated the country's pretensions to being a nation of baseball players. 'Canadians can't play baseball because baseball is a summer game and Canada has no summer. Canadians should stick to their native sports, namely, hockey and pelt trapping.'

Michael Bliss, the economic historian, is scarcely bothered by the alleged threat from the United States, whether in the form of economic domination or Jimmy Breslin's admonitions. It is obvious to Bliss that Canada can do little to diminish American influence. Cultural infiltration from the south cannot be preven-ted. Most artists and writers and musicians do feel culturally dominated by the United States, but it could hardly be otherwise. People in, say, Calgary, maintains Professor Bliss, not only have little sense of being different from Americans, but are untroubled by it. Canadian students would rather study at American universities, if they can get in. There was a time when Canada felt a certain justifiable pride in comparing itself with the United States. During the turmoil of the 1960s Canada provided a haven for draft dodgers and radicals. Compared to its southern neighbour, torn by racial strife and protest against the Vietnam War, Canada appeared calm and rational and confident. But now the American economy is reviving while the Canadian economy remains in severe difficulties. Canada is once again the poor neighbour.

'Think of Canada,' Bliss put it to me, 'as the Scotland of North America. Scottish identity isn't compromised by being part of the United Kingdom, and I don't believe we should be so terrified of closer economic or even political integration with the United States. Certainly western Canadians don't find the notion that alarming.'

No doubt many Scots would disagree with this assertion that their identity is not diminished by their political union with England, just as many Canadians would react with horror to the notion of ever closer ties with the United States, for there is a grain of truth in the frequently quoted maxim that Canadian unity consists in being thankful at not being American. Ironically, a large proportion of Canadians are of Scottish ancestry, and those who deplore the trepidation, frugality, and stern morality of all too many Canadians might not be far wrong in attributing these stupendously dull virtues to that heritage. Michael Bliss was not, of course, saying that there was no difference between the two North American countries, even though he would maintain, in common with nationalists who lament the development, that the differences diminish with every year. Canada is certainly more humane in its social policies than the United States. There is a collectivist and interventionist tradition that is alien to the go-getter individualism south of the border. As Mark had put it to me in Montréal, 'Canadians are prepared to surrender some individual rights in favour of communal ones. Our culture and cars and all that may be the same as in the States, but our attitudes are very different.' Canadians, especially as represented by their current Conservative government, may be yearning to import some of that entrepreneurial spirit into more lackadaisical Canada, but that the most crass and mindless manifestations of American individualism would be unwelcome has been made clear by the government's oft stated refusal to contemplate dismantling its welfare system in order to secure an agreement on free trade. Such entrepreneurial spirit has to be imported, for it is a consequence of the branch plant economy that Canadian businessmen are unwilling to take large risks. A Montréal businessman, originally from England, told me: 'Canadians are great at implementing other people's decisions. But they shy away from risks, from large concepts. For better or worse, there are few Canadian multinationals. Canadians lack aggression, and they're happy to allow the country to remain an industrial colony. Under Mulroney the doors have now been opened to outside finance and investment, but only if the work force doesn't come from outside Canada.'

As a fellow Englishman, it was hard for me not to share his impatience with Canadians' passivity. I have every sympathy with nationalist Canadians such as Robin Mathews and Abe Rotstein who are eager to maintain the integrity of Canada in the face of ever increasing economic and cultural domination by the United States. I fear it is a losing battle because Canadians simply don't care enough: such mighty and somewhat intangible issues seem remote to them. The invitation to catatonia must often seem hard to resist, and Canadians' political traditions expose them to such domination from outside. As has often been remarked, the United States, unlike Canada, experienced a revolution. It had to forge a new country on the back of an ideology, which Canada has never had to do. It was essential for immigrants to the liberated United States to become instant Americans, but Canada, sitting cosily in the lap of Empire, never felt a comparable pressure to mould its citizens in the service of an ideology. It is one of the most attractive and treasurable features of Canada that immigrants, even after many generations, are encouraged to preserve their ethnic inheritance within the broader, looser boundaries of Canadian identity. Canadians, secure in the world because they don't feel the peculiarly American urge to cajole and bully the world into becoming a mirror image of itself, are relaxed and diffident. They do not need to be aggressive because they do not experience irrational fears of invasion from tiny Caribbean islands. Canadians are realists in the world, preferring to pour oil on troubled waters rather than to lay mines in them; they are generous to immigrants, welcoming to refugees (at least in comparison with most other nations), respecting the strangeness of other peoples both within their own borders and in the world outside. Canadians are untroubled by their lack of clout. Indeed, they find it liberating. A New Yorker who had lived in Canada fifteen years ago had enjoyed her few years there: 'I remember Trudeau talking about Mao and radicalism, while his wife was hanging out with rock stars. In the States he'd have been impeached, but in Canada everyone said "That's cool" and went off to make maple syrup.'

Canadians are conservative in their mores, if liberal in their internationalism. They respect orderliness and continuity, they decline to jay walk except in Québec, yet they are not hidebound. As my acquaintance in Chicoutimi said: 'Canadians look forward. Of course we respect the past. If the past gives us great art and literature, so much the better for us. But your kings and queens and Napoleons – who needs them? In Canada we prefer to make life easy for ourselves. We don't want all that European formality.'

Diffidence and tolerance are attractive qualities but they don't do much for nationhood. There is a bovine quality to Canada that at times I found acutely depressing. Cosy, acquiescent, quick to complain but slow to act, Canada can seem somnolent, as though sedated by the awesomeness of its landscape. For that is the other major difference between the two countries. The people of Canada are pitted against their environment in a way that is barely comprehensible to most Americans. Margaret Atwood's famous observation that survival rather than winning is at the core of the Canadian experience surely contains a large measure of truth. When for most of the year you must battle against ice and wind, drought and crop failure, fog and isolation, there is little energy left over for conquering the world – not just territorially, but culturally. (Or as Michael Bliss put it, more brutally: 'What kind of identity is built on shivering in the cold?') In the cities it is easy to cope, but ten miles outside them you are on your own. There are those who find the wilderness exhilarating. I am not one of them. The expanses and vistas of Canada frustrate those who, like myself, often prefer the detail to the grand design. I relish virtuosity within confinement as much as, if not more than, the broad vivid brushstroke. Canada's mystique is its spaciousness, its northern emptiness. To me it is oppressive. You cannot bounce off the tundra: it receives no human imprint. It flattens my spirits; others', fortunately, are able to soar.

Canadians have learnt to tame the land for human ends by means of railways and dams, but they recognize the constraints of their environment. They know that the land makes Canada special, which is why they greet with indifference each latest economic invasion of their country, but react with fury when an American ship takes a short cut without saying please. There is no shortage of lakes in Québec, but when dozens of them are destroyed by acid rain emissions from the United States, they again respond angrily. Canadians may be despoiling their own country at a shocking rate – especially in the forests of British Columbia and the chemical dumps of Ontario – but they are increasingly aware of it and concerned about it. Respect for the land gives Canadians a sense of perspective, modest and humble, that contributes to the diffidence that can make visitors such as myself yearn on occasion for an injection of brassy rampant energy from south of the border. I do not mean to suggest that Canadians are flabby in their passivity. They may be mild-mannered in comparison with their more vulgar neighbours, but they are not without pugnacity and not without humour.

Canadians, berated for their stolidity, have produced their fair share of highly creative and individual talents. While it is true that Canadian culture is more often validated from outside the country than from within, and that Canadians are envious of each other's success, at least the world has not failed to recognize the marvellous gifts of singers such as Jon Vickers and Teresa Stratas, novelists such as Mordecai Richler and Margaret Atwood, and pioneering intellectuals such as Northrop Frye. On an earlier visit to Canada the high point was an evening I spent with Marshall McLuhan, during which we disagreed over the relative values of percepts and concepts, a discussion of more glitter than substance. Some of McLuhan's writings may be specious and vapid, but he did present us with a handful of insights that have changed the way we look at modern society – no mean achievement. Nor can I forget the sight of Glenn Gould, captured in an excellent CBC documentary, singing Mahler to a group of elephants. As Mordecai Richler put it to me: 'Canadians are less parochial than Americans because everything has always been going on some-where else.' Canada has also made more modest contributions to the enjoyment of the world: the satire of Mort Sahl, the song 'Born to be Wild', and the Rhinoceros Party, which proposed moving the Rockies to Central Canada and after twenty years of daft campaigns, has only narrowly avoided what its spokesmen describe as 'the ultimate humiliation of being elected to public office'.

When Canada stamps its foot, the world does not shake. But when Canada, beginning to shake off its diffidence, its inwardness, speaks loud and clear, the world echoes back, whether in its recognition of Canadian artistry or its appreciation of Canadian good-heartedness in an ever troubled world. Canadians should stop worrying, especially about their national identity. Were it not for its swollen-headed southern neighbour, identity would scarcely be an issue. We are what we are, hovering around our stereotypes, conforming, adapting, defying. Canadians are moulded by their pasts, which are wonderfully diverse, and by their land, and by their allegiance to regions that are as vast as nations. Patriotism, to be sure, is the vulgar notion that my country is the best country because I live in it, but it is surely time for Canadians to shake off the constrictions of their heritage, throw away the *fleur de lis* of Québec and the Union Jack of the Loyalist East, and relish to the full the honourable, unique, uncertain distinction of being, in invigoratingly various ways, Canadian.

Index

Stephen Brook lives in London and writes mostly on
travel and wine. He is working on a book about the
central European cities of Vienna, Budapest,
and Prague.